# TEACHING MODERN LANGUAGES

# Teaching
# Modern Languages

Edited by G. Richardson

CROOM HELM
London & Canberra

NICHOLS PUBLISHING COMPANY
New York

© 1983 G. Richardson
Croom Helm Ltd, Provident House, Burrell Row,
Beckenham, Kent BR3 1AT

British Library Cataloguing in Publication Data

Teaching modern languages.
   1. Languages, Modern — Study and teaching —
   Great Britain
   I. Richardson, G.
   418'.007'1041    PB38.G7
   ISBN 0-7099-2227-2
   ISBN 0-7099-2228-0 Pbk

First published in the United States of America 1983
by Nichols Publishing Company, Post Office Box 96, New York,
NY 10024

ISBN 0-89397-157-X
ISBN 0-89397-158-8 Pbk

Typeset by Leaper & Gard Ltd, Bristol
Printed and bound in Great Britain
by Billing & Sons Limited, Worcester.

# CONTENTS

# ACKNOWLEDGEMENTS

We would like to thank *Le Monde* for permission to use the material reproduced on pp. 140 and 160–1; *Québec Français* for permission to reproduce the cartoon on p. 132; and M. Philippe Olivier for his kind authorisation to use the material on p. 166.

Our thanks are also due to the Ministère de l'Education et de l'Information of the République des Seychelles for allowing us to use the figurines on pp. 172 and 174, and to Editions Gallimard for permission to reproduce the poems by J. Prévert on pp. 177, 178 and 180-1.

# FOREWORD

In planning this book we were not primarily concerned to provide a factual survey of modern language teaching in all its aspects, nor was it intended that the book should express the concerted views of any particular school of thought or the rationale of any one method.

Instead, having asked a number of acknowledged authorities within the field to write independently on some aspect of the subject of major interest to them and to all teachers at the present time, we were at pains to encourage and preserve the individual authors' originality of approach and independence of viewpoint. The result is a symposium of varied and wide-ranging essays.

At the same time these provide a comprehensive coverage of the most important issues in the field of modern language teaching today, and also reflect the broad lines and areas of agreement amongst the individual writers which will be immediately apparent from a reading of the book as a whole.

GR

# 1 AIMS AND OBJECTIVES IN FOREIGN LANGUAGE TEACHING

A.W. Hornsey

## Doubts and Certainties

> It is now conceded by all educationalists that the study of Modern Languages can confer far-reaching advantages on society in general and on the individual student. (IAAM, 1956, p. 19)

Only twenty-five years ago it was possible to write with such certainty. Discussion of the value of 'language studies' (even this label was not a subject for debate) and of the aims of the language teacher could be contained in four pages out of the three hundred in a major book on language teaching. In the half century since Morant had officially signalled the high status of French as a subject by including it in the curriculum of the secondary school but not in that of the elementary school, it seems to have become accepted that learning a foreign language unquestionably was worth while, even if Collins and others in the twenties and thirties had found it necessary to criticise the efficacy of the methods of teaching. This security and assumption of high status have not survived the years since 1956 and in discussing aims today it is important to understand why doubts have replaced certainties.

It was asserted that learning a foreign language brought gains in terms of enhanced career possibilities, cultural enrichment, linguistic understanding and character development. The consensus in the decade after the Second World War is quite remarkable and lists of such advantages can be found with slightly different wordings in Mallinson (1953), Hodgson (1955) and IAAM (1956). In concrete terms, the writers suggested that possession of a foreign language would increase the individual's prospects in commerce and industry and give access to the non-English fruits of research and development. It would enhance the experience of foreign travel and make the culture of another nation more accessible. It would improve linguistic awareness and grasp of the

1

mother tongue. The IAAM (1956, p. 20) even claimed that the struggle for accuracy in grammar and idiom would help to form enduring habits of careful thought. Even in 1956, late nineteenth-century beliefs about the nature of transfer were apparently still held.

The benefactors from all this were however only a limited group of children. The examples of work cited in Mallinson (1953, pp. 119 *et seq.*) will be recognised by experienced teachers as the products of learners of above average ability. The IAAM made this limitation quite explicit. They felt that acquiring only a smattering of a foreign language was futile and they were therefore conscious of a solemn responsibility to exclude less able children from the activity:

> It is our duty, however, to state here our conviction that any worthwhile success in language study demands a degree of ability rarely found in the lower streams of secondary modern schools. (IAAM, 1956, p. 21)

It is not here intended to debate such statements but to report them as an expression of views held by sincere people. The foreign language was a subject taken by a limited number of pupils in independent or grammar schools who stood a fair chance of becoming diplomats or international businessmen, who even in those days could anticipate participation in foreign travel and who would want to engage in personal contact with foreign cultures. Even if all these failed to materialise, then at least habits of careful thought were fostered. For some it was still possible that their future entry to university would be blocked by their not having evidence of foreign language attainment in their matriculation certificate. This at any rate was the ideal picture – even if it does not match too closely what I as a pupil in the 1940s perceived as the outcome of doing French for many of my contemporaries in a grammar school in a northern industrial town.

It was the appearance of F.M. Hodgson's book in 1955 which marked the beginning of a significant shift of emphasis. It is not simply a semantic nicety to point out that its title was *Learning Modern Languages*, whereas Vernon Mallinson's book two years earlier was *Teaching a Modern Language*. It is 'teaching' which appears in the title of all the books on method in Mallinson's bibliography, apart from two books by Michael West. Mrs Hodgson always made it clear that she was concerned primarily with the learner, with how we learn rather than how we teach. This shift from teacher to taught is a characteristic of the present situation in which we are forced to take into account variations in the ability and social background of our pupils and to attend closely to identifying materials and content appropriate to that variety. Mrs Hodgson wanted to know what it felt like to be a foreign language learner. It is perhaps sad that she chose the evidence of examination results to identify the problems but at least she posed the significant question: who is the learner?

Her second contribution derived from her refusal to accept the idea that some children were quite incapable of learning a foreign language:

> Since all these children have considerable competence in the handling of their own language . . . we cannot assume that they are incapable of learning a language as such. (Hodgson, 1955, p. 3)

It is quite possible that there are children whose progress in learning a foreign language in school is too slow or too limited to justify the time spent or who retain so little from lesson to lesson that progress is no longer the appropriate word; it is also possible to dismiss Mrs Hodgson's statement as a massive non-sequitur since learning a language artificially in a classroom is not the same as acquiring one's mother tongue. What is important is to recognise that she is asking a second significant question: who is to be the learner? And unlike the IAAM in 1956, but like many teachers today, she makes no exclusions on *a priori* grounds associated with general intelligence or previous attainment in other school subjects.[1] Children must be allowed to demonstrate by their attainment in the foreign language whether the activity is worthwhile for them and even then we need to try to take into account the enormous influence of motivation. The problem of making decisions about who is to learn the language is no longer solved for us by the IAAM's dutiful exclusion clause.

From Mrs Hodgson on, the story is clear, even if the certainties have evaporated. The rise of the comprehensive school, the widening of the range of children who take a foreign language, the demands of teaching mixed-ability groups and the changed status of the teacher (who in many schools has ceased to wield unchallenged authority and has to negotiate her position as a 'facilitator',[2] to use a current jargon word) – all these combine to make us ask why our subject features in the school curriculum, what we have to offer and who wants it in any case. In the debate about curriculum content, the foreign language is sometimes accorded a key position[3] but to justify this with the assertions of 1956 is no longer possible. Traditional courses are no longer a safety net; we do not know how to adjudicate between structures, situations and notions in debate on syllabuses; examination criteria are being re-assessed.[4] It is even fashionable to talk about a 'crisis' in language teaching.[5] I want to probe this position and to offer some tentative suggestions even if I must admit to being unable to give answers with the same air of certainty as my colleagues of twenty-five years ago.

**Constraints**

It is probably appropriate at this point to make my own position clear since it has changed considerably since I started to write about aims in language teaching some thirteen years ago (Hornsey, 1969). In particular, I am conscious that since publishing my reaction to the DHS document *The School Curriculum*,[6] I have become even more sure that, if all secondary children are to have a foreign language as part of their school learning experience, then the aim of gaining a communication skill must be secondary to the educational, humanistic aim of helping them towards greater linguistic and cultural awareness; I have come to this view because gaining a communication skill needs an investment of time and resources beyond what is available in school and even if the skill is acquired, it can only be maintained if it is performed and the majority of English speakers are not called upon in speech or in writing to perform in a foreign language. Four conditions derive from, or support, this belief.

First, there is no evidence that in Great Britain we could possibly teach the majority of the school population to understand, speak, read and write a foreign language at a level even approaching the needs of everyday communication, if the latter is understood as anything more than the simplest formulae of survival. The time available, the lack of intensity, the size of teaching groups and the absence of the kind of urge to learn a foreign language which might be present outside the English-speaking world together present virtually insuperable problems. The single aim of teaching French for communication (with the native speaker often held up as the model) to all children is as unrealistic and meaningless as if history or mathematics teachers were to define their aims in the hope that all their pupils will become A.J.P. Taylors or Einsteins.

Second, if language teachers can persuade their pupils to persevere in the subject, they need not feel frustrated by the very limited skill which their pupils acquire provided that, in acquiring it, they arrive at some understanding of a foreign culture and gain a modest insight into language itself. If they learn something of the validity of a different way of living and if work with a foreign language allows them to step back and look more objectively at language itself, then an important educational gain has been made. It is of course true that this gain is neither assessed nor rewarded in conventional language examinations.

Third, it is inevitable that slow progress in the skill area and the decline of novelty value will lead to frustration and that pupils will opt out. The numbers opting out will be considerably reduced if learners are engaged on courses which have clear and attainable short-term objectives so that they can have tangible indications of success and therefore wish to continue. If they leave the field, they will obviously not make the educational gains referred to above.

Fourth, a humanistic aim is not helped by compulsion. Pupils who are made to study the language while hating the experience may well develop attitudes of hatred towards the language, its speakers and their country. Since we cannot anticipate exactly who these pupils will be, they must all be allowed to taste the subject but then allowed to withdraw. It is better for them to return later, by choice, if more intensive courses are made available for older adolescents or adults at school or in tertiary-level colleges.[7] In short, the pattern of provision and aims within it at the secondary stage might be as in Figure 1.1.

It is not possible to specify how long each level will last. The beginners' level might be as short as one year or as long as three, but, whatever its length, it must aim to provide:

–   a useful survival skill, probably not based initially on structures or notions, although these remain important, but on situations likely to arise in a visit to a foreign country or in helping a foreign visitor here – telling him the way, getting to know him, serving him in a shop;
–   a clear and accurate base for those children who will want to continue their language learning beyond this level.

Figure 1.1:  Aims

| Level | Pupils | Content |
|---|---|---|
| Beginners | All pupils | 1. Learning some language skill<br>2. Learning about language<br>3. Learning about the foreign people and their lives |
| Middle school | Able and willing | Maintaining all three aims but paying considerable attention to the linguistic foundation necessary to advanced study, continued use of language as a service to their studies and future professional lives and interests (If this group is neglected, one wonders what will happen to language work in higher education and to national needs for foreign language expertise) |
| | Less able but willing | Continuing all three aims but graded objectives essential if any success is to be experienced in development of language skill |
| | Unwilling | Allowed to opt out with the possibility of returning later |
| Post O-level | Specialists | A-level courses |
| | Non-specialist | Continuation courses for those who will benefit by not losing what skill has already been acquired |
| | Others | Short, intensive, voluntary, beginners' courses, some of which will aim at special purposes |

This probably means a slow, thorough first year with emphasis on the survival skill and, thereafter, sets differentiated by attainment and/or motivation.

**Language as Skill**

In order to recognise what is involved in fulfilling the first aim, namely 'learning some language skill' (Figure 1.1), it is necessary to ask what learning a language means. The answer is complex but the complexity is unavoidable. It involves:

- penetrating a new set of meanings;
- assimilating deliberately a set of rules which the native speaker acquires tacitly and which make it possible for him to generate acceptable utterances and to recognise and understand the utterances of others;
- practising the skills of using the language (both productive and receptive) sufficiently to become tolerably fluent in their operation.

In short, the learner needs to be taught both form and message and to experience and use both a great deal. Thus, materials without any clear context or forms used randomly (neglect of correct use of gender or case, for example) will not meet this need and the aim will not be reached. Similarly, deliberate refusal to use the learner's mother tongue as a possible means of clarification or explanation of form or meaning will be counter-productive, just as over-use of the mother tongue will reduce the time given to practice of the foreign language. If teaching the language skill is one aim, then three clear conditions arise in planning lessons and work:

(1) a substantial part of every lesson will involve using the foreign language (in speech and/or writing) or receiving with understanding the message it conveys (by listening or reading). I doubt whether schools are places where reading and writing can be left out – to try to do so would be to ignore teacher and pupil fatigue, span of concentration and the need for variety;[8]
(2) explanations (in the mother tongue) will be needed to ensure clarity and in order to share lesson intentions with the learners so that they gain confidence from knowing what the lesson is about. I see no evidence that the majority of secondary school pupils can deduce all language rules from the examples used – there is never time to provide enough evidence;
(3) every opportunity will be exploited to put the language into a clear context and to provide as rich a variety of examples as possible. This means exploiting the foreign language assistant (even relative beginners might, for example, be helped by hearing simple exchanges between teacher and assistant), using any available radio and television material, playing records and tapes, showing films, taking learners abroad, arranging links with foreign schools, using readers and magazines for extensive reading, building up displays of posters and other media and

carrying out as much of the routine classroom business as possible (enquiries about absence, taking the register, etc.) in the foreign language.

## Language Awareness

The second aim (Figure 1.1), namely teaching children about language, does *not* mean running a course in linguistics, although the teacher might well find some help and guidance in popular books about language, for example Aitchison (1978), Brown (1959), Farb (1973), Hayakawa (1966). The intention is much more modest and for many teachers it is already an element of their work which they take for granted. It includes comparisons between the ways in which mother tongue and foreign language operate;[9] contrasting the various English present tenses with the one French one; showing how words which appear to be equivalent cover, in fact, a different range of meaning in one language from another – for example in the area of English 'bacon/ham' and German 'Speck/Schinken' (see Table 1.1), and even talking about features like word order (how do we know the difference between 'a Venetian blind' and 'a blind Venetian'?) or case (why do Germans apparently not distinguish between the prepositions 'in' and 'into'?). For younger pupils, attempts to use technical terms – tense, nouns, verb, accusative – might be confusing, but as the course progresses, the use and clarification of such terms cannot be avoided if we are not to exclude our pupils from access to much that has been thought and written about language. Later the teacher will aim to look at other features of language, such as style (the differences between

Table 1.1

| ←——Total range as displayed in a shop——→ | | |
|---|---|---|
| German Categories | Speck | Schinken |
| English Categories | bacon | ham |

fact and fiction, statement and persuasion, etc.) and register. Again, this does *not* mean plunging into stylistics or semantics but might be as humble as looking at the way language is used in the advertisements in *TV Times*, *Stern* or *Paris Match*. There is clearly room here for interplay between foreign language work and the practices of more enlightened mother tongue teachers.

## A Foreign Culture

The third aim (Figure 1.1) – learning about the foreign culture – is equally modest. Culture is not intended to mean only 'high' culture nor does it mean emphasis on the touristy or the quaint or on untenable generalisations. It will involve finding something out about how people live in the foreign country – not just random facts about the famous,[10] but the everyday world of people who in some ways are different from us but in many ways share the same human condition. The suggestion by Barry Jones[11] in his so-called 'jeu de poubelles' in which children are invited to speculate about the activities of a French person as indicated by the contents of his wastepaper basket or dustbin (used tickets, wrappings of food-tins, etc.) or in his attempts to link schools here and in France through the exchange of personalised tape messages are worth following for all learners. It is a pity if such work is relegated to 'French studies' for the less able who have failed to continue the language or if the study of French people is restricted to their manifestation in set literary texts for A-level.

## A Foreign Language for All

I have been at pains to avoid suggesting that a single aim in foreign language teaching will be appropriate to all secondary school children and I have separated humanistic aims from linguistic aims. I have also tried to avoid assuming that all children can or will attain a high level of linguistic skills, or, as a corollary, that we should ignore the limited number who both can and will. Nevertheless, I want to place on record my view that children should not be excluded from the opportunity to do a foreign language. It seems educationally indefensible to suggest that any secondary school pupil will not benefit in his future life as an adult from a sharpened understanding of language. Language will be a major controlling factor in his personal relationships with others, in his handling of the business of living (making applications, filling in forms, etc.) and in his ability to assess what is being done to his life by government, unions, the media or persuasive advertising. Clearly his school work in his mother tongue is immensely important, but his work in a foreign language can make its own unique contribution. Because it is not so integrally a part of himself, the foreign language is a language medium he can step back from. He can, so to speak, look in at it from the outside. He will of course not do so if his language work is exclusively concerned with mindless drilling or with language not even tenuously connected with any reality, nor will he gain much if it is judged that he is well employed exclusively at the level of colouring pictures or filling in clock faces. Teachers reading this may of course find it hard to relate such possible gains to some of their more difficult and recalcitrant pupils. Nevertheless the intention is essential and should be seen, in my view, as equivalent to the generally held belief that all children should be helped to read and write and count.

It is equally indefensible in the 1980s to base the planning of the curriculum on the assumption that the present generation of schoolchildren will live their adult lives in a monocultural society. It is certain that increased mobility of individuals and groups will lead to an even greater mixing of people of different race, colour and creed. Communities in which the members share beliefs, language and life aspirations will tend to merge, not necessarily with a complete loss of identity, into richly varied societies. The ability to tolerate differences will be essential – inability to do so can be seen in conflicts throughout the world today. Study of a foreign language and its associated culture is one of the clearest ways of bringing children face to face with difference and, in trying to accommodate the other person's ways of expression within their own attempts at communication, they gain a modestly limited sense of how that other person feels. There are French courses which unwittingly convey an impression that the French really think in English and then apply a set of prescriptions to encode the thought in their own language. When, for example, the foreign language is used exclusively for the mechanics of the lesson (exercises, question and answer work) and everything that matters (personal enquiry, remarks about yesterday's game or the latest joke in *Paris Match*) is expressed in or translated into English, it is hardly surprising if

French is seen to be an artificial thing unconnected with real life. In this respect too the showing of film material or the visit abroad or the informal use of the assistant would appear to be essential.

## Needs and the Language Skill

Thus I am saying that there are outcomes of learning a foreign language which at some level are valuable to all. Difficulty in asserting and defending this universal value is manifest as soon as one moves on to consider the skill of day-to-day communication. A minimal experience of the language is necessary for the realisation of the objectives of language awareness and recognition of difference but to engage in an operation which has the single aim for all of, say, achieving O-level standard or even the higher grades in CSE seems doubly unrealistic.

Such a goal is unrealistic because it is too remote and too homogeneous. It neither attracts by offering realisable short-term successes nor does it take into account the vast differences in interests, abilities and backgrounds of the learners. The same problem is recognised by expert groups looking at the definition of criteria for a common examination at 16 +:

> Moreover to attempt to use a single instrument for evaluating achievement by children of all types, interests, abilities, backgrounds and intentions must necessarily have the attributes of a Procrustean bed. [12]

Second, the skill aim is unrealistic, because, in order to make it tangible, one has to be specific about objective criteria of attainment and this inevitably calls for a definition of 'needs'. General universal needs of the kind involved in language-sensitising or multi-cultural awareness are common to all and the aims derived from them form a rationale for the subject which is not dissimilar from statements of aims put forward by the defenders of subjects like history, science, mathematics or geography. But how does one define what a variety of secondary school children *need* of a foreign language or a skill? Is the teacher to aim at immediate needs of the learner now (an eleven-year-old in Wigan or Darlington, for instance) or the possible needs of the learner when he becomes an adult language user? If the former, then what is taught could be both ephemeral and careless of the likelihood that the learner will not go to the country for some years: if the latter, then how are we to make a reliable forecast? Is the hypothetical adult going to want the written or the spoken language? In recent years, it has been readily assumed by many that the spoken language must be the aim, but it could be argued that for many it is only through the written word that the contact will be maintained, if at all. If it is the spoken language, then what purposes will it need to serve? Travel? Finding a job in the EEC? Selling motor cars? Business – but what branch of business? And so the questions roll on and the conclusion must surely be that, in the heterogeneity of an ordinary state school, we simply cannot know in advance. We cannot, for instance, teach an eleven-year-old all that is involved in the notion 'persuasion' when we have no idea what kind of person he will be when he actually comes to the point where he wants to talk French persuasively. The dilemma is then clear: we have to limit outselves to teaching that which is most useful and general, a kind of 'langue fondamentale' ('le français fondamental' is the explicit basis of some courses) but the very neutrality of such language might rob it of particularly that excitement which the novice needs. It is frequently this difference between a school class where needs are not specifiable and an adult class where language is often taught with a special purpose in mind which makes the successful experience of the latter unrepeatable in the ordinary classroom. Figure 1.2 (a model for imaginary Japanese courses) illustrates the situation.

Even from such a deliberately oversimplified layout, it is apparent that at school level it will not be possible to avoid the risk of a kind of emasculated general language: the heterogeneity of the clientele does not allow for the pursuit of individual interests. Add to this the slow progress which the learner makes in his brief contacts with the foreign language in school and it is not surprising that pupils seem so unmotivated. A linguistic aim which might be achieved in five years' time is inappropriate for many and they fail – not because English people have no aptitude for languages (the popular image), but because the attitude is wrong. Motivation is lacking.

It is to this problem that I now want to turn.

Figure 1.2: Japanese Courses

| Language Learning Client | Forecast in 'Needs' | Course |
|---|---|---|
| Motor engineer and car salesman | 1. Social niceties ('lubricating' devices)<br>2. Language of motor engineering<br>3. Persuasive techniques in buying and selling | Common core language (basic fundamentals plus concentration on 1, 2, 3) |
| Trade official | 1. Social niceties ('lubricating' services)<br>2. Commercial terminology and special register of a selection of business areas<br>3. Some political and financial language | Common core language (plus 1, 2, 3) |
| Student who intends to study Japanese literature and culture (largely in the written form) | 1. Study (at times contrastive) of everyday and literary language<br>2. Selection of cultural social discourse<br>3. Diachronic study in history of culture and history of the language | Common core (plus 1, 2, 3) |
| O level | Elements of language with the widest possible distribution: *cry* not *sob*, *you* not *thou*, *perfect* not *pluperfect*, *car* not *sedan*, etc. | Common core (plus ? a blandly neutral language? the language needs of a child?) |

**Attitude and Motivation**

An awareness of the nature of symbolic representation; a better understanding of oneself and others and a resulting modification of personal conduct;[13] the acquisition of an essential tool for gaining further knowledge (namely language itself)[14] – all these benefits derive from the study of a foreign language, but it would be inconsistent, not to say perverse, to suggest that therefore such a study should be pursued by all pupils, only to have to concede that the undertaking is beyond the scope of the majority and then to be satisfied with the small number who continue to learn languages in our schools beyond the elementary stage.[15] To avoid such unhappy satisfaction we have to consider attitude because, although it is notoriously difficult to identify and describe what this is, it becomes clearer that this is the reason for the high drop-out rate, rather than the unquestioned assumption that all English-speaking schoolchildren lack linguistic aptitude. Many of our pupils simply do not wish to learn a foreign language and our task is not to compel them to do so but to organise the experience so as to increase their wish to do so. We need to motivate them to continue and we can begin by making goals explicit, comprehensible and realisable in the short, rather than the long, term. Pupils of average and below average ability might be confused by goals like 'learning the partitive' and unimpressed by those like 'finishing the book' but it should be possible to share goals with them in terms they do understand and which have a recognisable and meaningful outcome. It is possible that we can do no better than signal attainment by awarding certificates, and a movement towards graded certificated objectives is very active (GOML).[16] I want however to suggest objectives where attainment is marked strongly by the pupil's being able to recognise his success because he realises he can do something he could not do before.

The first shared objective in French between teacher and pupil could for example take the following form: 'after eight weeks I shall bring a native French speaker to our French lesson and you will be able to introduce yourselves to him and also find out from him who he is and where he comes from'. The visitor could be the French assistant or a French person known to live in the locality. The teacher will be able to use such an objective to define his syllabus because it is clear what language will be needed: the learners will need to be able both to answer and to ask questions about identity (*s'appeler*), about age (*avoir*, numbers), dwelling (*habiter*), family (*frère, sœur*, etc.), location (*c'est dans le nord de l'Angleterre*) and geography (*c'est une grande ville*) as well as being able to recognise some French locations (*dans le Midi*) and to use a limited range of greetings and introduction vocabulary (*bonjour, enchanté*). When the meeting does take place, the learner will know only too clearly whether he has achieved anything and, if he has done so, he will be very conscious of his success, a feeling which is potentially highly motivating.

Further goals can then be proposed and agreed between pupils and teachers preparing for an exchange of tape-recordings with a French-speaking school (pupils will send personalised messages to their opposite numbers using their own mother tongue but will need to understand the foreign language message they receive – the language of everyday routine, of evening and weekend activities, as well as that of the first objective); preparation for a trip abroad (asking the way, recognising buildings, using shops and cafés); preparation for the viewing of a film or video-tape. Later in the course, objectives might include: telling a joke in French with the joke (or selection of jokes) as a text for language work; composing, with help from the teacher, a detective story in four or five episodes to be duplicated and then offered as reading with illustrations to a younger class; compiling statistic-like dossiers of the class's likes and dislikes – hobbies, sports stars, film stars, pop singers, cars, clothes, etc. – to be transmitted to the French school (*aimer, détester, préférer*, etc.); collecting and even trying out some simple French recipes. These are only suggestions; the publication of a comprehensive set by an adviser or a group of teachers is long overdue. The characteristic of all of them is that the language is given a context and used for recognisable purposes, and what is achieved is clear even to the least able. It is possible that on such a basis language work can be maintained longer than in many cases at present and general language and cultural benefits will accrue.


**Conclusion**


My approach in this essay has been tentative as I have tried to reconcile my own inner convictions with the views of the many teachers I meet in my professional life. It has been necessary to move away from traditional assumptions and to argue that learning a foreign language in school is only partly a question of acquiring a skill and that it has a strong claim to a place in the curriculum on humanistic grounds. The intention throughout has been to support four standpoints:

(1) the necessity of recognising not one but three separate and mutually supporting aims; the sharpening of language awareness; the recognition and tolerance of different cultural traditions; the acquisition of a communicative skill in a foreign language;

(2) the assumption that all children can gain by the experience of language learning but to different extents within the three aims and to different levels;

(3) the assertion that the gain will be devalued if the language skill is completely neglected while admitting, and the dilemma is obvious, that compulsion to pursue this skill is probably self-defeating;

(4) the idea that sets of goals have to be developed which are recognisable to pupils as well as teachers so that the former can see that they are succeeding and be motivated to continue.

Once we free discussion of the role of the foreign language in the school curriculum from the single, apparently straightforward but blatantly unattainable, goal of turning all our pupils into fluent speakers and accept in its place differentiated aims (humanistic as well as linguistic), we will no longer have to live with a false conception of massive failure. Instead of concern about a 'language-teaching crisis', there will be a recognition of the unique educational value of the subject and energy can be devoted to the important task of finding the best ways of achieving our aims.

## Notes

1. Identification of a special aptitude for learning a foreign language, or even evidence that such a thing exists at all, are areas of knowledge where there is still much debate. In any case attitude might ultimately be more important than aptitude. A useful, if elderly, introduction is to be found in E. Halsall, 'Linguistic Aptitude', *Modern Languages*, vol. L, no. 1 (March 1969). See also D. Wood, 'Language Aptitude Tests as a Preliminary to Intensive Language Courses', *Report of the Working Party on Resources for Language Learning* (CNAA, April 1979).

2. Subjects concerned with the environment and with social problems have gained ground and they lend themselves more readily to the perusal and discussion

of data with the teacher acting as 'facilitator'. The 'teacher-centred' activity of the typical foreign language lesson is called into question or even regretted. Cp. R.J. Hares (1979), pp. 1–2.

3. See *The School Curriculum* (DES, HMSO, London, March 1981), Section 43.

4. Cp. A. Hornsey, 'Communication Skills and the Training of the Secondary School Foreign-language Teacher', CILT publication (in preparation). See also D. Wilkins (1976) and C.J. Brumfit, 'Notional Syllabuses – a Reassessment', *System*, vol. 7 (Pergamon, 1979), pp. 111–16.

5. A conference was held at King's College, London, on 20 November 1976 which was actually entitled 'The Crisis in Modern Languages in Secondary and Higher Education'.

6. See A. Hornsey, 'Why a Modern Language?' *No, Minister* (Bedford Way Papers 4, University of London Institute of Education, 1981), also John McNair's thoughtful article in *Modern Languages*, vol. LVIII (4 Dec. 1977), in which he refers to the scant extent to which modern languages find a place in curriculum models proposed by thinkers like Phenix and Hirst but in which he too values highly foreign language study as a major contribution to learning about language itself.

7. Cp. my proposed scheme in 'A Foreign Language for All: the Questions to be Answered', *Modern Languages in Scotland*, vol. 1 (May 1973).

8. Cp. A. Hornsey, 'The Written Word in Oral Language Teaching', *Babel*, vol. 11, no. 2 (July 1975).

9. 'Foreign language' could be 'foreign languages' and there is some attempt in the London area to offer pupils short 'taster' courses in several foreign languages instead of offering only one. Although I am not a supporter of this innovation, I do think it merits critical consideration. Cp. D. Cross, 'Organisational Changes in Foreign Language Teaching', *Modern Languages*, vol. LVIII, no. 2 (June 1977).

10. In May 1968 one CSE Board set the following as a multiple-choice item on a French background paper:

3.  Brigitte Bardot owns a luxurious villa at a) Nice b) Biarritz c) Chantilly d) St Tropez

11. See also B. Jones, *Nala Journal*, vol. 7 (1976). For further discussion and ideas: 'Teaching European Studies', *Education*, vol. 151, no. 5 (Feb. 1978); *Modern Languages and European Studies* (CILT reports and papers no. 9, 1973); and *Modern Languages in Scotland*, vol. 4 (May 1974).

12. See National Congress on Languages in Education (1981), *16 + Criteria in Modern Languages*, 3/10 (papers of working party).

13. Cp. P. Phenix (1964), whose curriculum model includes symbolics (symbol as communicator of meaning), synnoetics (understanding of oneself and others) and ethics (personal conduct).

14. P.H. Hirst (1974).

15. Department of Education and Science (1981), Section 48.

16. Cp. A. Harding, B. Page and S. Rowell, *Graded Objectives in Modern Languages* (CILT, 1980).

# References

Aitchison, J. (1978) *Linguistics*, Teach Yourself Books, London
Brown, R. (1959) *Words and Things*, Glencoe, Illinois

Department of Education and Science (1981) *The School Curriculum*, HMSO, London

Farb, P. (1973) *Word Play*, Cape, London

Garner, E. (1981) 'Aims and Objectives' in *Teaching Languages in Today's Schools*, CILT, London

Hares, R.J. (1979) *Teaching French*, Hodder and Stoughton, London

Hawkins, E. (1981) *Modern Languages in the Curriculum*, Cambridge University Press, London

Hayakawa, S. (1966) *Language in Thought and Action*, Allen and Unwin, London

Hirst, P.H. (1974) *Knowledge and the Curriculum*, Routledge and Kegan Paul, London

Hodgson, F.M. (1955) *Learning Modern Languages*, Routledge and Kegan Paul, London

Hornsey, A. (1969) 'Why Teach a Foreign Language?' *Bulletin, 18* (9) (University of London Institute of Education)

Incorporated Association of Assistant Masters (IAAM) (1956) *The Teaching of Modern Languages*, University of London Press, London

McNair, J. (1977) 'Modern Languages in Today's Curriculum', *Modern Languages, LVIII* (4) December

Mallinson, V. (1953) *Teaching a Modern Language*, Heinemann, London

Phenix, P. (1964) *Realms of Meaning*, McGraw-Hill, New York and London

White J. (ed.) (1981) *No, Minister* (Bedford Way Papers 4), University of London Institute of Education

Wilkins, D. (1976) *Notional Syllabuses*, Oxford University Press, London

# 2 AN INTRODUCTORY OVERVIEW OF METHODS AND METHODOLOGY

## G. Richardson

Wilkins (1974) makes the point that 'there is no single, "best" way of teaching foreign languages. We can neither select one of the number of well publicised methods that is proposed to us, nor, by taking account of the undoubted weaknesses of each of them, can we arrive at a more satisfactory alternative' (p. ix). So far as the language teacher is concerned, indeed, not only is there no 'best' method, in that 'he cannot decide *a priori* that the audiovisual, the audiolingual, the structural, the grammar-translation or whatever other method is the one that he must use', but 'it is not certain that it matters very much which "method" he adopts as the basis of his teaching' (ibid., p. 57).

In another very real sense the successful language teacher is unable to limit himself to one method only, used to the exclusion of all others. Just as no one method is the 'best', so no one method is all things to all teachers or all pupils at all times. It is just possible, though unlikely, that the extremists among the advocates of the Grammar-Translation Method or of the Reform Method may have limited themselves to the one set of techniques only, but the majority of language teachers are aware of two things: first, that 'the method, in the sense of a set of materials organized into a fixed pedagogic sequence, requiring the use of classroom techniques which embody a certain view of language learning, is not the sole determinant of language learning' (ibid., p. 57), and second, that a method which is appropriate with one class on one occasion will not necessarily suit the same class at another time, nor another class during a similar lesson. Few teachers would pretend that there is one universally applicable method, equally suitable for use last period on Friday afternoons or on the first day back after the summer holidays. For most of us our 'method' is as personal as our idiolect, and just as the one is the sum total of our accents, dialects (geographical, social and professional), modes, registers and fashions of speaking, susceptible to instant modification in the light of our interpretation of the present situation or context, so the other is the ensemble of our techniques, tricks of the trade, ways of presenting material and of analysing and structuring the content of our subject, which likewise is under constant review and modification as we move from one situation to another even within the framework of the one lesson and the same room.

For the purposes of a historical review, however, it is perfectly possible to identify four or five distinct methods, each based (sometimes unconsciously) upon a different view of what language is and how it may be taught. It is important to remember, however, that few teachers nowadays would subscribe exclusively to one method only. Equally, it needs to be said that all of these methods have left a hidden legacy, of which teachers are often unaware. Those who would have said in the 1930s that they tried to use the 'Compromise' Method were in reality using a translation method some of the time at least, as we shall see, and teachers who set out verb paradigms and case endings in tabloid form are in fact using, temporarily at least, a grammar-based method, though they might hotly deny this and point to their textbook or other materials as 'proof' that they habitually used, say, an oral or an audio-visual approach.

## The Grammar-Translation Method

The most famous – though not the earliest – of the protests against this method of teaching modern languages was first published in 1882. For anyone writing exactly one hundred years later it would seem entirely appropriate to return to an analysis of 'Der Sprachunterricht muß umkehren!' (Viëtor, 1882) for an indication of what was the situation in language teaching at the time.

What Viëtor describes is the application of the methods used in the teaching of Latin and Greek to the teaching of modern languages. The typical textbook begins by introducing the parts of speech and the terminology of grammatical analysis so that the rules of the grammar – not the language itself – may be taught. Verb paradigms and declensions are set out in tabloid form; there are vocabulary lists to be learned, and then the lexis and the grammatical rules can be combined in order to translate a large number of exercises in which the mother tongue is to be rendered into the target language. There was little or no attention paid to pronunciation; the assumption throughout was that language consists of written words, and of words moreover which exist in isolation, as though they were individual bricks which could be translated one by one into their foreign 'equivalents' and then assembled according to the grammatical rules into sentences in the foreign language.

It seems that the underlying justification for such a method rested upon the belief that what was being taught – and what should be taught – was not the language itself, which was relatively unimportant, but the faculty of logical thought. As Dr R.W. Hiley (1887) put it:

> The prime object of scholastic education is the training of the mental faculties. Hence a youth is put to hard and dry studies, often confessedly distasteful, though the whole of them may be forgotten when he enters practical life. The mental training is never forgotten; on the contrary, the powers so developed gain in grasp and tenacity. Training by the ear will never do this. (p. 308)

Gilbert (1953) has collected a fascinating number of examples of this belief in English schools:

> The methods in general use in Public Schools were, in fact, those which Müller suggests: a study of formal grammar with some philology, much translation from English into the foreign language . . . At Newcastle Grammar School French is taught in precisely the same way as the ancient languages – the method is sound; grammar, not vocabulary, being first considered. (p. 2)
>
> German was considered however to provide a more valuable discipline for the mind than French. (ibid.)

(Was this because German has more inflections, to identify which required a greater capacity for 'logical thought'? Thus, *'of the boy* will be genitive, and the masculine form of the definite article "goes" *der, den, des, dem*: therefore *des* since *Knabe* is masculine singular. But *Knabe* is a weak noun, therefore its genitive ends in "*n*" – so *of the boy = des Knaben*.')

Viëtor (1882) was certainly well aware of the fact that his strongest opposition came from those who believed that the learning of a language trained the faculties and provided a valuable mental discipline: 'Doch ich sehe schon wieder das formale Prinzip im Hintergrund, und flüchte mich auf den Boden der Tatsachen zurück' (p. 6).

Even if the learning of a language by the Grammar-Translation Method *had* trained the mind in logical thought when dealing with translation, however, there is little evidence to suggest that this faculty would have been transferable to other walks of life than the language classroom. Montaigne points out that philosophers do not always act as philosophers in their domestic lives; and the public schoolboy's modest ability in Latin prose translation did not guarantee that the scholar's 'logical thinking' would later transfer to the sphere of colonial administration. 'And there is no doubt much truth in what Robert Browning says: "Learning Greek teaches Greek, and nothing else; certainly not common sense, if that have failed to precede the teaching!"' (Jespersen, 1904, p. 7)

The modern objections to the method, however, rest on linguistic and pedagogic grounds. They are nowhere better summarised and expressed than in Hodgson (1955), who points out that translation presupposes a competence in both languages, and asks

> when is the awareness necessary for translation to be obtained, if a considerable part of the limited time available is devoted to an exercise which constantly brings to the fore the patterns of the mother tongue . . . instead of being devoted to exercises which compel the pupils to meet and use in significant contexts the structures they need to possess? (p. 104).

Prose translation is a rigorous test of mastery of a language, but by definition it is a test of what has been learned, and cannot be a means of acquiring that mastery.

There are other, equally potent, objections to the use of translation as a teaching method. The most valid, to my mind, is that translation attempted before both languages have been mastered is not translation but transliteration, and the danger is that the learner will imagine – even be encouraged to imagine – that utterances in L1 can be separated into isolated words, each of which has an exact equivalent in L2. Thus Gilbert (1953) points out that a typical textbook of the era 1840–90 contained the usual disconnected sentences in English for translation into French, and that they were set out thus:

| Virtue | is | | more | precious | than | riches |
|---|---|---|---|---|---|---|
| art. virtu (f.) | est | | | précieux | art. | richesse (pl.) |

Similarly Jespersen (1904):

> Finally, sentences of this kind give the pupil quite an erroneous notion of what language is on the whole, and of the relationship between different languages. He is too apt to get the impression that language means a collection of words which are isolated and independent, and that there must be a corresponding word in his native tongue for each new foreign word that he learns. These words are then shoved about without any real purpose, according to certain given rules . . . (p. 16)

and Harding (1967):

> Any method of teaching which gives pupils the notion that word-for-word equivalents in one language can convey the meaning of sentences in another, is failing to teach an understanding of language in its widest sense. (p. 49)

It is this conception of language that leads directly to the present-day candidate's rendering of *What is the matter?* as *Quelle est la matière?* and the statement of his age as *Je suis seize*. It is a poverty-stricken view which is fundamentally false, and which has even graver effects and consequences. It would be bad enough that pupils should think that this 'translation' is possible between languages; even worse is the corollary that this is in fact all a foreign language consists of; that there is no more to language learning than rendering one written word in English by another written unit in French. But the worst effect of all is on the pupil's motivation: the activity is *rébarbatif* because he cannot do it; frustration, boredom and indiscipline follow.

Even among the more able pupils, who may be able to achieve a higher level of success at this activity, there is the feeling that this is all there is to language learning – this is all French or German lessons consist of. It is not a very rewarding or satisfying activity, and it was precisely this aspect of the old method that was singled out by Viëtor for attack first. Language learning should be fun, and bring some joy and pride in achievement with it. Quoting Goethe, he puts it thus: 'Wehe jeder Art von Bildung, die auf das Ende hinweist, statt auf dem Wege zu beglücken!' (Viëtor, 1882, p. 27), which might be translated (though not transliterated) as something like 'Shame on education if it seeks only to attain a given end, and brings no joy on the journey.' Jespersen (1904) shared the same view; we should 'teach in the right way, then there will be life and love in it all' (p. 9).


**The Reform Method**

There was from the inauguration of this method and the first statements of its rationale complete confusion as to what it should be called. Thus Jespersen (1904, p. 2) confesses to some embarrassment since it already had so many names – 'New' or 'Newer', 'Reform', 'Natural', 'Rational', 'Sensible', 'Correct', 'Direct', 'Phonetical', 'Imitative', 'Analytical', 'Concrete', 'Conversation', 'Anti-classical', 'Anti-grammatical', 'Anti-translation'. Viëtor (1882) makes it quite clear in his title and foreword that he thought of the method as a *reform*, but the tendency in this country has been to adopt – perhaps too loosely – the name Direct Method or Oral Method, so that Harding (1967) for instance can refer to 'The new Direct or Reformed Method of teaching languages' (p. 7). The Direct Method was really only a part of the new method, and refers strictly speaking only to the teaching of new vocabulary by *direct* association (hence the name) between the new noun or verb and the object or action it represented, but since the Reform Method is nearly always referred to as the Direct Method in England, I propose to use the common terminology from now on.

Whatever name the new movement is called by, there was never any doubt as to what it stood for. Gilbert's definitive and exhaustive survey of the topic (Gilbert, 1953, 1954, 1955) renders any other detailed analysis superfluous, but the manifesto of the new revolution by Viëtor (1882) will bear re-examination as a vigorous and militant statement of the case. Gilbert (1953, p. 4) classifies the reformers into two groups, 'according as they laid most emphasis on reading or on oral work', but it would seem from Viëtor's work that by 1882, at least, the two mainstreams of the opposition to the formal Grammar-Translation Method had combined.

All the reformers were vehemently opposed to the teaching of formal grammar. Viëtor (1882) says:

This study of grammar is a useless torture! It is certainly not understood, therefore it can have no effect as far as the moulding of the intellect is concerned, and no one could seriously believe that children could learn their living German tongue from it. (p. 4)

And even if you succeeded in ramming into his head the best of grammars and the most comprehensive of dictionaries, what he would have learned would still not be the language! (ibid.)

Instead, the grammar is to be acquired inductively, by inducing the rules of how the language behaves from the actual language itself.

Another method is coming to the front in all teaching, a method which trains the child to observe, to classify its observations, to draw its own conclusions, so that finally, when the time is ripe, the scientific system will raise itself, as it were, in a natural way on the foundations of the observations already made. The golden rule is 'Never tell the children anything that they can find out for themselves.' (Jespersen, 1904, p. 127)

To this end, the centre of language teaching will be the reader: 'The emphasis in language teaching must be laid on the reading of connected passages' (Viëtor, 1882, p. 22).

Viëtor was by training and inclination a phonetician, and therefore the other main emphasis of his method was on the spoken language. He constantly quotes his masters Sweet and Sayce:

Language consists of sounds and not of letters. (ibid., p. 4)

But, above all, a language consists – except for lexicographers – not of words, but of sentences. (ibid.)

No foreign language will ever be learned simply by committing to memory long lists of disconnected words. Even if we know all the grammatical rules as well, yet when it comes to the point, we shall soon give up trying to string words together and to understand the replies we get. (ibid.)

It is not surprising, therefore, that the new method laid great stress on correct pronunciation of the target language from the very beginning, insisted on the primacy of the spoken word and abundant practice of complete sentences, and advocated that writing should be forbidden in the early stages of learning L2. Viëtor and Jespersen both favoured the use of phonetic script instead of the conventional orthography in the initial stages, and the tendency lasted on well into the twentieth century. (See, for example, Hedgecock, 1926, last reprinted 1957.)

Translation into the target language was banned. 'Translation into a foreign language is an art which is quite unsuitable for the school pupil,' said Viëtor (1882, p. 24). Instead, the aim of the instruction was to plunge the learner into a flood of L2 exclusively, to compel him to think in L2 as soon as possible, and to this end even translation from L2 into L1 was later minimised – it would have re-introduced the mother tongue and thereby given rise to interferences and drawn attention to the possibility of translating instead of thinking directly in L2. Translation from the foreign language was not ruled out altogether – certainly not by the German pioneers, who used it extensively. But the later disciples of Viëtor in England took a much more extreme view, and for them recourse to translation of any kind was very much a last resort, and explanations of new vocabulary, as of points of grammar, were almost invariably given in the foreign language.

Jespersen (1904, chapter V) lists and describes the half-dozen ways which the Direct Method advocates developed in order to explain new words without translating them. The first of these was, of course, by direct association between the new word and the idea it stood for, for example 'Voilà *un livre*, voici *la craie.*' When this was no longer thought possible – and that was not for a long time, because as their later critics scathingly but justifiably pointed out, some of the more extreme Direct Methodists had cupboards and drawers stuffed with *Realien* which they insisted on bringing out and displaying instead of translating simply into English – they would point to a picture of the object. They used definition-type explanations (for example '*un meunier* est un homme qui travaille dans un moulin'); made great use of opposites (for example '*court* est le contraire de *long*'); relied on conveying meaning by placing the new word in a series of contexts (for example 'Voilà une cravate *bleue*: voice une jupe *bleue*: voice une chemise *bleue*') and only finally, reluctantly, allowed the similarity of the word in L1 to be played on (for example '*locomotive* veut dire la même chose en Anglais').

The shortcomings of the method are already becoming obvious, and will be dealt with more fully in the next chapter, but it is only fair to say that the Direct Method was not always as it is sometimes popularly represented, nor did its advocates always believe or practise what is sometimes ascribed to them.

It is sometimes believed, for example, that the Direct Method school condemned translation of all kinds at all times. Now although it is true that the English extremists, for instance, often refused to speak a word of English in their lessons, even giving expositions of grammar in L2, this was a later development rather than part of the original *credo* of the reformers. What Viëtor was attacking was only translation *in eine fremde Sprache* – into the foreign language – and he makes it clear that he at least saw an important role for translation into the mother tongue as an aid to understanding and as a test of comprehension:

> At school the teacher reads a short passage slowly and clearly and as often as necessary, while the pupils' books remain closed. The teacher translates into the vernacular those words not already known and whose meaning is not obvious from the context, leaving the full translation to be evolved by the class . . . others then read and translate . . . When the teacher has thus made doubly sure that the pupils understand the meaning of individual words . . . (Viëtor, 1882, pp. 23–4)

Gilbert (1953) points out that the earliest advocates of the reader as of central importance certainly saw translation into L1 as an essential part of the learning process (pp. 4–5), and most of them believed with Jespersen (1904) that 'the same piece is then translated word by word by the teacher . . . and afterwards in the same way by the pupil' (p. 89), although in his view 'Translation is omitted as soon as there is no danger of miscomprehension' (ibid.).

It is sometimes said, also, that the major fallacy of the Direct Method school was a belief that L2 could and should be learned in the way by which L1 was acquired, that is

> by a sort of total-immersion technique which did not grade or structure its material adequately, and which apparently saw no contradiction in comparing the *acquisition* of L1 (by a highly motivated learner with a pupil–teacher ratio of 1 to 1 or better) with the *teaching* of L2 (to an unmotivated class of 35 pupils,

within a school situation and a framework, in those days, of perhaps five 40-minute periods per week). (Richardson, 1981, p. 1)

Now whilst there might appear to be some evidence for this view in Gouin (1880, chapter XI), and in quotations from the Direct Methodists taken out of context (for example 'in theory he [Max Walter] would like to approach as near as possible to the "natural way of language learning followed by the very young child when learning his mother tongue"' (Gilbert, 1954, p. 12) and 'On the other hand, the natural way of learning languages is by practice. That is the way one's native language is acquired' (Jespersen, 1904, p. 110)), in fact the Direct Methodists were far too well acquainted with the nature of language ever to think that this was possible. Their emphasis on phonetics and their abolition of translation from L1 to L2 showed clearly that they well understood that L2 simply could not be learned entirely in the same way as L1, if only because of the interference of the different sounds and structures already acquired as L1.

What the Direct Methodists really had in mind was that their pupils could be exposed to L2 in something approaching the way in which the child was exposed to L1: as Franke puts it in *Die praktische Spracherlernung*, 'He [the child] uses language as the form of his thought – concept and word are learned together. It is a process of learning in and through the language' (Gilbert, 1954, p. 10). Franke's next sentence makes it quite clear that he knew the difference between acquiring L1 and learning L2: 'But we have far less time and opportunity in schools than the little child has in learning his mother tongue – we must replace quantity by intensity' (ibid.). Jespersen too, cited above, merely had in mind that the pupil should acquire the structures unconsciously before being required to learn the grammatical rule for them:

The pupil becomes acquainted with the elements and absorbs them, as it were, into his soul in their entirety before he is consciously able to separate and account for the single parts and their special relations; he forms complete sentences without knowing which is the subject and which the object; he gradually finds out that he has to give each part of the sentence its correct endings without knowing anything about tense or case (Jespersen, 1904, p. 111), [just] as the English boy who has often heard superlatives like *hardest, cleanest, highest* etc. does not need any rule to be able to construct forms like *purest, ugliest, dirtiest* of his own accord. (ibid., p. 116)

There is far more justification for the charge that the Direct Methodists failed to grade and structure their material adequately. What they 'seem to have missed completely is the principle of selection, grading, and controlled presentation of linguistic items, first vocabulary and then structures. They did not make word counts, nor did they arrive at the idea of a basic vocabulary; they did not grade the structures of the languages they taught for controlled and systematic presentation' (Harding, 1967, p. 7). They plunged their pupils directly into a flood of living language which was quite bewildering for some pupils, and chose reading passages of such difficulty and complexity that they were forced to do two things which were pedagogically unsound and a contradiction of their ideals: they were forced to translate every word several times in order to ensure comprehension; and they thought it necessary to embark upon excessive repetition, sentence by sentence, which must have been boring to the majority of pupils. Gilbert (1954) says that this trend runs throughout the whole of the nineteenth century: 'Jacotot, Hamilton, Robertson, Prendergast and many others all chose passages which were excessively difficult, and worked through them slowly in their different ways' (p. 13).

The trend did not end with the nineteenth century. As late as the mid-1930s the writer was reading in class, in his second year of French, material which he was later to reject as far too difficult for possible use in the O-level examination of the 1960s. Yet this was the latest edition of J.E. Mansion's *Contes et Récits*, first published in 1911, which had by then been 'still further simplified' as to style and vocabulary (Mansion, 1934, Preface, p. 5).

Yet even here the best of the Direct Method teachers were aware of their deficiencies, and made some efforts to correct them: although Walter's material, for instance, was impossibly difficult for his first-year syllabus, his second-year is much more satisfactory and interesting. Jespersen (1904) too understood that

There must be gradual progress in difficulty, that is, the material for instruction must be arranged in stages from very easy to more and more difficult things (p. 14), [and] Now since it is also better, as we have said, to learn five absolutely necessary words than

twenty-five of less importance, it is of course the duty of the
editors of text-books in large part to revise the selections which
they reprint, so that that which is of linguistic value for the pupils
may be cultivated at the expense of everything that is unusual or
odd. (p. 31)

The failure of the textbook writers and editors to do as Jespersen
suggests perpetuated well into the twentieth century the major
defect of the Direct Method – this lack of selection and grading.
This should not be allowed to detract from what is otherwise an
amazing achievement: as Gilbert (1954) says of Walter, he

> attained, both in the theory and practice of language teaching, an
> ultra-modern position. We are still trying to realise in practice
> what he recommends in theory, and so largely carried out, even
> in 1888, in his classroom teaching . . . A close reading of
> Walter's and Klinghardt's pamphlets would go far to dispel three
> illusions widely entertained about the early reformers; namely,
> that their teaching was superficial and not thorough, that they
> neglected grammar, and that they never used translation and so
> confused their pupils. None of these criticisms is true, at least of
> the German reformers. Many eyewitness accounts have,
> moreover, been given of their classroom teaching, all of which
> testify to its soundness and practical success. (p. 15)

## The Compromise Method

It is important to keep the 'three illusions' (above) specified by
Gilbert very much in mind when assessing the contribution to
language teaching of the so-called 'Compromise Method'. The
Direct Method was not in itself superficial or lacking in
thoroughness, although there were and are of course teachers (of all
schools of thought) whose work lacks depth. The early Direct
Methodists did not neglect grammar, nor did they ban all
translation – if some of their later, more extreme, disciples did, one
could with equal validity argue that extremists of the other school
also neglected the true teaching of grammar and that they banished,
say, all oral work in the foreign language – though this might be
thought today to be of more importance than translation.

The difficulty lay in the fact that a successful teacher by the

Direct Method needed a competence in his language, a stamina and energy, an imagination, a capacity for working himself and his pupils hard, and the ability and time in which to create his own materials and courses – since these were not yet available – which were beyond the capacities of all but a very gifted few. But this does not invalidate the method itself, nor should it have been made the grounds for calling for a modification of the method, or one 'so clearly developed that it could be used by the average or less than average teacher with the average or less than average class' (Harding, 1967, p. 8). If the method was good and sound in itself – and it was – then teachers should have been encouraged and adequately trained to use it, as they were in Austria and Prussia, and they should have been supplied with the courses and materials necessary for an implementation of it. Instead the next development, in England at least, was a reversion to a grammar-translation approach with as much attention being paid to oral work as could conveniently be achieved. This of course varied from teacher to teacher, and still does; it is to be feared that whilst the Palmers and Collinses of the world used the new-old, simplified and much more structured and selected materials in a way which brought in the maximum amount of oral work possible, many other teachers (perhaps less confident in their mastery of the language, or less convinced of the necessity for its use in the classroom, or simply less extrovert in their personality) would revert to the old translation methods and the formal grammar teaching of the pre-revolutionary era.

Some would maintain that during the period between the two world wars a large number of teachers 'modified' the Direct Method so as to meet the practical requirements of the conditions in their own schools and, whilst continuing to implement the main principles of the Direct Method, that is, to teach through oral practice in the language and to ban all translation into the target language, nevertheless discarded with success some of the more extreme ideas of some of the later enthusiasts for the method. Thus Palmer (1917, p. 84) had referred to the 'fallacy' of the Direct Method, namely that it was possible to explain everything without recourse to translation into L1. As he rightly pointed out, some of the Direct Method explanations of the extremists were time-consuming, cumbersome and unacceptably ambiguous; it was sometimes said that a Direct Methodist would spend much of a lesson jumping over desks and flapping imaginary fins rather than admit that *un saumon* meant *a salmon* in English. It had always been self-evident, also, that concepts like *cependant* and *néanmoins* should be translated without more ado rather than made the subject of 'explanations'. But it should be pointed out that this was not the 'fallacy' nor indeed any part of the Direct Method as applied so successfully by the school in Germany, where translation into L1 had always been used extensively. And if 'In the period between the two world wars a considerable body of language teachers in this country successfully adapted the Direct Method to the practical requirements of work in the schools' (Harding, 1967, p. 10) it needs to be added that before the First World War the unmodified Direct Method proper (that is, devoid of the extreme ideas of some later, English, adherents) had been proved to be just that, namely successful in meeting the practical requirements of the schools. (See Gilbert, 1954, p. 15, quoted above).

What was proposed by H.F. Collins (1934) and approved by, for instance, the Incorporated Association of Assistant Masters (1929, p. 75) was

> a compromise method, one that does not scorn to explain a real difficulty in lucid English, but one that never loses grip of the foreign language, that uses it whenever possible and aims at pronunciation, conversation, and grammatical accuracy in written work . . . Each lesson should aim at affording some practice in all these sections: to isolate any must tend to destroy linguistic fabric. If we are teaching German, let us teach as Germanly as possible; let us consciously create in our classrooms a German atmosphere. Let Henry become Heinrich and Mary Marie, and let them all hear class directions in the language they are trying to acquire; but let them proceed step by step under the wise guidance of a teacher who will not befog them in the name of some pedagogical shibboleth and, when passive voice and modal verbs come along, will not put them off with meaningless German explanations when clear English, in a few minutes, would make foundations secure. (Collins, 1934, p. 419)

Collins' coursebook (Collins, 1929) had appeared five years previously and might therefore be assumed to embody this teaching philosophy and to provide the kind of teaching materials which the new method would require. (It will be remembered that one of the major difficulties encountered by the early Direct Methodists was that there were no such materials available to them, and that when they began to produce their own these were insufficiently structured, impossibly difficult in the early stages, and lacking in selection and grading.) Collins' books are highly structured, carefully graded, and provide for ample repetition and practice. They were used with signal success by Collins himself, who was a sincere believer in the necessity for oral work in abundance, and by a generation of disciples of the Direct Method who used them – *faute de mieux*, perhaps, because there were no other courses available which were thought to offer as much as they did.

The paradox was that Collins knew from personal experience, and none better, the nature, potentialities and limitations of the Direct Method.

> The purely Direct Method can be safely adopted provided the right type of teacher and class is forthcoming. The method by its very nature presupposes a teacher of immense vitality, of robust health, and one endowed with real fluency in the modern language he teaches. He must be resourceful in the way of gesture and tricks of facial expression, able to sketch rapidly on the blackboard, and, in the long teaching day, he must be proof against linguistic fatigue. (Collins, 1934, p. 419)

Yet an examination of his coursebooks would not suggest that Collins had any connection with Oral or Direct Method, nor that this was merely a 'compromise' with the ideal. Any Direct Method element in the teaching had to be supplied by the teacher; the books themselves merely supply reading passages, explanations of grammatical rules, exercises, vocabulary lists and verb paradigms which could all, of course, be 'learned' without a word of meaningful French being spoken. And whereas the original reading passages of the old Direct Methodists had been too complicated, too difficult, too French, Collins writes in a simplified, diluted style which can only be described as contrived French, scrupulously avoiding anything extraneous to the point being taught, for example:

'Bonjour, Marcel. Marcel, où es-tu?'
'Je suis dans la salle de classe.'

'Es-tu l'élève?'
'Oui, Monsieur, et vous êtes le professeur.'

(Collins, 1929, I, p. 1)

bringing into the passage every irregular plural if that is the grammatical point being taught (ibid., p. 34), and dragging in numerous uses of both *pouvoir* and *vouloir* when *they* are the point at issue.

Because of this it is *possible* to use the passages to teach grammar inductively, but this is difficult when on the page immediately following there is much grammatical jargon, a statement of the rule, and tabloid grammar in the shape of verb paradigms and tables of irregular verbs.

Most significant of all, there are vocabularies of both kinds at the back of the books, and from the very first lesson of Book I there are sentences and a connected passage in English to be translated into French. This was not a compromise with the Direct Method: it was a reversion to Grammar-Translation.

## Audio-visual and Audio-lingual Techniques

A description and a critique of these are developed in a subsequent chapter; the aim of this section is no more than to locate them in the history of language teaching, and to suggest how much they owe to Direct Method traditions, and in what respects they may be fundamentally different.

The point is often made that the modern-language teaching 'revolutions' each tended to have their bases in what is thought to be a new view of the nature and function of language (for example Richardson, 1981, p. 1). So it may be said that the Direct Method was based on the then new science of phonetics and on the views that language was sounds, not letters; that the unit was the sentence, not the word; that translation into the foreign language was inappropriate and harmful and had nothing to do with the *learning* of L2; that a language can be learned without the formal rules of grammar and that grammar should therefore be taught by inductive methods.

To the great credit of the Direct Methodists it must be said that they started from this new 'philosophy' of language, which they stated clearly and logically from the outset (Viëtor, 1882;

Franke, 1884) and whose tenets they then applied systematic-ally, consistently, and with great thoroughness to the teaching of foreign languages. (See for instance the activities of the 'Neuphilologenverband', mentioned by Gilbert, 1954, p. 11). Perhaps the support for and the success of the methodologies which followed the Direct Method revolution would have been longer-lasting if they too had always begun from a carefully thought-out and clearly stated case, and proceeded with equal clarity of thought and similar conviction to their associated rationale and related teaching philosophy.

Clarity of thought in the expression of their rationale is precisely what is most lacking in the movements which came after the Direct Method. Harding (1967), whilst approving in the main of the 'Oral or Compromise Method' (pp. 12, 36) also points out that 'the difficulty is that the result remained something of a compromise, *without a clearly defined theory of its own*' (my italics) (ibid., p. 55). And the position with regard to audio-visual and audio-lingual techniques is no better.

It is generally accepted that these techniques have their threefold base first in behaviourist psychology and the belief that learning a foreign language consists of 'acquérir avant tout un ensemble d'habitudes, un certain nombre de réflexes, qui permettront de communiquer' (Jerman, 1965, p. 41); second in the science of linguistics; and third in technological developments which have made possible the application of linguistics and psychology to the classroom teaching of languages.

What one would have liked to see is a clear statement of the rationale, followed by a logical application of its tenets via the new aids now available, and with a clear understanding of the principles being applied and of the role, purpose and limitations of those new aids. In practice, the position reflects anything but logicality and clarity.

The confusion of thought underlying the audio-visual rationale has been fully dealt with elsewhere (for example by Cammish (1975, pp. 220–1) and by Richardson (1966, p. 113; 1975, pp. 194-8; 1981, pp. 1–2). The latter points out that there seem to be contradictions both as between one advocate and another, and within the thinking of individual experts themselves.

The most unfortunate consequence of this is that if the acknowledged experts cannot agree as to the rationale of their method, either with one another or with themselves, then their confusion and illogicalities may be communicated to the practising teacher, who may then be unable to use the method because he does not understand it, or may become sufficiently perplexed and frustrated to abandon it after introducing it.

At least the teachers who abandoned the Direct Method could not claim that they did so because of a faulty exposition of the method. The ideas underlying the method had been clearly stated and, in the hands of gifted practical teachers, proved to be successful. What discouraged some teachers was their own lack of the physical stamina and nervous energy which the Direct Method demanded, and the lack of suitable materials for the implementation of the method.

What is most interesting to speculate upon is what might have happened if the Direct Methodists had been able to dispose of the sophisticated linguistic research and technological advances which have since the Second World War given teachers the tape-recorder, frequency-counts and scientifically graded materials. 'The Direct Methodists had some excellent ideas; in fact, they were right most of the time' (Harding, 1967, p. 54). They were indeed. 'But their ideas were rather extreme and need modifying in practice. This modification is what the Compromise or Oral Method attempted to undertake' (ibid.).

As was stated above (pp. 30–4), it is difficult to see how the Compromise Method (if that is what was exemplified in Collins' textbooks) did attempt that modification. Whether the Oral Method did, depends on one's definition of that essentially personal variant of the Compromise Method – that is, on the extent to which one was prepared to compromise on the amount of oral work undertaken; on the ways of teaching vocabulary; on the place of translation not only from but into the foreign language.

Yet if the Direct Methodists had possessed the equipment and the scientific research and the materials underlying the audio-visual theories, there would have been no need for any compromise. There is a school of thought which maintains that all the sound ideas of the 1980s were in fact inherent in the Reform Method of a hundred years previously, and the next chapter will examine the methods used by the Direct Methodists in greater detail, and endeavour to point out how many of these are still highly relevant today, and how close the pioneers were (sometimes unconsciously, or by intuition only) to what we have come to regard as some of the truths about language teaching.

# References

Cammish, N.K. (1975) 'Using A/V Materials' in A.W. Hornsey (ed.), *Handbook for Modern Language Teachers*, Methuen, London, pp. 219–28

Collins, H.F. (1929) *A French Course for Schools*, Macmillan, London, Part I 1929, Part II 1930, Part III 1931

———— (1934) 'Modern Languages' in (Lord) Eustace Percy (ed.), *The Yearbook of Education 1934*, Evans, London

Franke, F. (1884) *Die praktische Spracherlernung auf Grund der Psychologie und der Physiologie der Sprache dargestellt*, Altenburg, Heilbronn

Gilbert, M. (1953, 1954, 1955) 'The Origins of the Reform Movement in Modern Language Teaching in England', *(Durham) Research Review, 4, 5, 6*

Gouin, F. (1880) *L'art d'enseigner et d'étudier les langues*, referred to in the third edition of *The Art of Teaching and Studying Languages*, translated by H. Swan and V. Bétis, George Philip, London, 1892

Harding, D.H. (1967) *The New Pattern of Language Teaching*, Longman, London

Hedgecock, F.A. (1926) *The Active French Course*, University of London Press, London

Hiley, R.W. (1887) in *Journal of Education, IX*, 308, quoted by Gilbert (1953), p. 4

Hodgson, F.M. (1955) *Learning Modern Languages*, Routledge and Kegan Paul, London

Incorporated Association of Assistant Masters in Secondary Schools (1929) *Memorandum on the Teaching of Modern Languages*, University of London Press, London

Jerman, J. (1965) 'Audio-Visual Methods in Modern Language Teaching' in B. Dutton (ed.), *A Guide to Modern Language Teaching Methods*, Cassell, London, pp. 3–83

Jespersen, O. (1904) *How to Teach a Foreign Language*, George Allen and Unwin, London

Mansion, J.E. (1934) *Contes et Récits*, Harrap, London

Palmer, H.E. (1917) *The Scientific Study and Teaching of Languages*, Harrap, London

Richardson, G. (1966) 'A Survey of Five Audio-Visual Courses', *Modern Languages, XLVII* (3), 112–13

———— (1975) 'Criteria for Good Teaching Pictures' in A.W. Hornsey (ed.), *Handbook for Modern Language Teachers*, Methuen, London, pp. 193–204

———— (1981) 'A Hundred Years of Language Revolutions' in G. Richardson (ed.), *Modern Language Teaching in the 1980s* (Aspects of Education 25), University of Hull Institute of Education, Hull

Viëtor, W. (1882) *Der Sprachunterricht muß umkehren!* O.R. Reisland, Leipzig. The references in English are from the unpublished translation by A.D. Christie and G. Richardson

Wilkins, D.A. (1974) *Second-Language Learning and Teaching*, Edward Arnold, London

# 3 'DIRECT METHOD' TEACHING

## G. Richardson

The early German pioneers of the Reform Method have left detailed and well documented accounts of their theories and of their practical teaching; so too have their English counterparts. We know from their pamphlets, lectures, books and conferences what Walter and Klinghardt in Germany, Widgery and MacGowan in England, believed and taught. (See Gilbert, 1954, pp. 9–18; Jespersen, 1904, chapter V; Viëtor, 1882, pp. 23–5.)

They all insisted on the primacy of phonetics as a basis for language teaching; on the importance of oral practice and the necessity for making the reader the centre of instruction; on the principle of direct association between the thing referred to and the new word in the foreign language; on the teaching of grammar by inductive methods, and on the avoidance of the written or printed word until the pupil's pronunciation was so sound that it would not be influenced by seeing how the words were spelt.

Gilbert (1955, p. 9) considers that by 1912 the movement had perhaps reached its peak, and although the impetus provided by the pioneers continued throughout the 1920s and even, despite the call for a 'Compromise Method', in isolated instances into the mid-1930s, the 'Direct Method' lesson of the 1930s, of which the writer had personal experience, was in many ways very different from those of thirty years previously. The emphasis on accurate pronunciation was still there, though the daily lesson no longer began with five minutes' practice of the sounds of French in isolation, often from vowel charts such as Viëtor's. Isolated practitioners still retained these, just as occasionally one would encounter a teacher who used phonetic transcription only, for the first term or two (Hedgecock's 'Active French Course' had a phonetic transcription of the first ten lessons, and was certainly in use up to 1957, when it was last reprinted), but it was much more common now for the pronunciation practice to take the form of an elementary conversation – on the weather, the date, time, school day, last Saturday's football match, etc. – which was at the same time a 'warm-up' session in which the class attuned its ear to the sounds of French and switched from the memories of the previous lesson to the French atmosphere of the present one. Several things were understood by the class from the outset: only French would be spoken in the lesson; all answers had to be in the form of complete sentences; what was important was not the provision of a mathematically correct piece of information in one's answers, but the composition of a reply that no one else had yet given. Thus 'Quelle heure est-il?', posed at exactly 10 a.m., would elicit the answers 'Il est dix heures'; 'Il est dix heures deux'; 'Il n'est pas encore dix heures'; 'Mais si! Il est dix heures passées!'; 'Il est dix heures moins une'; 'Il est presque dix heures'; 'Il est dix heures du matin'; and so on.

So long as a single hand remained up the teacher would go on accepting answers, and commending them, in rapid succession. Certainly classes fortunate enough to be introduced to this technique never had the impression that a 35-minute period of oral work divided among 35 pupils worked out at one minute per pupil, which would have been manifestly ludicrous. Every question was listened to by everyone; everyone instantly prepared at least one answer in his mind. No one was allowed to sit back when his answer had been given; nor was the excuse that someone else had just said the sentence you had prepared kindly received. (There was a robustness of manner, a ruthlessness even, that went with the indispensable Direct Method vigour referred to by Collins (see p. 33) and which ensured that language lessons were very hard work for all concerned.)

Such rapid-fire questioning would reveal the class's pronunciation weaknesses, and after a time the teacher would start to remedy these, either individually – for example 'C'est ça! Mais répéte: *une!*' or in chorus, for example 'La classe – répétez: *une!*', but in either case without reprimand and without impatience, relying on the pupils' ear and powers of mimicry for a closer imitation of the teacher's own perfect [y].

It will be seen from the above that for these teachers, as for Viëtor, language still consisted 'of sounds, not letters', and that the unit of language was still considered to be the sentence, not the isolated word or even phrase. We shall return to a consideration of these ideas when we have seen how the Direct Method teachers dealt with a reading passage.

**Exploiting a Reading Passage**

The teacher would first read through the whole passage, fairly slowly, giving the class time to get the main gist of the story or description, without being expected at this stage to understand completely. Then he might read it again, with the class repeating each phrase, and practise a few phonetic difficulties. Then he would read the first paragraph, if short, or the first sentence or two only, and ask individuals to repeat them. Finally he would ask, 'Quels sont les mots que vous ne comprenez pas?' (Not, be it noted, 'Est-ce qu'il y a des mots que vous ne comprenez pas?' since that might have inhibited a shy pupil, or one too proud or too insecure to ask something he thought he was expected to know already.) The implication was that of course there were difficulties in the passage, but that all the class had to do was ask for an explanation of them, when it would be given.

As soon as a pupil replied, 'Je ne comprends pas X,' or 'Que veut dire X?' the teacher would give a 'Direct Method' explanation, using two or three or more of the techniques outlined in the previous chapter (see p. 26), so as to make absolutely sure that all the class understood. Nothing was ever translated into English except perhaps abstract concepts like *malgré, parce que, cependant*; and even here translation was the last resort. There must have been much imperfectly understood material, and there was indeed no insistence on knowing *exactly* what was intended by such words – it was thought to be enough to know approximately what they meant, and the context in which they might be used. The similarity with the *explication* stage of an audio-visual unit, with its equally ambiguous insistence upon comprehension without the intervention of the mother tongue if at all possible, and without direct translation (except in the very early stages of TAVOR) is obvious, and merely another example of the surprising modernity of much of the Direct Method rationale.

So far, this virtual banning of translation of any kind is the only departure from the Reform Method as practised by, say, Walter. (See Gilbert, 1954, p. 14.) There is the same insistence on the reading passage as the centre of the lesson, the same frequent repetition sentence by sentence, the same insistence on high standards of pronunciation, the same unconscious learning – simply by hearing it spoken so frequently – of language material which was later to prove invaluable. All the classroom business being conducted in French, the difference between *tu* and *vous*, between *livre* and *cahier*, between definite and indefinite article, were absorbed from the outset without grammatical explanation and without conscious effort.

The next stage in the lesson, too, was pure Walter: 'Finally, they know the whole sentence off by heart and can answer the questions rapidly' (Gilbert, 1954, p. 14). This teacher's next command was 'Repassez le morceau! Vous avez deux minutes!' In those two minutes, the class knew, they had to learn as much of the passage as would be necessary to enable them to understand and answer any question the teacher might ask. In a word, they had to learn it off by heart – not parrot-fashion, not so that they could repeat the whole thing word by word given their cue, but so that they could on demand instantly frame a complete sentence embodying the material studied.

At the end of the two minutes – or a little less – the teacher would ask, 'Pour la dernière fois: il y a des mots que vous ne comprenez pas? Vous n'avez qu'à le dire!' Even at this stage, when all should have been known, he was prepared to undertake another explanation if necessary. What he was not prepared to tolerate was that any pupil should remain silent about a difficulty, and thus allow him to embark upon his question-and-answer routine whilst there was still a single word which was not understood.

The questioning was exhaustive, and exhausting. A simple sentence like 'Au rez-de-chaussée il y a une petite boulangerie, fermée depuis sept heures du soir' would give rise to questions like

Où est-ce qu'il y a une boulangerie?
Quelle sorte de boulangerie est-ce?
Est-ce une grande boulangerie?
Où se trouve la boulangerie?
La boulangerie est au premier étage?
La boulangerie est ouverte, n'est-ce pas?
Depuis quand la boulangerie est-elle fermée?
Est-ce que la boulangerie est fermée depuis sept heures du matin?

And the answers being in complete sentences meant that at least a dozen pupils would be able to reply with expressions like

Il y a une boulangerie au rez-de-chaussée.

C'est une petite boulangerie.

Non, ce n'est pas une grande boulangerie – c'est une petite boulangerie.

C'est une boulangerie fermée.

La boulangerie se trouve au rez-de-chaussée.

Non, la boulangerie est au rez-de-chaussée.

Non, elle est fermée.

La boulangerie est fermée depuis sept heures.

Non, la boulangerie est fermée depuis sept heures du soir.

In addition, the whole class had had to listen to every question, understand it, and prepare at least one correct answer for themselves, since all the teacher's questions were directed to the entire class, never to an individual nominated in advance of the question.

It is obvious how extremely modern the technique was. What the Direct Methodists were doing, had they but known it, was drilling a series of structures and enforcing repetition of vocabulary items which they were concerned to teach. Moreover, they were doing it in the most efficient manner available to them, the language laboratory not yet having been invented. Indeed, it is possible that this live, interesting, even exciting exchange of sentences in the foreign language with another person was a better way of learning than is nowadays the recording of student responses on the student tape in the laboratory: Rivers (1964, p. 163) points out that 'language communication involves a relationship between individuals and not merely the repetition of phrases and practising of structures', and to those who would point out that these pupils' replies were unnatural, forced, artificial – because no one normally replies in complete sentences – three replies are possible.

In the first place, this was the only way available to the teachers of the day of *compelling* the student to practise the structure or the lexis. To have accepted more 'natural' answers like 'Oui', 'Non', 'Au rez-de-chaussée' would have been profitless. They can come when the language has been learned.

Second, the complete sentences did not strike the *class* as artificial, cumbersome, or unnatural, if only because they had not as yet learned any other way of expressing these ideas. To them, these sentences were correct French – as indeed they were – created by themselves, from what they had learned. They really were speaking French, and thinking in French, and the sense of achievement was enormous. To the English beginner, everything that is French is fresh and new – a fact which has to be taken into account when 'teaching' literature, since the beginner is not always able to spot the clichéd, the hackneyed, the doggerel, simply because to him, hearing it for the first time, it is new, original, attractive. As Jespersen (1904, pp. 26–7) says, 'that which amuses a French child of five or six years may often amuse an English child of ten or eleven or even more, because in the foreign language it gets the charm that is always connected with the unknown'.

And finally, if anyone could be excused for finding the exercise boring, it would be the teacher, who was not interested in the content of the class's replies nearly so much as in their form. But the class certainly was not bored. So far as they knew, they were putting valid, living French together, and they were thereby acquiring the most valuable gift that any teacher could give his pupils – the complete conviction that even at their stage, with so much still to learn, they can 'do it'; that they are in control, and really speaking French, without any need to ask for a word or ever to drop into English. We might now label the process mere 'rehearsal' instead of 'performance' ( a point to which we return on p. 48), but to them it was the real thing.

**The Teaching of Grammar**

The teaching of grammar in the class of which the writer had personal experience was a strange compromise. The course book in use was similar in layout to Collins' famous 'French Course for Schools' in that the grammar was carefully graded and presented systematically, with numerous examples of the point at issue contained in the text of the reading passage, but a clear statement of the rule in English following the passage, and verb paradigms to be learned.

The method of this individual teacher was to draw the attention of the class to the examples of the new rule in the text, in French, and then to formulate the rule, again in French, and to follow this by abundant oral practice of the rule in action. The previously established question-and-answer routine, and the insistence upon every answer being in the form of a complete sentence, made drilling easy. The structure 'il faut quelque chose à quelqu'un pour + (infinitive)', for instance, was consolidated by forcing the entire class to answer, one after another, such questions as

> Qu'est-ce qu'il me faut pour écrire?
> Qu'est-ce qu'il me faut pour faire du café?
> Qu'est-ce qu'il vous faut pour aller d'ici à la gare?
> Qu'est-ce qu'il me faut pour voir clair?
> Combien de temps vous faut-il pour aller à l'école?

and the writer has no recollection of such rules in English (nor, it must be said, of the formulation given to them in French!) but only of what the structure sounded like in use in a correct context.

In retrospect it seems likely that the Head of Department was a believer in the Compromise Method, and that this class teacher was one of the last survivors of a more Direct Method, who was resolved to put his own gloss on the methods recommended, whilst continuing to use the only course book available. Be that as it may, grammar was not neglected, and verb paradigms were certainly learned for homework, and tested – in French, of course – next day by written answers to instructions like 'Ecrivez la deuxième personne du pluriel du présent du subjonctif du verbe . . .' Doubtless the conditions laid down by Collins (1934, p. 419) for a successful use of the Direct Method were fulfilled in this case; the teacher was quite exceptional and the class were what Collins calls 'bright'. They had also learned a great deal of complicated grammatical analysis, in English, in preparation for the 'scholarship' examinations before proceeding to secondary school, and in addition to being 'bright' they were highly motivated and extremely competitive.

In such circumstances of course any method would be successful in achieving its aims: in this case however what was learned by the method seemed to transfer successfully to totally different techniques whose aims were quite different. Thus, the structure learned as 'Il faut + expression of time à quelqu'un pour faire quelquechose' was still there and ready for use when a year later the class was called upon by a different teacher to translate from L1 into L2 for the very first time. 'A voyage which Magellan's companions had taken a year to accomplish' emerged instantly as 'Voyage pour faire lequel il avait fallu aux compagnons de Magellan un an', and was rightly annotated as 'clumsy' in the margin. But the important thing was that the question of admitting defeat, or of asking for a word, or of trying to use a dictionary or an E-F vocabulary, just did not arise. What had been acquired was something more valuable even than the very commendable body of French that had been learned, namely a view of language and of language learning and of language use which was already incorruptible.


**Free Composition**

For all the Direct Methodists the natural follow-up from a lesson in the coursebook was a free composition. Having established their question-and-answer routines from the outset, they had almost immediately at their disposal the possibility of an oral free composition; all they had to do was to ask the right questions in the right sequence, and insist on the replies being in complete sentences, as they always had. They were highly skilled, however, in framing their questions so as to elicit the most useful reply, and they were not afraid of 'feeding' the correct reply to the class in the questions asked.

Thus, if their aim was that the pupils should be able first to say, and then to write, for example, 'Nous allons jouer au football cet après-midi,' their question would not be 'Qu'est-ce que vous allez faire cet après-midi?' (since that might have suggested a reply beginning 'Nous allons faire . . .') but instead 'Quand est-ce que vous allez jouer au football?' or 'Qui va jouer au football cet après-midi?'

The free composition lesson would begin with exhaustive question-and-answer work of this kind, to which the class were already well accustomed from their reading-passage lessons; far more questions would be asked, and far more answers received, than could figure in the final composition. Then a selection only of the questions would be asked again, and this time the replies would be written up on the blackboard by the teacher, or by a pupil who could write fast enough. The whole composition was then learned off by heart by repeated reading aloud of a section at a time, and written up for homework. Pupils were discouraged from adding to the agreed composition, and forbidden of course to look anything up in a dictionary. This 'free' composition was in fact rigidly controlled, and consisted only of writing out what had been heard many times, seen written already, and learned by heart.

It was in a direct line of descent from the Direct Method pioneers and their insistence on oral work first, and then on writing only what had been heard and said: 'The pupil must only write down what he has spoken and read correctly' (Walter, quoted by Gilbert, 1954,

p. 15). 'Never allow any child to read or write any exercise that he has not heard, not repeated, not assimilated' (Gouin, 1892, p. 138). It was based also on two other tenets basic to a correct view of what free composition is; first that any attempt to think of an English sentence and then to translate it into French is doomed to failure; and second that statistical accuracy in the composition was less important than using an approximation, or if need be of saying something quite different, so long as it was correct French.

The Direct Method question-and-answer technique came under fire from the 'mental discipline' advocates, who complained that such a method 'spoon-fed' the pupils, making things too easy for them. It had not yet been accepted that no teacher can make things 'too easy' for his charges, and Viëtor's riposte that if we really wanted to make things difficult for a class, why not call in their pens and paper and issue stone tablets and chisels? (Viëtor, 1882, p. 9) had not struck home. In fact, this criticism continued to be voiced for many years to come: one of the commonest criticisms levelled at Richardson and Fletcher's (1951) *Histoires Illustrées*, which re-introduced the old Direct Method technique, was that it gave the pupils the correct sentence 'on a plate'.

## Modernity of the Direct Method

The essential modernity of the Direct Methodists' views on the teaching of grammar has been referred to elsewhere (see pp. 25 and 42, and Richardson, 1967, pp. 7–9). What is particularly interesting however is the extent to which the Direct Methodists had thought out their theories in detail, and arrived at an expression of their beliefs which differs only in vocabulary from ours today.

It is plain that Viëtor for instance was highly critical of mechanical, repetitive drills which could be completed without thought on the part of the learner (Viëtor, 1882, p. 22), though he would not have called them repetition or mechanical drills. Similarly Jespersen (1904, p. 119) comes very close to our concept of a substitution drill in all but name:

> For instance, the teacher can write on the blackboard a sentence like 'Je donne un sou à Alfred' and get the pupils to conjugate it through all the persons. In the beginning he might also write down all the forms of the verb, one under the other; they are not

to be committed to memory, but merely furnish a scheme, which the pupils are to fill out by inserting the correct pronouns before, and *un sou à Alfred* after the verb. Then the next step is to let the pupils use other words instead of *un sou* and *Alfred*, so that pupil A says, for instance, 'Je donne un centime à Paul', B 'Tu donnes un franc à Jean' and so on.

Equally modern were the Direct Method views on the necessity for correct pronunciation, on the primacy of the spoken word, on the learning of grammar inductively, on the avoidance of translation as far as possible, and so on.

Yet it seems valid to argue that the Direct Methodists were equally modern in their approach to a much wider and more important issue, namely that of the motivation of their classes. In this connection they were in part working in the dark, or unconsciously; Viëtor wished to ease the burden of learning on the young pupil, and Jespersen too believed that language learning ought to be fun rather than a chore or a discipline, but their thinking preceded by half a century and more the linguistic and psychological research which has begun to reveal what it is that impels the learner of L1 to acquire his mother tongue.

Eric Hawkins (1980, 1981) has analysed the theory of the 'speech act' enunciated by Austin (1962) and developed by Searle (1969), and related this to the 'two levels of communication' described by Dodson (1978). He points out that in a true speech act the issuing of an utterance is at the same time the performance of an action, and that 'The motor that propels language acquisition seems to be the drive to "do things with words" as Austin puts it' (Hawkins, 1981, p. 210). If the language transacted serves no function for the learner, does not enable him to achieve some purpose, to 'change the world' in some way, it does not consist of speech acts and is for Searle not 'serious language':

'Only "serious language"', Searle says, 'consists of speech acts having "force". I contrast "serious" utterances with play acting, teaching a language, reciting poems, practising, pronunciation, etc.' (Searle, 1969, p.57). Exchanges in the foreign language classroom, then, for Searle, are not 'serious' language. They may have propositional content or reference and be susceptible of grammatical analysis but they are not uttered with intention to mean. (Hawkins, 1981, p. 210)

Similarly 'Dodson contrasts pupils "using" language (to show teachers that they can use it) and "making use" of language (to communicate a message)' (ibid., pp. 211–12).

What is spoken in the foreign language classroom, then, is merely a 'rehearsal' (of utterances devoid of 'function' and merely being practised in case the need to use them in a true speech act should ever arise), not 'performance'. And the difficulty with such 'rehearsal' utterances is that in them 'the language uttered does not *stick*; it is not retained and has to be repeated tomorrow and tomorrow' (Hawkins, 1980, p. 76).

> And might it be the case that for the average learner the foreign language will not stick unless (as happened when the mother tongue was acquired) it is used to transact real speech acts, conveying personal meanings that matter to the learner? (Hawkins, 1981, p. 244)

Yet to provide the opportunities for meaningful 'speech acts' which will enable the learner to fix the language in his mind is incredibly difficult: 'Much more difficult is to set up situations and activities in which the learner really wants to do things with words' (Hawkins, 1981, p. 245), and may well prove almost impossible for at least two reasons. In the first case, the physical conditions of the classroom and the administrative restrictions of the school may render it unfeasible; and in the second, it may be that in the learning of L2 the speech act in the foreign language is the ultimate objective and the last stage, which may be impossible until the 'rehearsal' stage has been gone through.

Hawkins is aware of this, of course: as he says, 'Dodson (1978) suggests a two-level categorisation: medium-orientated and message-orientated utterances' (Hawkins, 1981, p. 246) and 'sees level 1 (concentrating on the medium) as an essential preliminary to level 2 though ineffective in itself' (ibid., p. 213).

Hawkins also makes it quite clear, in defining his 'four levels of personal meaning or "depth"' (ibid., p. 246) that level 1 is concentration on the medium, level 2 is message *relaying* as rehearsal for eventual performance, level 3 is conveying a personal message but still with an element of rehearsal, and level 4 is 'the level of true "speech acts": real performance'.

This involves:

*Production:* Activities in which the pupil takes the initiative (as in learning the monther tongue) to satisfy his own felt needs and, *because he is faced with a native speaker*, has a compulsion to speak the foreign language. Utterances at this level have 'force', in Searle's terms, and . . . are more likely to lead to retention for that reason. The best example is, perhaps, the pupil, genuinely lost in Paris on his first school visit, who asks the *agent* the way to the Gare St Lazare. He will never forget the ensuing dialogue! (ibid., p. 248)

Now whilst agreeing that 'utterances at this level have "force" . . . and are more likely to lead to retention for that reason', one wonders whether 'retention' could have been altogether absent from the preceding levels 1–3, if the pupil was in fact capable of making his speech act (at level 4) when he got to Paris. In any case, it is generally agreed that level 4 is the ultimate stage in language learning, and the other levels are indispensable: 'The foreign language "apprenticeship", below 16+, is fully justified *as a preparation* or springboard for later rapid acquisition, even if few level 4 transactions are possible' (Hawkins, 1981, p. 268). In very few walks of life is it possible for the trainee to serve his apprenticeship exclusively on the job; most would-be navigators have to spend considerable time plotting imaginary courses on Admiralty Chart 5103 ('Not to be used for navigation; for instructional purposes only') before taking a vessel to sea, for instance, though the motivation which attaches to the 'real thing' is of course very much greater.

In the light of the above, one marvels all the more at 'the extent to which the earlier pioneers successfully progressed *à tâtons* towards important concepts which we, who have the advantage of having inherited their ideas and of having developed our own sophisticated linguistic techniques and modern technology, are only now beginning to expound' (Richardson, 1981, p. 5). They would not have agreed that 'spoken language at this level *must be addressed to a native speaker*' (Hawkins, 1981, p. 268) nor that 'Any use of the foreign language *to an English speaker* involves "suspension of disbelief" to which many pupils react strongly in adolescence' (ibid.). Their classes *had* a teacher who seemed, paradoxically, a 'native' speaker in everything but the accident of birth – that is, an extremely competent linguist who refused to speak English to them at all. Nor did the (willing!) 'suspension of disbelief' present any problems to them: they accepted unquestioningly the fact that all learning within a school must be to some extent artificial, pretence, and make-believe, with conventions that must be accepted if the system of organised learning is to function at all. Knowing that they would not have the opportunity of speaking to a Frenchman for at least another four years, if ever, they were very happy to settle for the nearest approach to that ideal they were ever likely to get.

True it is that adolescents in 1983 'react strongly' to a request for a 'suspension of disbelief', but the generations of the 1920s and 1930s were motivated and conditioned by all sorts of different, often undesirable, forces, and they did *not* react in this way. Their teachers of course are proof against any criticism that their method would not work today: one works within the parameters one is set, and within theirs they achieved considerable success:

> It must be said that in the main this theory works. Pupils so taught do in fact remember the basic grammar when they go abroad and, if they stay there long enough, develop a considerable capacity to speak the language. The theory leaves great opportunity for the enterprising teacher to develop conversational work, use BBC broadcasts, indulge in dramatic work or conduct school parties abroad. Some of the language teaching that has been done in this way has been very successful. (Harding, 1967, p. 56)

In another important way the Direct Methodists were implementing ideas and techniques which were only clearly expressed a hundred years later. Hawkins (1981, chapter 9, 'Foreign language learning in school: rehearsal or performance?') points out that

> We should do everything we can to awaken and develop insight into pattern while providing as much opportunity as possible for pupils to alternate their formal studies of language structure with activities which call for the expression of personal meanings and the solving of personal problems . . . the second objective will be attained if we can devise activities in which the pupils' attention is not focussed on the form of the message but on a real concern

with achieving some result by use of the language *which could not have been achieved by the use of English*.

Now this is precisely what the Direct Methodists achieved (perhaps unconsciously) by their question-and-answer technique: the 'insight into pattern' was provided by the repeated drilling of structures (for example, p. 43: 'il faut quelque chose à quelqu'un pour + infinitive') to the point at which they became automatically available, and at that point the pupils were no longer concentrating on the form of their utterance, but on how to say something interesting to themselves and original in the sense that no other pupil had already said it, whilst using the structure being practised. Another good reason for the Direct Methodists' insistence on complete-sentence answers, and for their skilful 'feeding' of structure and lexis to the class in the question being asked! The teacher who asked 'A quelle heure vous levez-vous le matin?' instead of, perhaps, 'Dites-moi ce que vous faîtes le matin avant de venir en classe!' freed the pupils from the need to think of the structure – all they had to do was to concentrate on the expression of time relevant to their own case and to their own interests, and make the pronoun transposition.

It is perhaps excessively old-fashioned and reactionary to wonder whether the modern insistence upon taped dialogues of French being spoken at educated native speaker speed, or upon O-level oral examinations, for instance, being conducted as 'natural' conversations instead of consisting of complete-sentence answers to specific questions (as they were up to about 1955) has in fact achieved much that the Direct Method had not already attained nearly a century ago. 'Ne parlons plus de cela,' as Mme de Sévigné said, 'j'y pense, pourtant, et il le faut,' and elsewhere (Richardson, 1981, p. 5) I have even gone so far as to suggest that, given the inescapable classroom situation, the Direct Method techniques (such as Gouin's famous 'series', for instance) were as near an approach to doing what Hawkins very rightly would like to see done, as any of us is likely to achieve within the conventional framework of school or college.

# References

Austin, J.L. (1962) *How to do Things with Words*, Oxford University Press, Oxford

Collins, H.F. (1934) 'Modern Languages' in (Lord) Eustace Percy (ed.), *The Yearbook of Education 1934*, Evans, London

Dodson, C.J. (1978) *Bi-lingual Education in Wales*, Schools Council, London

Gilbert, M. (1954, 1955) 'The Origins of the Reform Movement in Modern Language Teaching in England', *Durham Research Review*, 5 (6)

Gouin, F. (1892) *The Art of Teaching and Studying Languages*, translated by H. Swan and V. Bétis, 3rd edn, George Philip, London

Harding, D.H. (1967) *The New Pattern of Language Teaching*, Longman, London

Hawkins, E.W. (1980) '"Force" and "Awareness" in Language Learning', *The Incorporated Linguist*, 19 (3), Summer

———— (1981) *Modern Languages in the Curriculum*, Cambridge University Press, Cambridge

Hedgecock, F.A. (1926) *The Active French Course*, University of London Press, London

Jespersen, O. (1904) *How to Teach a Foreign Language*, George Allen and Unwin, London

Richardson, G. (1967) 'Wilhelm Viëtor – a *philosophe* for the New Language Revolution?' in G. Richardson (ed.), *A New Look at Modern Language Teaching* (Aspects of Education 6), University of Hull Institute of Education, Hull

———— (1981 'A Hundred Years of Language Revolutions' in G. Richardson (ed.), *Modern Language Teaching in the 1980s* (Aspects of Education, 25), University of Hull Institute of Education, Hull

———— and Fletcher, W. (1951) *Histoires Illustrées*, Edward Arnold, London

Rivers, W.M. (1964) *The Psychologist and the Foreign Language Teacher*, University of Chicago Press, Chicago

Searle, J. (1969) *Speech Acts*, Cambridge University Press, Cambridge

Viëtor, W. (1882) *Der Sprachunterreicht muß umkehren!*, O.R. Reisland, Leipzig. References in English are from the unpublished translation by A.D. Christie and G. Richardson

# 4 THE AUDIO-LINGUAL AND AUDIO-VISUAL 'REVOLUTION'

## N.K. Cammish

It was possible for a modern linguist to be trained as a teacher in England in 1960 and to enter the profession never having heard of audio-lingual and audio-visual courses, never having seen a language laboratory, and believing that in using a few slides for oral composition work, one was being really avant-garde. Over the next ten to fifteen years, however, a revolution in teaching methods and materials seemed to sweep through the language classrooms of the country: audio-visual and audio-lingual courses were apparently in use almost everywhere and shiny new language laboratories were installed. By 1980, however, in many schools the tapes and film-strips were mouldering sadly in stock cupboards and language laboratory equipment stood dusty, derelict and forlorn. The 'revolution' in some classrooms had left barely a trace and all was as before; in others, new bandwagons were rolling. In the schools and institutions where audio-visual and audio-lingual courses continued to be used, the methods and materials had mostly been extensively modified and very often the techniques used would have been regarded as heretical by the early exponents of the 'revolutionary' methods. Once again, a so-called revolution in language teaching methods had apparently failed.

This contrasted sadly with the euphoria with which audio-visual and audio-lingual techniques and the language laboratory associated with the latter had been greeted when they first appeared. In 1966 Brian Dutton could write of 'the enormous potential of the language laboratory', and say, 'I should . . . dispel any impression that the language laboratory is not entirely desirable – it is, and if language teaching is to achieve fluency and quasi-native accuracy in the learner, it is well-nigh essential' (Dutton, 1966, pp. 19–20). It seemed as though the panacea had at last been found: 'In the seven weeks that the language laboratory has been functioning at the college, he had already noticed a marked improvement in the boys' fluency and self-confidence', we were told by a report on a teacher's reactions at Bradfield College (*Times Educational Supplement*,

53

1965). From merely reading with interest touched with scepticism the early reports on the use of audio-visual courses in *Modern Languages* (see for example Ingram and Mace, 1959), many teachers rushed eagerly to buy *TAVOR Aids*, the CREDIF courses *Voix et Images de France* and *Bonjour Line*, and the Harrap-Didier AV courses in French, German or Italian. Others were converted by the audio-lingual courses coming from the USA such as the *ALM* materials and *Entender y Hablar*. All at once, for the first time, modern languages departments in schools demanded extensive capital investment: film-strip projectors, tape-recorders and language laboratories had to be purchased and black-out facilities and electric points installed. Instead of buying merely thirty-five textbooks to equip a class it was a question of the far more expensive boxes of film-strips and sets of tapes.

The language-teaching journals, conferences, in-service courses and initial training programmes all reflected the excitement. Not all teachers, however, were carried along on the wave of enthusiasm, of course. The die-hard grammar-grind traditionalists continued to teach rules and do proses, whilst those teachers who had already built up successful techniques for an oral-aural approach were often suspicious of what seemed to them to be a '*Son et Lumière*' irrelevancy in the case of audio-visual courses or a 'Battery Hens' syndrome where audio-lingual courses and language laboratories were concerned.

### Audio-lingual Materials

Most audio-lingual materials at that time consisted of short, recorded dialogues for the pupils to commit to memory by means of repetition (the 'mimicry-memorisation' technique) and sets of recorded pattern-drills with a strict stimulus-response format. The tapes could be used either on a tape-recorder in the classroom or in a language laboratory. This extensive use of tapes and equipment was revolutionary for the teacher of languages but it was the underlying philosophy of the approach which was considered the significant factor. The audio-lingual approach, with its roots in behaviourist psychology, was based on the assumptions that foreign language learning is basically a mechanical process of habit formation, that it is more effective if the spoken form precedes the written form, and that analogy is superior to analysis as a basis for acquiring control of linguistic structures. The stress on oral proficiency, the idea that quality and permanence of learning are in direct proportion to the amount of practice done, the carefully structured drill-sequences and the use of natural dialogue all appeared to offer much to the teacher wanting to use an oral-aural approach and to produce pupils who could actually use the foreign language to communicate.

There was, however, a great danger inherent in the audio-lingual approach. As Belyayev (1963) points out – 'If the formation of habits is considered the main thing, the basic method of teaching becomes repetition, speech activity is standardised, and students turn into parrots which can reproduce many things but never create anything productive or new' (p. 78). This is rather a different result from that sought by exponents of the method such as Lado (1964), who aimed to produce by repetition and pattern-drill pupils who would handle the foreign language in the same unconscious way as one handles one's mother tongue – 'under a normal speech set the speaker has his attention chiefly on the content, and he manipulates the mechanics of expression largely through bundles of habits below the threshold of awareness' (p. 34). Lado states categorically that it is not the memorisation of individual sentences upon which the method depends, but the establishment of linguistic habits by practice in the manipulation of sentence patterns in a variety of situations (p. 93). Having once achieved mechanical mastery of a particular pattern, the pupil should then go on to open-ended, creative utterances where he uses the pattern accurately but is concentrating on communicating what he actually *wants* to say. In her critique of the audio-lingual approach, *The Psychologist and the Foreign Language Teacher* (1964), Wilga Rivers warns that the mechanical process of habit formation applies only to the development of the lower level of manipulative skill – 'both pattern drill and language laboratory practice should be auxiliary and subordinate to practice in natural, face-to-face situations, contrived in the classroom, in a relaxed atmosphere' (p. 40). Unfortunately, despite these warnings, many pupils grew better and better at pattern practice but were unable to use the patterns fluently in normal speech situations (see Hayes, 1965). The tapes were used, the practice was being done, so what was going wrong? It was not that the teachers really expected the tapes somehow to work miracles by themselves, although perhaps subconsciously a few of them did, but because the final and most important stage of the teaching process was often omitted: that of exploiting the new structure in an open-ended, creative way. Audio-lingual materials certainly would produce nothing but parrots if they were not used correctly.

**Audio-visual Materials**

Audio-visual materials were open to the same sort of misuse. The 'revolutionary' elements were the tapes and film-strips and the concept of the global-structural approach to language learning. The early courses consisted of taped dialogues accompanied by film-strip pictures. After a mimicry-memorisation phase, when the pupils repeated each aural stimulus whilst looking at the appropriate picture, and after the drilling of the new sentence patterns, the teacher was expected to exploit the material – 'Dans la méthode de St Cloud-Zagreb, les moyens mécaniques ne sont qu'un point de départ; le professeur demeure l'âme du cours. Il exerce ses élèves à utiliser les notions apprises spontanément et dans des situations sans cesse renouvelées' (Renard, 1963, p. 97). Unfortunately there was a tendency to regard audio-visual materials as a teaching method or process in themselves, rather than as a teaching aid, and because the early courses provided little more than the basic tapes and film-strips, teachers were inclined to stop short after repetition and a little pattern practice and to consider the work of the unit finished. The course producers certainly made suggestions for transposition and exploitation of the new lexis and structures but provided little material with which to do it. As a consequence, faced with the usual pressures to push ahead to cover the course in the time available, many teachers neglected the final, vital phase.

This neglect of the exploitation phase seemed to occur whether the course was conceived structurally or situationally. A structurally conceived course, such as TAVOR Aids for example, provided a series of mini-dialogues, each one containing an example of the new structure being learned. The teacher, however, had to produce all the other ideas and materials needed for further practice of the structure and for its use in open-ended, realistic communication. The demands of the situationally based courses were even heavier: because the dialogues were more natural and contained less built-in repetition of the structure being learned, the teacher had far more work to do even in the initial phases of using the material.

Gifted and energetic teachers, of course, used the early audio-lingual and audio-visual courses with great success. For them, the repetition and pattern practice phases of both types of course were just the beginning: the tapes, drills and pictures were just aids on which to build. With A-V materials, for instance, selected pictures in situationally based courses could be used to exploit not only the new lexis and structures of the unit but to recycle previously learned items and to move forward to open-ended question and answer work, oral composition and extended dialogues. They designed their own supplementary materials: exercises, work-sheets and workbooks.

Even these teachers however sometimes had doubts and others were disillusioned and dissatisfied. There were many problems associated with the new courses and new technology, some more serious than others, ranging from everyday practicalities in the classroom to fundamental questioning of the basic tenets of A-L and A-V techniques. All this, of course, was during the same period when teachers were trying to cope with a host of other challenges engendered by the re-organisation of secondary education: teaching languages across the ability range, devising courses for the less able, and developing techniques for mixed-ability classes. Added to this was the arrival in secondary school of children who had started French in the primary school during the Pilot French Scheme. All these changes made great demands on the teachers, quite apart from the challenge of the new courses and methodology.

## Some Problems of Early A-L and A-V Courses

### (a) Hardware and Software

The new materials necessitated extensive use of equipment with all the associated problems of black-out, extension leads and transport of tape-recorders and projectors from classroom to classroom. Most schools coped with this by providing specialist Language Rooms but teachers still had to set up projectors and find the place on a tape before they could start teaching, and equipment could, of course, easily break down. Projector lamps could explode, tapes could tangle, and in those days such equipment was not the ordinary, everyday part of life it is now. As for the even more complex language laboratory, breakdowns could be common and might necessitate calling in a technician from the other side of the Pennines! The hardware therefore involved extra time, worry and responsibility for the modern languages teacher and for those reasons alone, in some schools its use simply faded away. In institutions which provided a technician to deal with modern languages equipment, teaching staff could concentrate on developing new materials and techniques and the success rate was higher. Such institutions tended to be in the further or higher education sectors, however, not in the secondary sector.

The software was also problematical. In the early days there was very little commercial material available and some of it, especially that for use in the language laboratory, was of the 'bandwagon' variety, produced very rapidly in answer to market needs. The main source of difficulty was that most courses failed to provide materials for exploitation of the teaching points, and, in their anxiety to stress oral and aural skills, provided the teacher with little help for developing the other skills of reading and writing. This was why the second generation of A-L and A-V courses – the 'Compromise' courses (see p. 67) – were so gladly welcomed by teachers.

*(b) Research Reports*

Most of the research appearing in the period 1960–80 was not encouraging to users of A-L and A-V materials. Although successful small-scale experiments were reported, larger projects had either inconclusive or negative results.

Among the small-scale experiments, Freedman's elegantly designed piece of research (Freedman, 1969), comparing the learning of a structure in the language laboratory with learning the same thing by means of a lecture and fifteen minutes' classroom practice, proved conclusively that the language laboratory technique was the more effective. The York study of the effectiveness of the language laboratory, however (Green, 1975), showed that, exploited in the normal school situation in the most typical way, the language laboratory was no more effective than a single tape-recorder in the classroom when the same materials were used with both, *over a period of three years*. This study was a salutary reminder about the Hawthorne effect for those who enthused about the efficacy of language laboratories after only a few weeks' use.

Two pieces of research done in the USA were even more

depressing, as they both indicated that not only was the language laboratory not the panacea it had been greeted as, but that audio-lingual materials themselves were not achieving results superior to more traditional teaching methods. The Scherer and Wertheimer experiment at Colorado University appeared to show that students gained little from the use of A-L materials (Scherer and Wertheimer, 1964). The results of the experiment, 'in spite of the neck-to-neck finish', says Hilton (1969), 'impart no zest. Interested teachers will more likely feel a flat disappointment that an elaborate experiment, in a sphere that is of importance to them pro-fessionally, should yield answers which imply that there is little point in endeavour' (p. 98). At the end of the first year of the experiment, the students taught with A-L materials were better at speaking and listening than the control group but inferior in reading, writing and translation into both L1 and L2. By the end of the second year, they were still better than the control group in speaking but poorer at writing and translating into English and merely equal to the control group in reading, listening and translating into German. The experimental group was, however, superior to the control group in attitude.

The overall results were disappointing to devotees of audio-lingual methodology but as there appeared to be room for criticism of the design and control factors in the experiment (see Hilton, 1969), it could be rejected as inconclusive. Criticism included the points that the A-L group had not started to use the language laboratory until the course had been running twelve weeks; that the experimental and control groups had been merged at the end of Year 1, so that the tests at the end of Year 2 were measuring only the residual effect of the first year's teaching; that the experimental materials had been written and used largely by novice teachers whereas the traditional group had been taught with established materials and by teachers who, even if novices, had themselves ex-perienced as pupils the methodology used; and finally that the 'traditional' method used with the control group would certainly have had an overlay of reform techniques – even the strongest traditionalists no longer teach exactly as their nineteenth-century predecessors did.

Certainly then, doubts could be cast on the validity of the Scherer and Wertheimer results, but a bigger shock lay in store: the results of the large-scale Pennsylvania Project (P.D. Smith, 1970), which were traumatic to the research team and caused a furore in the modern languages teaching field in the USA. The experiment attempted to compare the traditional grammar/translation method (TLM) with the 'functional skills' (FSM) and the 'functional skills and grammar' (FSG) approaches. Among the FSM and FSG classes, the research team considered separately those using simply a tape-recorder in the classroom, those using an audio-active model of language laboratory and those using an audio-active-comparative one. The conclusions after one year were that traditional classes not only did better on reading and writing tests but equalled the FSM groups in speaking test results. The language laboratory was shown to have no measurable effect on achievement. At the end of the second year of the experiment, there was no significant difference between the three groups in either listening, speaking or writing tests. The TLM and FSG groups scored equally in reading tests; the FSM, or strictly audio-lingual group, scored lower. There were no significant differences between the groups using a tape-recorder in the classroom, an audio-active laboratory or an audio-active-comparative laboratory. Judging by these results (Smith, pp. 164–7 and pp. 236–9), it appeared that not only were audio-lingual methods proving no more successful than traditional ones, but that it does not really matter which methods or facilities the teacher uses, the results will be the same.

The Pennsylvania Project report (ibid.) points out wryly that 'The attempt to replicate small studies on a bigger scale does not come out the same' (p. 337, Appendix F) and we know that once we go beyond the small-scale experiment, it is very difficult to control all the variables. In the Pennsylvania research, not only was the teacher variable uncontrolled, but no detailed classroom records were kept. The project leaders frequently observed the teaching going on, but their observation check-lists could have been more precise. Different methodologies can be properly compared only if we have careful records of what actually goes on in the classroom and as Recommendation 5 of the Pennsylvania Project says, it is necessary that 'future research involving teaching strategies or classroom procedures attempt to precisely and objectively measure [sic] the instructional process within the individual classroom' (ibid., p. 239). The teacher factor, however, is probably the most important one – 'The difference between two teachers is, on average, greater than the rate of difference between the treatments one tries to impose' (ibid., p. 342, Appendix F).

Despite the criticisms of the research design and despite the contention that because of the impossibility of controlling all variables in large-scale experiments, the results of such experiments must always be inconclusive (Freedman, 1971, p.36), the confidence of teachers in the USA was shaken by the project. Chomsky's dictum that language is not a habit-structure to be acquired by practice with audio-lingual materials, with or without a language laboratory, was apparently proved at grass-roots level.

Audio-visual techniques were also being questioned, mainly by experiments testing the validity of the visual element. Obviously the pictures in an audio-visual course can provide a context of situation, can act as a cue for a particular statement or question, and can, unless tied very closely to a particular phrase, serve as a basis for general question and answer work. What they cannot do, except in the case of concrete vocabulary, is to 'represent' language closely enough to ensure that the learner understands without other help what he hears on the tape. Pictures cannot always convey even general concepts, and far less so, particular ones expressed in particular linguistic forms. Unfortunately the authors of the first A-V courses, intentionally or not, conveyed to teachers the impression that the pictures *did* 'represent' the dialogue heard on the tapes: 'le sens général se devine sans peine grâce à l'image qui se substitue à la traduction et la rend inutile' (Kamenew, 1962, p.iii) and 'A chaque image du film, correspond donc un groupe sémantique qui en est l'expression sonore. Ce groupe, l'élève doit d'abord en entendre la structure sonore et, en même temps, en percevoir la signification' (CREDIF, 1962, p.xi).

This misleading impression was reinforced by the insistence in some A-V 'methods' that the *explication* phase should follow, not precede, the repetition phase in the learning progression. A teacher's blind faith in the efficacy of the visual element in conveying meaning could lead to parrot-like, meaningless repetition by the pupils. The use of the mother tongue to help comprehension was indeed suggested by the authors of some courses, but excessive use of English seemed alien to the other general aims of the materials. Experiments by Guénot (1962 and 1964), and Mialaret and Malandain (1962) showed just how dangerous it was to rely on the visual element to establish meaning, especially with younger pupils. The intervention of the teacher and a re-ordering of the recommended progression of phases in the teaching were necessary as several writers pointed out (for example Cammish, 1966 and 1975, and Harris, 1975). The research reports and the course critiques were depressing for those who had thought that the film-strip in A-V courses was a breakthrough in conveying meaning: it was merely a useful aid and not a panacea after all.

### (c)  Pupils as Parrots

As we have already seen, the early A-L and A-V materials were often considered to constitute a complete 'method' in themselves. As Professor Hawkins (1981) says of A-V courses – 'Had the early materials been described merely as an aid in the presentation of language, a great deal of confusion might have been avoided' (p. 175). As it was, there was a tendency to neglect or even omit the manipulative and creative phases which must follow the presentation of new material. Hawkins uses the terms 'assimilation' and 'emancipation' for these stages and says, 'These two crucial steps, which demand more subtle classroom skills on the teachers' part than the straightforward presentation stage, are the nub of language teaching' (pp. 174–5). It was precisely here, where the ordinary teacher needed ideas and materials, that the new courses left him to his own devices. The gifted teacher worked hard to build up, on the basis of the dialogues and drills of the course, his pupils' ability to transfer what they had learned to countless new situations; his less gifted colleague thought he had completed his task when the dialogues were memorised and the drills practised.

Even the pattern-drills themselves, in A-L courses, and, where they were provided, in A-V courses too, were a great cause for concern. The concept of language learning as a mechanical process of habit formation had led to the mindlessness of the mechanical pattern-drill which of course encouraged the 'parrot complex'. Meaningful use of language, involving intelligence and creativity, seemed to have no role in the drilling of structures. The reaction against the mechanical drill in the late 1960s and early 1970s, and the attempts to develop 'meaningful' or 'contextualised' drills, was a welcome later development (see pp. 64–7).

From observation of the early and sometimes abortive experiences with the new courses sprang a reaction against the limitations of mechanical repetition and mechanical drilling. Valdman (1966) says of audio-lingual methods: 'we have come to remember belatedly that parroting basic sentences and performing mechanical pattern-drill is not communication, that is, the natural use of language in an authentic cultural context'. He goes on to say (p. 105) that 'skilful elicitation of authentic conversation' is what is needed. That 'elicitation' required imagination, effort and energy, and the courses in the form in which they existed offered little help and were in fact both inadequate and misleading. Dissatisfied teachers either turned back to the long-established grammar-based textbook or hoped for better things in the second-generation so-called 'compromise' A-L and A-V courses which were beginning to appear.

## The 'Second Generation' Courses and Materials

Some deficiencies of the early A-L and A-V courses were remedied by the appearance of supplementary publications, which provided not only materials to help the teacher exploit each new group of lexis and structures but the reading and writing exercises which had been lacking. One has only to compare the original '*Livre de l'élève*' of the TAVOR A-V course (Kamenew, 1962) with the lively and useful pages of Derek Slade's workbooks '*Le Français . . . de France – Etudes de la Méthode TAVOR*' (1968 *et seq.*), to see the difference such new materials could make for the ordinary teacher. The publisher's comments on the workbooks show how exactly the workbooks aim to solve some of the problems of teaching with the original TAVOR materials:

> The pupil learns to read and write accurately what he has learned orally, not by mere repetition but through fresh scenes and themes illustrated with new realistic pictorial material . . . The student is encouraged to write his own exercises and saynètes . . . The active and creative participation of the student is required when working from these studies . . . a wide range of material that lends itself to many kinds of imaginative exploitation. (Slade, 1970, back cover)

Other help for teachers appeared in articles suggesting exactly how the original A-V materials could be used and exploited in order to achieve creative use of language. Derek Slade (1970) and G.D. Marrow (1970), for example, offered excellent advice on supplementary materials, planning and exploitation. Cole (1966) had already stressed the importance of variety of approach, especially during the repetition phase, and shown the need for newness, surprise and uncertainty. Even more importantly he had stressed the need for personal involvement and the fact that language, to be used meaningfully, has to be a cue for action: the importance of exploitation and follow-up with the new materials was clear.

Heretical ideas were developing: some teachers cut up and re-assembled the long and difficult-to-handle TAVOR film-strips. The material for repetition was so long that almost a complete school period could be taken up on repetition alone: variety and exploitation were fostered by taking a few film-strip frames at a time. Harris (1975) suggested that the film-strip pictures and recorded dialogues should not be the first experience of the new grammatical items in a unit. Oral presentation and practice of a new structure would precede the showing of the film-strip:

> Once the new grammar had been introduced, presentation of the film-strip *without* the tape-recording would enable the teacher to teach some of the new vocabulary, convey the gist of the 'story' of the unit and present some of the newly acquired grammar in contexts which would now have a greater chance of making sense. (p. 233)

The tape would be used only later to clinch the work already done, with the pupils 'in a much better position to understand it than they would have been had the recording constituted the *initial* experience of the language'. As Harris says,

> The pleasure of hearing an authentic French voice uttering recognizable speech can only have a positive effect on motivation; whereas listening to *new* language, which may at best be ambiguous, in circumstances which may and usually do preclude a high standard of acoustics, can be confusing and motivationally damaging. (p. 233)

Harris' heretical suggestions not only re-ordered the teaching phases of the A-V 'method' but omitted the mimicry-memorisation phase, previously seen as the nub of A-V teaching. If the teacher wants to give his pupils 'the ability to handle the component grammar and lexis in a flexible way', then, says Harris, 'there is no obvious reason why memorization should be other than incidental' (p. 234).

New developments were also taking place in the field of pattern-drills. As we have seen, the mechanical drills of the early A-L approach were being criticised as being not only boring and mindless but also counter-productive if used beyond the elementary, initial introduction to a new structure. The 'meaningful' or 'contextualised' drill controversy can be seen reflected in articles in the modern language teaching journals over the period 1967–72 (Beile and Beile, 1971; Buckby, 1967 and 1970–1; Cole, 1969; Cook, 1970; Edener, 1972; Newmark and Riebel, 1968; Oller and Obrecht, 1968; Sager, 1969; Scarborough, 1968–9; D.G. Smith, 1969–70; and Swallow, 1971). It was hoped that contextualised drills would concern the pupil with *meaning*: he would have to concentrate on the message and answer *appropriately* rather than automatically as in a purely mechanical drill, and hence be brought a step nearer to real communication. For example, a mechanical drill, practising *aller à la* ⸺, *aller au* ⸺, at the *brassage* stage, might take the following form, with the stimulus serving incidentally as master answer to each preceding example:

| Tape stimulus | Student response |
| --- | --- |
| Je vais à la boucherie. | |
| Gendarmerie. | Je vais à la gendarmerie. |
| Je vais à la gendarmerie. | |
| Cinéma. | Je vais au cinéma. |
| Je vais au cinéma. | |
| Discothèque. | Je vais à la discothèque. |
| Je vais à la discothèque. | |
| Théâtre. | Je vais au théâtre. |
| Je vais au théâtre. | |
| Supermarché. | Je vais au supermarché. |
| etc. | etc. |

A 'meaningful' drill, practising the same structure, might be constructed as follows:

| Tape stimulus | Student response *(master answer follows in each case)* |
| --- | --- |
| Il faut acheter du pain. | |
| Où vas-tu? | Je vais à la boulangerie. |
| Il faut acheter des gâteaux. | |
| Où vas-tu? | Je vais à la pâtisserie. |

Il faut jouer au football.
  Où vas-tu?                    Je vais au terrain de sports.
Il faut parler à la police.
  Où vas-tu?                    Je vais à la gendarmerie.
Il faut acheter des cigarettes.
  Où vas-tu?                    Je vais au bureau de tabac.

It is obvious in the 'meaningful' drill, although the answers are identical in form with those in the mechanical drill, that the student is involved with something more than a 'mechanical process of habit formation'. He has to *understand* the situation set out in the stimulus and make an *appropriate* reply; he has to respond to a question form in a conversational way; he has to use his commonsense; he is unable to doze off and reply mechanically. Admittedly, there is the difficulty in 'meaningful' drills that the pupil may produce some perfectly valid answer which is not that supplied by the master answer. The pupil may reply 'Je vais au supermarché' when asked where he would go for bread, or 'Je vais au stade' when asked where he would go to play football. Even very careful writing of drills cannot eliminate entirely the possibility of variation in pupils' answers in this sort of drill. This problem arises, however, only in the language laboratory where the master answer, confirming and reinforcing or, alternatively, correcting, has to be pre-recorded on the tape. In the classroom, the problem is non-existent: the teacher can accept a whole range of possible answers, and in fact, pattern-drilling in the classroom, allowing open-ended questions as it does, is probably the nearest to real communication that drills can achieve. The following snippet of classroom interaction illustrates the value of the open-ended drill.

*Teacher:*  Imaginez un peu! Il faut acheter quelque chose à manger. Où vas-tu?
*Pupil 1:*  Je vais à la boulangerie.
*Teacher:*  A la boulangerie? Oui. Et toi, Jacques?
*Pupil 2:*  Moi, je vais à la pâtisserie.
*Teacher:*  Ha! tu aimes les gâteaux, eh? Et toi?
*Pupil 3:*  Je vais au supermarché.
*Teacher:*  Au supermarché! Bien! Et toi, Angèle?
*Pupil 4:*  Je vais au café.
*Teacher:*  Bonne idée! Tu vas au café! Et toi?
*Pupil 5:*  Je vais au restaurant.
*Teacher:*  Encore une bonne idée. Et toi, Marie?

The 'contextualised' or 'meaningful' drills duly appeared in new materials as they were published. Visuals and sound-effects were sometimes used as part of drill stimuli and role-playing was introduced into the drill format. The new pattern-drills still practised structures but in a far more lively and meaningful way. The essence of the drills in the early A-L material had been, as Cook (1970) said, 'that the learner's response is forced into a rigid mould' (p. 7); open-ended drills in the classroom, where the structure is controlled but lexical items used at will, seemed the only answer to the demand that the learner should use the foreign language innovatively even at the practice stage; the 'contextualised' drill in the language laboratory came somewhere between the two.

It was compromise, rather than development, which came where A-V courses were concerned, and it can be seen reflected in such series as the *Longmans A-V Course* Stages 1 and 2 and the Downes and Griffith *Le Français d'Aujourd'hui, Première et Deuxième Parties*. These courses were a serious attempt to marry the oral approach and the new technology with the more conventional textbook approach. As the preface to *Le Français d'Aujourd'hui* states:

> Experience of the exclusively audio-visual approach has left many teachers in doubt as to its validity. Difficulties, either unforeseen or else deliberately minimised in the first enthusiasm for a new idea, have proved real. The main ones are: the transition from speaking to writing; the problem of homework . . . ; the danger of monotony and parrot-like repetition; the difficulties caused through the absence of pupils or teacher; and, above all, the undeniable fact that purely 'Audio-Visual French' is extremely demanding for the teacher.
>
> This course has been written in an attempt to provide a compromise of traditional and modern which is most suited to the majority of pupils and teachers in grammar and secondary schools. (Teacher's Handbook, *Première Partie*, p. 2)

The 'compromise' courses offered teachers the materials for developing reading and writing skills which they had found to be lacking in the early A-V courses. The written word was no longer held back for a long period and there were plenty of reading passages and written exercises. The traditionalists who had never considered for a moment accepting the enormous change in approach engendered by the drills of the A-L materials or the global-structural learning of the A-V 'method' could buy and use these 'compromise' courses without surrendering what they held dear. Despite the aims of the authors of the courses, it was possible to use them in a very traditional way and many teachers did just that, leaving the film-strip and tapes in the stock cupboard and using the pupil's book in much the same way as they had used traditional textbooks in the past.

The grammatical progression in these courses tended to be attractive to the traditionalist, who was wary of progressions based on new insights about frequency, liveliness of dialogue and value in survival situations. As Jerman (1967) pointed out, 'Longman's course, on closer examination, turns out to have a startling resemblance to another course published by the same firm, Whitmarsh's *First French Book* . . . The items to be taught are staged and sequenced in very nearly an identical manner' (p. 81).

It was with these 'compromise' courses that the term 'audio-visual' broadened to include a wide range of modern language teaching materials instead of denoting only the strict methods of '*Voix et Images*' or '*TAVOR Aids*'. Jerman might well say of the Longman course, 'Is it truly audio-visual or are we being offered a menu (*à prix élévé*, if we take all the dishes) of Whitmarsh '*à la mode, sauce audio-visuelle (facultative)*?' (ibid., p. 82) but this sort of course has certainly proved attractive to large numbers of teachers.

Other courses developing at the same time tried to avoid the problems of the old A-V materials without actually compromising. The following review of Pamela Symond's *French through Action* describes one such effort:

> Instead of producing film-strips and tapes and then merely hoping that the teacher will use them well, that he will involve the child in using the language to express himself as he talks, works and plays in a variety of classroom activities, Pamela Symonds has made sure that it is practically impossible to teach narrowly with her course. Because it is an integrated assembly of lessons and various teaching materials, it is impossible to use the film-strips and tape in every lesson as some teachers tend to do with other courses, and it is impossible to restrict one's teaching to the repetition phase of audio-visual work and fondly believe

one's task is done. The outlines and ideas in the teacher's manual, the materials in it, the pupils' workbooks and the flannel-graph pictures are essential to the course and the film-strips and tapes are only one part of the materials. They are used to widen the scope of the language experiences presented to the children, by bringing into the classroom sights, sounds and situations from beyond the school walls. By producing this course which uses a variety of materials, which suggests all sorts of activities and which shows exactly how they are to be used in the different phases of teaching, Pamela Symonds is helping to drive home the truth that a primary school child should learn a foreign language through activity and meaningfulness, and *not* through being treated as a moronic parrot. (Cammish, 1967, p. 116)

The well known and widely used Nuffield/Schools Council courses: *En Avant*, *Vorwärts* and *Adelante* showed as they evolved over the years the same desire to offer a wide variety of materials, including variety in visual aids; plenty of materials to develop reading and writing skills as well as the aural/oral ones; and plenty of materials for exploitation of the new structures being learnt. Whether or not Kamenew or Guberina would regard these courses as 'audio-visual' or not is another matter.

### Why did the A-L/A-V 'Revolution' Fail?

It is easy to pick out weak points in the early A-L and A-V materials, pointing to the belief in them as a panacea, the imposition of '*the* method', to the problems concerning the validity of the visual element in A-V courses, the defects of pattern-drills and the lack of materials to help foster creative use of language. It is easy to quote Wilga Rivers (1964) – 'Language communication involves a relationship between individuals and not merely the memorisation and repetition of phrases and the practising of structures' (p. 163), and to say that the audio-lingual/audio-visual 'revolution' failed because the materials as they stood were insufficient to foster creative language use. Some would argue, as does Richardson (1967) that the new courses were no revolution at all but simply the old ideas of an oral/aural approach re-appearing with a technological 'top-dressing'. Cynics may argue that the sixties and seventies did witness a revolution but that any revolution based on a refusal to employ the traditional grammatical techniques of language teaching is bound to fail because the majority of teachers are, consciously or unconsciously, committed to those techniques.

It is however perhaps in the most recent ideas about how languages are learned that one can find the real explanation of why audio-lingual and audio-visual materials were not the great success they were expected to be. We must, however, be careful, for as Spolsky (1979) says:

> the structural linguists worked effectively to replace a system based on one limited view of language (the translation method) by an equally rigid and psycholinguistically invalid approach (the audio-lingual method). When this system too turned out to be inadequate, there were many who thought that all that was needed was to come up with a new one based on the latest theory of language. (p. 167)

If however the current 'creative construction' theory of language learning is valid, then the reasons why A-L and A-V courses, and, incidentally, many other approaches and techniques, did not achieve their aims do become clearer. The concept of L1 language learning advanced by Chomsky suggests that when the child is exposed to language, an innate hypothesis-forming mechanism in the brain helps him or her to internalise a set of grammar rules from the linguistic evidence presented. This 'language acquisition device' (LAD) gradually organises speech data until the child can understand and speak the language accurately. If this theory is true of L1 learning then, despite certain differences between L1 and L2 learning, one can ask whether L2 acquisition by children can also be characterised by the child's gradual acquisition of his own linguistic rules and further, if it can, what the implications are for modern language teaching methodology.

Certainly the roles of repetition and pattern practice and indeed the whole concept of learning by habit formation would be irrelevant, but exposure to large amounts of language 'data' would be vital –

> the learner must initially be exposed to an input of linguistic data upon which to base his hypotheses about its grammar;

subsequent stages involve hypothesis-testing and revision in the light of further data. If second-language learning is accepted as being this kind of process, it becomes the teacher's task to enable it to take place in the classroom. (Newman, 1980, p. 179)

The teacher must not only present the raw data, the language, so that the pupil can internalise its rules gradually but must learn to accept error as part of the learning process. The rich linguistic environment, as Ingram says, must be 'structured to facilitate the child's perception and internalisation of the rules since it seems that at each stage he is ready to perceive and acquire certain structures rather than others' (Ingram, 1976, p. 74). Part of the teacher's task must be to avoid teaching sequences which go counter to the 'natural syllabus'. Research has already provided some initial insights from L1 learning and informal L2 learning which give indications of what the progression in the 'natural syllabus' may be, and it will be interesting to see what is produced in the future.

This idea that perceiving patterns may be more important in L2 learning than practice and that an emphasis on perception of patterns and verbal play with the language may be more useful than pattern-drill was expressed by writers such as Cook as long ago as 1969, but it is only with the demise of the orthodox A-L and A-V courses that this sort of approach has become more current.

Another answer to why the so-called AV/AL revolution failed may however lie in our instinctive search for the panacea, for *the Method* which will solve all our problems, once and for all. Audio-visual and audio-lingual courses worked well for some teachers in some situations; for others, they were either unsatisfactory or even disastrous. Freedman (1971) could be right when she says:

> Perhaps it is time to stop looking for the elusive 'universal method' for teaching foreign languages, and instead to begin thinking in terms of different techniques for different aspects of language learning. It may well be that it is only possible to hope for a large number of different techniques, each one appropriate to a particular type of learner and a particular type of teacher, in a particular language learning situation, where particular problems arise from the conjunction of particular native and target languages. (p. 38)

An eclectic and empirical approach may well produce the best overall results for a wide variety of teachers and learners, as long as that approach has the steady long-term and short-term aims of meaningful communication.

## References

Beile, W. and Beile, A. (1971) 'Assessing Specific Language Laboratory Drills', Parts 1 and 2, *Modern Languages*, 52 (2), 54–63, and (3), 104–12

Belyayev, B.V. (1963) *The Psychology of Teaching Foreign Languages*, trans. R.F. Hingley, Pergamon, London

Buckby, M. (1967) 'Contextualization of Language Drills', *Modern Languages*, 48 (4), 165ff.

———— (1970–1) 'Another Look at Drills', *Audio-Visual Language Journal*, 8 (3), 111–17

Cammish, N.K. (1966) 'A Survey of Two Audio-visual Courses: Bonjour Line', *Modern Languages*, 47 (4), 161–4

———— (1967) 'Surveys of A/V Material: French through Action', *Modern Languages*, 48 (3), 115–17

———— (1975) 'Using A/V Materials' in A. Hornsey (ed.), *Handbook for Modern Language Teachers*, Methuen, London

Cole, L.R. (1966) 'Some Basic Aspects of A-V and A-L Theory and Techniques', *Audio-Visual Language Journal*, 4 (1), 28–31

———— (1969) 'The Structured Dialogue: an Attempt to Integrate Structural and Situational Approaches to Language Teaching', *International Review of Applied Linguistics*, 7 (2), 125ff.

Cook, V.J. (1969) 'The Analogy between L1 and L2 Learning', *International Review of Applied Linguistics*, 7, 207–16

———— (1970) 'The Creative Use of Language', *Audio-Visual Language Journal*, 8 (1), 5–8

CREDIF (1962) *Voix et Images de France, Livre du Maître*, Didier, Paris

Dutton, B. (1966) 'Language Laboratories', *The Teacher* (Audio-Visual Aids Supplement), 29 April

Edener, W. (1972) 'The Development of Oral and Written Skills by Free Expression', *Modern Languages*, 53 (1), 18–22

Freedman, E.S. (1969) 'An Investigation into the Efficiency of the Language Laboratory in Foreign-language Teaching', *Audio-Visual Language Journal*, 7 (2), Summer, 75–95

———— (1971) 'The Road from Pennsylvania – Where Next in Language Teaching Experimentation?' *Audio-Visual Language Journal*, 9 (1), Spring, 33–8

Green, P.S. (ed.) (1975) *The Language Laboratory in School: Performance and Prediction: an Account of the York Study*, Oliver and Boyd, Edinburgh

Guénot, J. *et al.* (1962) 'Etudes sur l'évolution de l'aptitude des sujets à lire les vues fixes et introduction à une étude sur la lisibilité des vues fixes', *Etudes de Linguistique Appliquée*, 1, Didier, Paris

Guénot, J. (1964) *Pédagogie audio-visuelle des débuts de l'anglais*, Chapter 4, SABRI, Paris

Harris, D. (1975) 'Pictures and Recorded Speech in A/V Courses' in A. Hornsey (ed.), *Handbook for Modern Language Teachers*, Methuen, London

Hawkins, E.W. (1981) *Modern Languages in the Curriculum*, Cambridge University Press, Cambridge

Hayes, A.S. (1965) 'New Directions in Foreign-language Teaching', *Modern Languages Journal*, *49* (5), 282–93

Hilton, M. (1969) 'A Scientific Experiment?', *Audio-Visual Language Journal*, 7 (2), Summer, 97–101

Ingram, D.E. (1976) 'Something there is that doesn't Love a Wall', *Audio-Visual Language Journal*, *4* (2), 71ff.

Ingram, S.R. and Mace, J.C. (1959) 'An Audio-Visual French Course', *Modern Languages*, *40* (4), 139ff.

Jerman, J.A. (1967) 'Survey of A-V Material: Longman's Audio-Visual French – Stage 1', *Modern Languages*, *48* (2), 80–2

Kamenew, V. (1962) *Cours audio-visuel de Français (Préliminaire), Première Série, Livre du professeur*, TAVOR Aids, EFVA, London

———— (1962) *Cours audio-visuel de Français (Préliminaire), Première Série, Livre de l'élève* (revised edition), EFVA, London

Lado, R. (1964) *Language Teaching*, McGraw-Hill, New York

Marrow, G.D. (1970) 'Teaching with "Voix et Images de France"', *Audio-Visual Language Journal*, *8* (2), 75–83

Mialaret, G. and Malandain, C. (1962) 'La perception du film fixe chez l'enfant', *Etudes de linguistique appliquée*, *1*, 95ff., Didier, Paris

————, ———— (1962) 'Etude de la reconstitution d'un récit chez l'enfant à partir d'un film fixe', *Enfance*, *15*, 169ff

Newman, E.M. (1980) 'The "Creative Construction" Theory of Second-language Acquisition and its Implications for Language Teaching', *Modern Languages*, *61* (4), 175ff

Newmark, L. and Riebel, D.A. (1968) 'Necessity and Sufficiency in Language Learning', *International Review of Applied Linguistics*, *6* (2), 145ff

Nuffield Foundation/Schools Council (1966 etc.) *En Avant!* E.J. Arnold, Leeds

———— (1967 etc.) *Adelante!* Macmillan Education, Basingstoke

———— (1968 etc.) *Vorwärts!* E.J. Arnold, Leeds

Oller, J.W. and Obrecht, D.M. (1968) 'Pattern Drill and Communicative Activity: a Psycholinguistic Experiment', *IRAL*, *6* (2), 165ff

Renard, R. (1963) *La méthode audio-visuelle et structuro-globale de St Cloud-Zagreb*, Fonds Raoul Warocqué, Mons

Richardson, G. (ed.) (1967) Editorial in *A New Look at Modern Language Teaching*, (Aspects of Education 6), University of Hull Institute of Education, Hull, pp. 5–9

Rivers, W.M. (1964) *The Psychologist and the Foreign Language Teacher*, University of Chicago Press, Chicago

Sager, J.C. (1969) 'The Language Laboratory and Contextual Teaching Methods', *International Review of Applied Linguistics*, 7 (3), 217–29

Scarborough, D.R. (1968–9) 'The Contextualised Drill Fallacy', *Audio-Visual Language Journal*, *6* (2–3), 85–8

Scherer, G.A.C. and Wertheimer, M. (1964) *A Psycholinguistic Experiment in Foreign Language Teaching*, McGraw-Hill, New York

Slade, D. (1968 etc.) *Le Français de France – études de la méthode TAVOR*, Methuen, London (each workbook tackles a different theme, for instance *Thème 6: La vie quotidienne*, 1971)

———— (1970) 'Teaching with TAVOR', *Audio-Visual Language Journal*, *8* (2), 71–4

Smith, D.G. (1969–70) 'Contextualisation: Towards a More Precise Definition', *Audio-Visual Language Journal*, 7 (3), 147–52

Smith, P.D. (1970) *A Comparison of the Cognitive and Audio-lingual Approaches to Foreign Language Instruction* (The Pennsylvania Project), Centre for Curriculum Development, Philadelphia

Spolsky, B. (1979) 'The Comparative Study of First and Second Language Acquisition' in F.R. Eckmann and A.J. Hastings (eds.), *Studies in First and Second Language Acquisition*, Newbury House, Rowley, Mass.

Swallow, T. (1971) 'Why drills?' *Audio-Visual Language Journal*, 9 (2), 97–9

*Times Educational Supplement* (1965) 'Spreading the Gospel', 5 March

Valdman, A. (1966) 'Towards Self-Instruction in Foreign-language Learning', Chapter IV in G. Mathieu (ed.), *Advances in the Teaching of Modern Languages*, vol. 2, Pergamon, London

# 5 FOREIGN LANGUAGES AT THE POST O-LEVEL STAGE

F. Corless and R. Gaskell

## A Climate for Change

Over the course of the last fifteen years or so, the post O-level provision in foreign languages has attracted considerable attention. The reasons for this are not hard to find. Some fall within the sphere of general trends in education: the transition to comprehensive schooling; the development of sixth-form and tertiary colleges; a consequent increase in the number of students staying in full-time education after the age of 16 with ambitions other than a place on a traditional university course; an awakening of interest in the establishment of a broader curriculum at the post O-level stage. Other reasons relate more directly to the teaching and learning of foreign languages: a recognition, reinforced by the movement of Britain into Europe, of the need to produce businessmen and scientists who have a good command of another language to complement their professional skills; a gradual change in objectives and teaching methods, particularly in the early and middle years of secondary education.

The purpose of this chapter is to examine the ways in which those concerned with the teaching and testing of foreign languages at the post O-level stage have responded to this changing climate. The chapter opens with a brief study of the A-level syllabus and scheme of examination in the light of three publications which represent the movement for curriculum reform. Next, the purposes of advanced language study are analysed and a classroom methodology based on the systematic exploitation of authentic texts is described and exemplified. The chapter closes with a discussion of the reading programme and some comments on the management of teaching and learning.

**The Impetus for Reform**

At the end of the 1960s, the A-level syllabus and scheme of examination were much the same as they had been when the GCE was instituted two decades earlier. Indeed, in 1969, all the A-level boards offered the same elements of examination: translation from and into the foreign language; essay in the foreign language; dictation and oral test; appreciation of literature including works on 'background' (Schools Council Working Paper 28, 1970, pp. 9–10). The bright teenager's response to such a diet was, with hindsight, predictable. In the following few years, when most other subjects were maintaining or increasing their numbers at the 16 to 18 stage, the numbers of those studying foreign languages declined (Schools Council 18 + Research Programme, 1977, p. 15).

The growing impetus for a reform of the post O-level curriculum in foreign languages is reflected in the pages of three publications which span the 1970s. The first two emanated from the Schools Council and were produced within the context of proposals for a new pattern of studies at the sixth-form stage (Schools Council Working Paper 28, 1970; Schools Council 18 + Research Programme, 1977). The third was produced by a group of teachers and lecturers whose concern was to develop and extend the earlier work (French 16–19 Study Group, 1981).

To provide an accurate summary of these three publications in a few sentences would be an impossible task. What may be said, though, first of all, is that their essential criticisms of the traditional A-level pattern concentrate on five areas: the fragmentary quality of the programme of studies; the low status accorded to the development of skill in speaking the foreign language; the dominance of prose translation as a teaching and testing device; the constricting nature of a reading programme comprising four or five set texts; the privileged status of the literary register of language. At a more positive level, each of the three publications states more or less directly that an advanced language course should both equip the students with a usable set of skills and contribute to their development as individuals; all of them emphasise, to a greater or lesser extent, the need to draw on the students' existing interests and to increase their knowledge and understanding of the foreign culture. Whilst these publications differ in the detail of the reforms they propose, there is substantial agreement amongst them on essential principles: an integrated approach to the study of language and culture through the use of a wide range of texts in a variety of styles and registers; an increase in the status of oral production; the specific development of listening and reading skills and a complementary emphasis on the growth of what have come to be called study skills (identifying the key ideas, making notes, summarising, etc.); the investigation of a range of alternatives to prose translation as a test of written production; the introduction of a wider reading programme, largely based on contemporary texts, including both literary and non-literary material; the participation of teachers in a more flexible system of examination and assessment.

Since the first of these three proposals for reform was published in 1970, it might be expected that more than a decade later, A-level syllabuses and schemes of examination in French and German, for example, would look rather different from those of 1969 outlined above. Two boards do now offer a radically different alternative syllabus in French, as will be discussed later. However, scrutiny of what the English examination boards lay down in their mainstream syllabuses for 1983 reveals that whilst the monolith of 1969 has begun to crumble, it is still standing fairly solidly in its place. One apparent gain is that listening and reading comprehension have established a firm place in the 1983 syllabuses, the former having in some cases replaced dictation. However, the material used in one or two instances for the listening test – a passage to be read out by the teacher – raises serious questions as to authenticity. What is more, the range of marks awarded for the listening and speaking skills – from 16.67 per cent to 27.5 per cent – has not increased substantially since 1969 (Schools Council Working Paper 28, 1970, p. 9).

The three major components of the traditional A-level pattern – translation into English, translation into the foreign language and the study of literature and 'background' through set texts – retain their time-honoured places in the mainstream syllabuses. However, there have been some significant changes. Prose translation is required by all boards in French, though in the German syllabuses of two of the boards a use-of-language exercise is offered as an alternative. Translation into English is also required by all boards, though some state that passages in a non-literary register will be set. In the sphere of literary studies, there is now a greater emphasis on contemporary texts, though the traditional 'literary history' framework still looms large. Two boards now offer optional cultural studies topics in addition to literary set texts. In three further instances, it is possible for students to work on set texts entirely in the field of cultural studies; in another, some work in a non-literary area must be undertaken. One board, most enterprisingly, offers students the opportunity of doing a dissertation on a non-literary topic as an alternative to a literary set text; another provides scope for an individual study on a cultural topic, but this will only be 'taken into account' by the examiner.

Both the alternative French syllabuses – offered by London and the Southern Universities Joint Board – place a similar premium on practical objectives: a high standard in the command of the foreign language in terms of all four skills: a sound knowledge and understanding of varied aspects of French life and culture. Both boards stress the integration of language and content; both, directly or implicitly, place emphasis on the development of study skills: consulting source materials, making notes, organising ideas. As far as content is concerned, London prescribes a range of broad topics on aspects of contemporary France. The SUJB, on the other hand, whilst requiring the production of an individual project on an approved topic, leaves the choice of materials to teachers and students. Both boards offer the opportunity for some work in the literary field. In the examination, both boards set an essay in the foreign language, a language exercise/guided composition, a listening comprehension, a translation from French of non-literary material and an oral test; the SUJB still sets a dictation and London tests both reading comprehension and translation from English. What is particularly striking is that both boards assign about a third of the overall marks to tests of the listening and speaking skills; and the total number of marks awarded for tests *within* the foreign language amount in one case to 60 per cent and in the other to 65 per cent.

The main point to emerge from this brief review of current A-level syllabuses and schemes of examination in French and German is that the·present situation is one of flux. What is therefore required, as a priority, is a classroom methodology that will enable teachers to achieve practical, realistic objectives as well as preparing their students for examination within the context of a traditional or a progressive syllabus. But first of all the purposes of post O-level language study need to be defined with some care.

**The Purposes of Post O-level Language Study**

During the late 1970s, a crucial shift of emphasis became gradually apparent at all stages in the teaching and learning of foreign languages. Increasingly convinced that there is more to using a language than being structurally correct, methodologists and teachers came to see *communication* as the central purpose of foreign language learning. In practical terms, this involved far more than giving extra marks or classroom time to listening and speaking activities: indeed, it implied a root and branch re-appraisal of objectives, materials and working methods which is still going on.

The principal source of this new perspective was the work carried out under the auspices of the Council of Europe in order to develop a language teaching system suitable for teaching all the languages used in the Council's member countries (for example van Ek, 1975). In Britain, this work made its initial impact in the teaching of English as a foreign language (for example Abbs, Ayton and Freebairn, 1975) and in some broadcast courses in foreign languages for adults (for example British Broadcasting Corporation, 1974). More significantly, perhaps, for the school system, it helped to provide a sound theoretical basis for the graded syllabus movement as it began to gather momentum (Harding, Page and Rowell, 1980).

This new perspective, as the work of the French 16–19 Study Group (1981) demonstrated, was relevant to courses at advanced levels as well. Their report, whose spirit is reflected in the views expressed in this chapter, was based on the belief that a working knowledge of a foreign language could only be acquired by direct experience of the language itself, at work in authentic contexts. It considered the kinds of language sample students should be encouraged to work with, the tasks they should be required to undertake and ways in which their command of the language could be evaluated so as to measure, and stimulate, the development of communicative skills applicable outside the classroom.

A foreign language course founded upon communicative principles should equip an eighteen- or nineteen-year-old student to do some quite ordinary things, largely neglected in traditional courses: to understand and comment on a radio or television news bulletin, for example, to take notes during a discussion or conference, to pass on information or decisions to another person in the foreign language or his own, to engage in a telephone conversation, to scan a document or manual for a specific purpose, to identify a point of view in the course of a conversation with a native speaker, to see what a salesman or an advertisement is up to, even to present a persuasive argument. It can be seen at once that in a course with a communicative basis, the language skills – listening, speaking, reading and writing – are not distinct but interdependent, almost every act of speech or writing being a response to something heard or read.

At a more specific level, it is not difficult to compile a list of everyday *situations* in which a linguistically well equipped school leaver should be able to operate with a degree of confidence: bank, post office, travel agency, airport and so on. Indeed, it is with just such situations that elementary graded syllabuses, together with the initial proposals of the Joint Council for 16 + National Criteria (1981), are concerned. Even at advanced levels, learning to cope with routine circumstances is important. But a situationally based syllabus is fundamentally impracticable, and much too restrictive, partly because it is impossible to predict with any accuracy the situations which adult language users will encounter. It is also evident that most communication is not simply determined by its context: in a hotel dining-room, for example, the foreign visitor may engage the waiter in conversation about his job or his family, or discuss the previous night's televised football match with someone at the next table.

What is required, therefore, by the learner is a flexible control of the foreign language. In part, this adaptability will derive from mastery of the *grammatical system* and from possession of an adequate *vocabulary*, things with which the language teacher is very properly concerned. But whilst grammar may enable the learner to build sentences, and vocabulary provide the blocks to build them with, they are no more than the means of saying something, of conveying concepts, without which communication would be impossible. Already in the mid-seventies, the documents produced under the aegis of the Council of Europe, discussed by Wilkins (1976), were proposing that syllabuses should focus less upon language items and forms, more upon the *notions* that language transmits, many of which – location, time, sequence, cause, for example – are in constant use in speech and writing.

Whereas the traditional grammar book or vocabulary list may have found a place, under 'idioms' perhaps, for some at least of the notions referred to here, for what language says, they were not at all concerned with what language *does*. What speech and writing do, essentially, is to set up relationships between speaker or writer and listener or reader, According to this *functional* view, every time a person advises, commiserates, protests, apologises, refuses, and so on, he or she is imparting an attitude or a desire, attempting in some respect to influence another, or others. This intention, moreover, is reflected in the manner in which the person speaks or writes. In order to communicate effectively, the foreign language student needs to learn to use language appropriately: to recognise indignation, insistence, sympathy; to find, in a given context, the right words with which to be indignant, insistent or sympathetic.

Effective communication, then, means among other things finding words or forms to convey ideas, and giving messages a character suited to their purpose. But it also implies an adequate control of the ideas themselves. Learning in any area of the curriculum depends upon the capacities referred to as *study skills* (for example Tabberer and Allman, 1981). To process information and ideas, and to respond to them, a learner must be able, for example, to identify the significant features of what is read or heard, to analyse and classify, to see connections, to interpret implications, to detect bias or inaccuracy. Activities such as selection or re-organisation, emendation or interpretation, summary or adaptation, call upon and develop skills that underlie all language-based learning. In these study-skill activities writing has a vital place. For whilst it is true that foreign language users may rarely write to someone else, except in a letter, they may quite frequently commit their thoughts to writing for their own benefit: taking notes, recording and sorting information, preparing ideas for a conference or discussion. In the process of learning the foreign language, moreover, writing is an essential means of focusing upon items or principles, of structuring the language and retaining it.

Every genuine act of listening or reading entails understanding the ideas, intentions or mood of another person. Every act of speaking or writing is purposeful: it engages the speaker or the writer as a person. Language students will, consequently, achieve a measure of confidence in communicating only if learning provides them with opportunities to co-operate with one another in tackling practical linguistic tasks, to share ideas and experience, to find out more about themselves, each other and the world by means of the language. The contribution that an advanced foreign language course can make to the intellectual and emotional development of teenage students need not be insisted upon. The language class, then, is not simply a place where language is practised; it has also to be a place where language is used.

Finding out about the world means, in the case of a foreign language student, exploring aspects of the way of life and thought, aspects of the culture of the country concerned. A film or television programme seen, a magazine or newspaper read, a native speaker conversed with, each constitute an excursion into foreign territory. Language samples drawn from authentic sources may, if they are chosen with care, provide valuable glimpses of a country as the student is likely to perceive it and relate to it. There is in principle much to be said for the 'classe bilingue' in which geography, history or contemporary society are studied in the appropriate foreign language (Brown, 1973). For it may well be that a language is absorbed more readily when learners' attention is directed towards what is being said, when the targets set lie not simply within the language but beyond it. Whatever shape the post O-level reading programme may take, a topic which will be discussed later, there is no doubt that well chosen, arresting case studies, as part of the language course itself, can stimulate interest, can provide insights which study of other subject areas – geography, history, politics, cultural studies – or above all life in the foreign country, can transform into a more profound understanding.

The professional world outside the classroom needs linguists, but it does not need many foreign language specialists whose expertise is confined to a language or two. Of much greater interest to employers are qualified technicians, accountants, engineers or salesmen with an efficient working knowledge of one or more languages. Post O-level foreign language courses cannot, clearly, cater for precise professional needs; but courses with a communicative basis are capable of laying the foundations for language use in the world of work. In higher education, what is more, modern–language students are increasingly opting for courses of a vocational type, in which knowledge of a foreign language is seen as a support for other qualifications of a professional nature. Moreover, as historical, geographical and political studies establish themselves more firmly, together with modern linguistics, even in specialist language courses, the case for a post O-level programme modelled on traditional university courses, and dominated by literature and formal language skills, becomes correspondingly weaker.

The brief survey of language–learning objectives contained in this section serves to illustrate many of the inadequacies of the old A-level course and lends support to the criticisms levelled against it by the three publications referred to earlier (Schools Council Working Paper 28, 1970; Schools Council 18+ Research Programme, 1977; French 16–19 Study Group, 1981). There is now a growing demand that the fragmentary language course, often conducted chiefly in England and largely divorced from the foreign culture, with its emphasis upon translation and academic writing activities, should be replaced by something more in tune with the needs of students and the demands of the modern world. What is required instead is a coherent course, working essentially within and through the foreign language and based upon authentic language samples. This implies that knowledge of a language and how to use it for communicative purposes can be acquired only by direct contact with that language operating in a range of styles and for a variety of purposes. What such samples might consist of, how learners can gather language from them, systematise it and put it to work, is the subject of the next section.

## From Principles to Practice: the Exploitation of Texts

Texts, authentic pieces of language both spoken and written, are the essential fabric of the post O-level language course as it is envisaged in this chapter. Any genuine text, as originally constituted, is a message. It is vital that this message should speak convincingly to the students to whom it is presented; it must engage their attention, provoke a response, work upon the intellect, the emotions or the imagination, for the linguistic resources that a text offers are likely to be absorbed only if the message itself is of interest. That interest may derive from the fact that the text represents language in a form that learners are likely to encounter in the outside world: news broadcasts, weather forecasts, advertisements, the fashion column or the sports page, brochures or instruction manuals. Alternatively, a text may be a sample of language of a kind that students are likely to want to use for themselves, in conversation or in writing: describing an experience, recounting an anecdote, presenting an argument or an opinion. Recordings of live interviews or discussions, for example, not only provide information and ideas; they are also models of the ways in which speakers of the language use words, inflections and patterns to convey their thoughts and intentions.

The character of a text depends in part upon its degree of formality and upon whether it is spoken or written. But a text is shaped, too, by its purpose, by the job it was composed to do. Recognising this, the French 16–19 Study Group (1981, pp. 10–11) proposed the classification of texts into five categories broadly functional in nature: *conversational* pieces, whose dominant purpose is social interaction, the exchange of views, impressions and ideas; *narrative* accounts, whether in speech or writing, characterised generally by past tenses and the expression of temporal relationships; *informative* material, whose function is essentially to convey facts and whose lexis is relatively specialised; *descriptive* tracts, often rich in terms of structure and vocabulary, which convey impressions and emotions; finally *persuasive* texts, which are intended above all to influence the thoughts or actions of listener or reader. The classification of texts is pedagogically useful: check-lists such as that provided by the French 16–19 Study Group (1981, p.61) are a means of providing a balanced linguistic diet. However, it needs to be borne in mind that relatively few texts are in practice pure examples of the categories listed above, so that a narrative may contain elements of persuasion or description; it may directly or indirectly report conversation. Moreover, linguistic texts frequently rely upon, or are supported by, non-linguistic material such as pictures, maps, diagrams or tables.

The treatment of a text within the language course will depend partly upon the communicative purpose of the piece concerned. If its purpose is to inform or narrate, the initial exploitation will tend to concentrate upon establishing the facts or story-line; a descriptive or poetic passage may call for a more reflective approach, designed to sharpen responses and awareness; with a persuasive text, the reactions of the reader or listener may be examined, the devices of the persuader analysed. Frequently, the teacher will wish to direct attention simply to the function of a part of the text, or an aspect of it, to the way in which, say, comment, advice or protest is expressed, so as to enable students themselves to comment, advise or protest in an appropriate manner.

To serve students' linguistic and educational needs, a language course has to be viewed not as a collection of separate tasks but as a series of interrelated and mutually supportive activities; texts consequently cannot be treated in isolation one from another. A thematic approach entails grouping texts, as most recent textbooks have done, according to their subject-matter. A programme organised in this way pays dividends in terms of language learning: careful selection and ordering of texts enables language acquired from one text to contribute to the understanding and exploitation of another. The thematic approach promotes meaningful use of language patterns and vocabulary. It also tends to restore to texts some of their original force: the learner sees each less as an exercise and more as a message inviting reflection and response. Theme-based materials encourage purposeful application of study skills, communication between learners and, not least, exploration of a foreign way of life and view of the world.

A collection of texts, thematically related, might take as its starting point something of evident practical value, such as a set of spoken and printed weather forecasts. Initial treatment of the weather theme could be extended by the exploitation of one of those newspaper reports of avalanches or climbing accidents which are a regular feature of holiday news. An oral account, recorded off-air, of the same incident or another, might be compared with the one taken from a newspaper. In these texts informative and narrative language will predominate, though they may acquire a persuasive dimension when the reporter warns of the dangers of 'ski sauvage' or of inadequate equipment. The teacher could add a conversational element by asking a foreign acquaintance to record a personal anecdote of an incident in which weather played a part. Then the collection might be completed with a literary extract in which, for example, a climbing accident is treated descriptively in a manner intended to touch the emotions and imagination of the reader. The exploration of a practical theme such as weather forecasts, part-time jobs or leisure activities, the meal table or the camp site may, therefore, take in a wide range of texts of different types.

Another type of thematic collection, not necessarily distinct from the practical, may focus on material that reflects the experience of the students. In the case of teenage language learners this might include sport, fashion or evenings out, family, friends, the opposite sex. Subjects such as these, if tackled without condescension and without undue intrusion into privacy, can provide opportunities for genuine communication, especially if experiences are exchanged by students working in pairs or in small groups. However, as the course progresses, the emphasis of the thematic approach may well fall upon the sort of social topics that provide the substance of intelligent adult reading, listening and discussion and that draws, perhaps, upon subjects dealt with in other areas of the curriculum; privilege and deprivation, property and crime, advertising and the media, work and unemployment. These are themes upon which students will have opinions and at least a little knowledge; their interest can be aroused by further information and ideas, if these are presented in terms of particular instances which, additionally, offer insights into the life of the country concerned.

So with three or four texts chosen thematically – a couple perhaps from a textbook or anthology, an extract from a favourite novel, supplemented by something topical – the teacher is set for two or three weeks' language work. But, given this raw material, by what processes and strategies is the subject-matter to be explored and the active use of the language to be acquired? The study-skill activities referred to earlier, such as re-organisation, interpretation or summary, are designed to systematise and refine the ways in which students deal with ideas, information, images and so forth. In a similar manner, language-learning activities will enable them to manipulate sounds, vocabulary items and grammatical patterns with some confidence and accuracy. In reality, however, language-learning activities are inseparable from study-skill activities: they interlock and support each other, the latter giving context and purpose to the former.

Intensive exploitation of a text can be viewed, linguistically, as a process by which elements of language are identified, understood, processed, worked over, added to the learners' available stock of language and subsequently re-applied. For the students, therefore, there has to be a gradual liberation from the constraints of a particular text as both its content and language progressively become their own. Each language text, according to its character, demands an individual treatment, but, as has been suggested elsewhere (Gaskell, 1977), exploitation activities may conveniently be assigned to three broad phases. In the first, the *discovery* of the text, the activities are intended to assist the learners in an exploration of its meanings and its linguistic fabric. Working alone, in a pair or a small group, the students should be led to unravel the text for themselves, not simply to respond to interrogation by teacher or textbook. During the second or *practice* phase, the students bring the language under control, establish or extend categories and principles, clarify rules and meanings, refine pronunciation and intonation patterns. But if this process is to lead to communicative use of the language, it must be seen to have some purpose, it must itself suggest applications and contexts for application. Finally, in the third stage of work with a text, the *performance* stage, each student is encouraged to apply, for his or her own ends, the language acquired and practised in the preceding two phases. In this final stage, traditional A-level activities – essay-writing, conversation, dictation, even translation – may find a place. But sustained speaking and writing activities should, as far as possible, reflect some of the ways in which language is used most characteristically outside the language class. The ultimate objectives of this final stage lie in the world beyond the classroom.

The approach to text-based language work outlined here recognises the systematic nature of language: particular items do have to be learned, principles have to be acquired through practice. But language must first be encountered in operation in typical contexts; then practice and performance activities must set the language to work again, in further contexts. Suppose, for example, that the teacher wishes to tackle a relatively straightforward text, such as a news item from a popular daily reporting, say, a climbing accident in the Alps:

## UN GROUPE DE SKIEURS 'SAUVAGES' EMPORTÉS PAR UNE AVALANCHE

C'est la première avalanche tragique de la saison blanche. A la veille des vacances de Noël, en dépit des risques, un groupe de huit bons skieurs de Bourg-Saint-Maurice (Savoie) skiaient, hier en début d'après-midi, sur une pente vierge, aux environs de deux cents mètres d'altitude au-dessus de la station des Arcs. Soudain l'un d'eux déclencha une coulée qui emporta . . .

The teacher has also, it is assumed, been able to record a radio news bulletin, and unearth an extract from a literary source, each telling a similar story. Schematically presented in Table 5.1 are some examples among the many activities that might be devised, and used selectively as appropriate, in relation to the radio and

## Table 5.1

| Discovery of the Text | Language Practice | Language Performance |
|---|---|---|
| **Overview**<br>• *Summarising/classifying* essential facts from oral or printed news story under headings: time, place, victims, etc.<br>• *Answering questions* on lessons intended to be learned from oral and/or printed text | **Vocabulary**<br>• *Matching* nouns from text with verbs likely to follow, or the reverse; completion of narrative using expressions assembled<br>• *Composing* brief paragraph using vocabulary on rescue theme | **Summary**<br>• *Re-narration* in shortened form, as for serious newspaper, of either spoken or printed news story; headings provided |
| **Information/Ideas**<br>• *Inserting* missing facts in transcript of spoken version, after study of newspaper article<br>• *Reconstituting* sequence of events from oral version on basis of sketch map of accident | **Grammar**<br>• *Contextualised composition* of sentences containing relative pronouns, based on sketches of people or things in newspaper story<br>• *Contextualised* question-answer to elicit conditional perfect: What would have happened in other circumstances | **Expansion**<br>• *Oral account*, as for news broadcast, of parallel event: journalist's notes provided |
| **Language Items**<br>• *Completing* summary of newspaper story from which patterns or elements expressing cause and effect are missing<br>• *Tabulating* vocabulary under headings: skiing, accident, rescue, weather | **Functions**<br>• *Contextualised role-playing* requiring identification of advice given in oral and printed versions, followed by advice-giving activity in pairs | **Adaptation**<br>• *Conversational outcome*: replying to questions by journalist as if from point of view of member of rescue team<br>• *Informative outcome*: gathering or inferring factual detail on incident from literary text; composing news item on this incident<br>• *Narrative outcome*: eyewitness account, oral or written, related by 'gendarme de montagne'<br>• *Descriptive outcome*: after analysis of literary extract, description of incident recounted in newspaper from a survivor's viewpoint, emphasising feelings and impressions<br>• *Persuasive outcome*: composition of brochure on dangers of skiing or climbing, and on precautions to be taken |
| **Interpretation/Response**<br>• *Listing* expressions revealing writer's attitude to events related, or identifying responses expected of reader<br>• *Evaluating* according to criteria provided why this story constitutes news | **Notions**<br>• *Contextualised pattern practice* on time relationships, linking together events of parallel incident presented in note form | |
| **Style**<br>• *Identifying* expressions characteristic of narrative text: adverbs, conjunctions, etc.<br>• *Reducing* spontaneous oral version in radio report, eliminating repetitions and redundancies | **Intonation**<br>• *Microconversations* to practice interrogative and declarative intonation: model sentence from oral text presenting accident to be modified for other accidents: road, fire, sea, etc. | |

newspaper reports and in accordance with the three phases of exploitation outlined above.

It can be seen that the first, exploratory, stage in the treatment of a text is intended to focus attention upon elements of content and of language, to explain or clarify these as necessary and to help students to remember them. Furthermore, this *discovery* phase may usefully be divided, as here, into two stages: a first approach, or overview, designed to establish the basic form, character and purpose of the text, then a close analysis of the text in greater detail. In the overview stage, in the early part of the course at least, students need guidance in their approach to a listening or reading task: indications such as headings, a summary chart or simply questions may provide reassurance, and help to shape the act of comprehension. Once students know what kind of text they are faced with, what its salient features are, to whom it is addressed and for what purpose, they can profitably tackle finer points: they may scrutinise facts, ideas, relationships between facts; they may identify categories of information, themes or arguments, interpret implications, detect the author's point of view. In addition, they will direct their attention, with the help of the teacher or with guidance provided in the teaching materials, towards linguistic features: vocabulary or grammatical items, the form or style of the text.

Once the language and content of the text have been unravelled and partly assimilated, the *practice* phase enables students to systematise what they have just acquired, to assign items of vocabulary to a familiar cluster, to sharpen up a rule or pattern, to see how a function such as advising or reproving may be expressed, how a notion such as causality, sequence or location may be formulated. But understanding principles is not enough; the principles must also be applied, several times over. However, unless items, patterns and rules are practised appropriately, within a given context, few of them are likely to be added to learners' active stock of language. In the practice phase, therefore, students must have something real or realistic to say or write, and they need to say or write it to someone for a purpose. Pair and group activities can increase the sense of realism and provide extra time for students to engage in practice.

It is in the final phase of the exploitation of a text, in sustained and increasingly independent language *performance*, that the approach outlined in this section finds its justification. Here students are re-applying language patterns and items, combining them with material they already possess, so as to say or write something considered and coherent. A final phase activity is generally in some sense an adaptation, but one in which the students are personally or intellectually engaged. At its simplest adaptation may entail summary or expansion of the original, or of related material. More often than not, however, a shift of some kind will be required: the form of the original may be preserved and the content modified; alternatively, the content may assume a new form, with a narrative being transformed, for example, into a conversation, into a poetic account or an informative piece. Text types, as Table 5.1 shows, not only characterise what the students read or hear, they also characterise what they say or write; they feature at the outcome as well as at the starting point of the language learning process.

In the approach to the use of language texts outlined here, the learner is seen as a user of language in an authentic and realistic sense; language is seen as something purposeful, implying and creating relationships between people. If learning tasks enable students to absorb, practise and apply pieces of language, ideas and information in ways that they perceive as related to what they want to do with the language, then they will learn with more enjoyment and more commitment; they will learn more effectively. If in addition they can, within the language class, share and exchange ideas, hopes, fears and experience, as in their everyday lives, then they are involved personally in their learning and the classroom is open to the outside world.

Collections of thematically related texts, exploited in the manner described here, will then form an effective focus for an advanced foreign language course. But this sort of work will need to be complemented by a systematic reading programme if learners are to extend and deepen their knowledge of the foreign culture. The nature of the reading programme and the development of the skills necessary to tackle it effectively are the topics treated in the next section.

## The Reading Programme

The post O-level reading programme has traditionally consisted of little more than the four or five texts studied for the examination. This has too often meant that the students' engagement with the foreign culture has been restricted to one small corner of the literary domain and that their experience of reading material in the foreign language has largely been confined to literary narrative. More-over, as a study of A-level questions demonstrates, the critical perspective adopted in testing and teaching has been one which falsifies the nature of literature by reifying it as literary history. The unsuitability of this approach when applied at sixth-form level has been discussed elsewhere (Corless, 1978). What is more, it denies, by its very nature, the contribution which literature can make to the personal development of teenagers. The reading of a novel or short story in the mother tongue can be seen as an act of pleasure, with the reader creating a secondary world in his own imagination from the cues provided by the author. Literary texts can justify their place in a post O-level reading programme in foreign languages if this act of imaginative engagement is seen as central, and if individual response opens the way for discussion of personal relationships, moral values and social issues as they arise from the texts.

Whatever might be their merits, however, literary texts represent only an aspect of the foreign culture. Depending on their background and interests, students will want to find out more about how the inhabitants of the foreign country lead their daily lives, how they use their leisure hours, how their society is organised, how it has grown to be what it is. With the exception of those of one board – which now offers an alternative French syllabus – the English A-level syllabuses in French and German now offer scope for a broader investigation of the foreign culture. Nevertheless, 'civilisation' must not be seen as a separate component of the post O-level course. Just as it is impossible to present an overview of the foreign literature in four or five books, it is equally unrealistic to expect students to draw even provisional conclusions about the geographical, social and economic character of the foreign country from a similarly limited range of set texts. The commitment to a broad reading programme is therefore an essential aspect of the approach to language work advocated in this chapter. If students have to study set texts – whether literary or non-literary – they can approach them with greater confidence and enjoyment if they are presented within the framework of a broad reading programme, which will, of course, occupy a reasonable part of students' private study time. However, the principle of a broad reading programme raises important questions, first about the choice of materials and second about the development of the students' reading skills.

The texts prescribed at A-level often seem to pay more regard to the tastes of teachers than to the needs and interests of those who will study them. If a reading programme is to arouse and sustain enthusiasm, teachers will need, at each point in the course, to select texts which respect their students' linguistic capabilities, cultural understanding and intellectual and emotional maturity. At the post O-level stage, 'civilisation' texts will be short more often than long, they will offer case histories rather than abstract generalisations and they will in the main be contemporary and not overloaded with jargon or technical language. Similarly, literary texts will most profitably be selected from the modern period and will offer students insights into human issues which they can relate to and talk about. If teachers plan their language work along thematic lines, the themes selected will open up avenues which a whole class or particular individuals can follow up in their reading. There are published lists available, particularly relating to French, which suggest a broad range of suitable reading material (for example French 16–19 Study Group, 1981, pp. 58–60).

The processes involved in fluent reading have been the subject of much research and speculation. One influential view of this complex of skills is that it is basically a 'psycholinguistic guessing game' (Goodman, 1973). In approaching a text, the fluent reader uses knowledge networks he already possesses, both linguistic and informational, in order to form hypotheses about what the text is saying; and once a hypothesis has been confirmed and the piece of information 'read', this will form the basis for further anticipations. Skill in reading, it is suggested, involves not greater attention to detail, but 'more accurate first guesses based on better sampling techniques, greater control over language structure, broadened experiences and increased conceptual development' (Goodman, 1978, p. 81).

Reading research has identified three 'higher-level' skills which the fluent reader employs: *skimming*, *scanning* and *reflective reading*. The skilled reader will *skim* a text, be it a book, a chapter or an article, in order to find out what it is about, whether he wants to read it closely; he will do this by looking at chapter or section headings, first and last paragraphs, key sentences, important words. He will *scan* a text when he wants to identify an item or items of detail (names, dates, events, reasons). What modern linguists refer to as gist comprehension usually involves one or other of these skills. *Reflective reading* will involve concentrating on a text at one or more levels. Adding a gloss to Gray's formulation (Clymer, 1972, p. 61), it may entail establishing the facts of an argument or narrative (reading the lines), making inferences about the text, reacting to it, linking it with one's own ideas or experiences (reading between the lines) and/or evaluating the text's worth or validity, appreciating form or use of language (reading beyond the lines). It should be stressed that the reader may engage with a text on more than one of these levels in a single act of reading: they are not necessarily separate and distinct.

Reading, therefore, is more than a receptive skill; it is an active, interrogative process. It will moreover be evident that the act of reading will be more efficient if the reader approaches a text with a clear reading purpose in mind. It may be assumed that most post O-level linguists have achieved a sufficient degree of competence in the foreign language and in basic mother-tongue reading skill to start to read in an interrogative manner. This being the case, the teacher will need, from the outset of the course, to guide their approach to extensive reading by setting regular reading assignments. In order to ensure that these are carried out effectively, he will need:

(1) to match material carefully to the students' linguistic competence and to their needs of interests;
(2) to consider which of the reading skills described above he wants to call on in the processing of a text (perhaps, for example, scanning followed by reflective reading);
(3) to guide the students' approach to a text by suggesting a reading *purpose* (to collect information, to unravel a sequence of events, to follow a line of argument) and by proposing an *outcome* (to make notes following given guidelines, to answer questions, to fill in a grid, to complete a gapped summary);
(4) to ease the students into more demanding texts by providing essential background information, glossing key vocabulary items, outlining the pattern, say, of an argument or narrative and by highlighting the structure signals which point the way through a text (Marland, 1977, pp. 125–6);
(5) to arrange for some assignments to form a basis for discussion – small group or whole class – or for writing, so that the students begin to reflect on what they read.

To exemplify some of the points made above, suppose that the students, in the latter part of their first post O-level year, are investigating the issue of road safety in France. The teacher may wish to complement work on selected magazine articles, radio and newspaper accident reports and relevant documentary materials by asking them to read, say, an edited version of the road accident which forms the basis of Paul Guimard's *Les Choses de la Vie* (1967, p. 35ff.). A Parisian lawyer, Pierre Delhomeau, is driving to Rennes for a meeting with a colleague:

La MG 1100 aborde à 140 le large virage du lieu-dit la Providence. Le profil de la route autorise cette vitesse. Le virage est convenablement relevé, la visibilité suffisante. Les pointillés jaunes qui délimitent les trois voies de la chaussée se rejoignent à l'entrée de la courbe . . .

Table 5.2

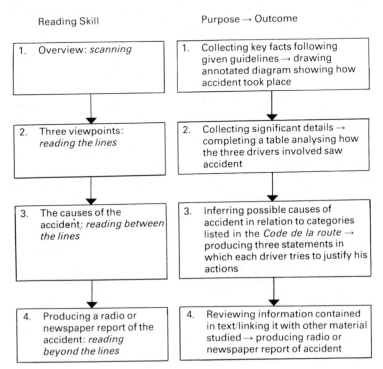

| Reading Skill | Purpose → Outcome |
|---|---|
| 1.  Overview: *scanning* | 1.  Collecting key facts following given guidelines → drawing annotated diagram showing how accident took place |
| 2.  Three viewpoints: *reading the lines* | 2.  Collecting significant details → completing a table analysing how the three drivers involved saw accident |
| 3.  The causes of the accident: *reading between the lines* | 3.  Inferring possible causes of accident in relation to categories listed in the *Code de la route* → producing three statements in which each driver tries to justify his actions |
| 4.  Producing a radio or newspaper report of the accident: *reading beyond the lines* | 4.  Reviewing information contained in text/linking it with other material studied → producing radio or newspaper report of accident |

After establishing the context and picking out and glossing any key vocabulary items which may impede fluent reading, the teacher might guide the student's encounter with the text as shown in Table 5.2.

The teacher would no doubt want to introduce each of these activities to the whole class, as well as presenting them on a work-sheet. At appropriate points in the sequence, he might equally wish to complement individual reading and note-making with pair, small-group or whole-class discussion.

In the example quoted above, an extract from a literary text is used as a means of adding an imaginative dimension to work on a cultural topic. The approach described, however, can clearly be applied to a wide range of non-literary material. If, for example, as part of their work on the theme of holidays, the students are confronted with an article ironically critical of the French enthusiasm for camping, they can be led – in a manner similar to that outlined above – from forming an overview of the article, to collecting the main arguments, to inferring the author's position and finally, with the help of other material on camping, to evaluating the article in the light of their own knowledge and experience.

The approach described may also be adapted to the close study of a literary text. After introducing Mauriac's *Thérèse Desqueyroux*, for example, by providing some background information on the Landes and presenting some basic facts about French judicial procedure, the teacher might first ask the students to read the book through for their own enjoyment, perhaps with an overview guide-sheet indicating things to look out for or points to consider. Small-group and whole-class discussion of initial reactions might be followed by further study of the text, either chapter by chapter or more broadly in terms of plot development, characters, themes, with key passages being selected for study in detail. Whichever approach is adopted, the teacher will need to help the students, perhaps by means of guide-sheets, in collecting information about places, events, relationships (reading the lines), in interpreting attitudes, values, motives (reading between the lines), in exploring social and moral issues and in appreciating imagery and form (reading beyond the lines). Throughout the course of their work on a literary text, as has been suggested elsewhere (Corless, 1978, pp. 165–6), the students will need frequent opportunities to share their findings and talk over their reactions in structured but unsupervised small-group discussion. There is in fact an important place, in the post O-level foreign language course as a whole, for learning activities which are organised by the teacher but carried out by small groups or pairs of students working independently. The organisation of the language class is the topic considered in the next section.

## The Management of Teaching and Learning

There is a substantial body of writing, perhaps best represented by the work of Barnes (for example 1976), which suggests that school-based learning is most effective when students participate fully in the learning process. This implies in particular that in order to relate new experiences to what they already know or believe, they need frequent opportunities to talk their way to knowledge and understanding. Barnes writes persuasively about the contribution that structured but unsupervised small-group activities can make in many areas of the curriculum.

In the advanced foreign language class, the students' concern is a double one: to acquire new knowledge or understanding and to make their own at least some of the language in which this is expressed. The active participation of the students is therefore doubly important. However, small-group activities are not the only alternative to whole-class work. The teacher of an advanced foreign language class needs to adopt a flexible approach to the management of teaching and learning, to vary group size according to the task to be carried out. At the beginning of a learning sequence, for example, the teacher may need to work with the *whole class* in order to provide background information about a text, to propose a way of approaching it and perhaps to introduce some key vocabulary items. Students may then need to work as *individuals*, reading or listening, making notes on ideas or language, doing written exercises. As the sequence unfolds, they may need to work in *pairs* to compare notes and develop ideas, to work through interactive exercises or carry out role-play. Alternatively, the students may need to gather in *small groups* in order to pool information, exchange opinions, establish a consensus. And at various stages, the teacher will want to draw the *whole class* together in order, for example, to check on points that have emerged from individual listening or reading, to review and develop the work that has been carried out by pairs or in small groups, to establish a language principle and direct controlled practice, to prepare related writing assignments.

The theme of this chapter has been that if students are to learn to communicate confidently, the language class must be a place where language is not simply practised but also used. With flexible management of learning activities arising from authentic texts, students may acquire and apply language in realistic ways; they may relate to each other and to the teacher through the language itself. The purpose of the advanced foreign language course, as it is conceived here, is therefore to bring that language into the classroom, then to put it at the disposal of learners for use in real life.

## References

Abbs, B., Ayton, A. and Freebairn, I. (1975) *Strategies*, Longman, London

Barnes, D. (1976) *From Communication to Curriculum*, Penguin Books, Harmondsworth

British Broadcasting Corporation (1974) *Kontakte*, British Broadcasting Corporation, London

Brown, M.W.F. (1973) 'The Mill Hill French Geography/History Scheme' in *Modern Languages and European Studies* (CILT Reports and Papers 9), Centre for Information on Language Teaching and Research, London, pp. 27–30

Clymer, T. (1972) 'What is "Reading"?: Some Current Concepts' in A. Melnik and J. Merritt (eds.), *Reading: Today and Tomorrow*, University of London Press/ The Open University Press, London, pp. 48–66

Corless, F. (1978) 'A New Look at Literary Studies in the Sixth Form Modern Languages Course', *Audio-Visual Language Journal*, 16 (3), 161–9

van Ek, J.A. (1975) *The Threshold Level*, Council of Europe, Strasbourg

French 16–19 Study Group (1981) *French 16–19: a New Perspective*, Hodder and Stoughton, London

Gaskell, R. (1977) 'Using Foreign Texts in Post O-Level Language Teaching', *Audio-Visual Language Journal*, 15 (1), 26–35

Goodman, K. (1973) 'Reading: a Psycholinguistic Guessing Game' in N.C. Farnes, *Reading Purposes, Comprehension and the Use of Context* (Reading Development Units 3 and 4), The Open University Press, Bletchley, pp. 78–84

Guimard, P. (1967) *Les Choses de la Vie*, Denoël/Collection Folio, Paris

Harding, A., Page, B. and Rowell, S. (1980) *Graded Objectives in Modern Languages*, Centre for Information on Language Teaching and Research, London

Joint Council for 16+ National Criteria (1981) *Draft National Criteria for French: French Working Party Report*

Marland, M. (1977) *Language Across the Curriculum*, Heinemann, London

Schools Council 18+ Research Programme (1977) *Studies Based on the N & F Proposals: Report of the Modern Languages Syllabus Steering Group to the Joint Examinations Sub-Committee of the Schools Council*, Schools Council, London

Schools Council Working Paper 28 (1970) *New Patterns in Sixth Form Modern Language Studies*, Evans/Methuen Educational, London
Tabberer, R. and Allman, J. (1981) *Study Skills at Sixteen Plus* (NFER Research in Progress 4), National Foundation for Educational Research, Slough
Wilkins, D.A. (1976) *Notional Syllabuses*, Oxford University Press, Oxford

# 6 LANGUAGE STUDY FOR THE SLOWER LEARNER

E.W. Hawkins

## Preliminary

Slower learners are newcomers to the foreign language classroom. Before we discuss the new problems they pose to curriculum planners and teachers, there are some preliminary things to be said about the circumstances which opened the classroom door to them.

The re-organisation of secondary education on comprehensive lines was never planned. The ending of selection at 11+ was something into which Local Education Authorities drifted unprepared and without any research into the implications of what they were doing. The drift began long before the Labour government issued its famous Circular 10/65. Already by 1963 some ninety local education authorities had introduced comprehensive education and it is estimated (Kogan, 1971) that by 1965 at least 12 per cent of all pupils in England and Wales were in some kind of comprehensive school. Anthony Crosland's circular merely accelerated the development. Although Margaret Thatcher withdrew Circular 10/65 in 1970 this did not halt the drift away from selection at 11+ which had become widely discredited, largely owing to the stark contrast in most areas between the opportunities offered in the two kinds of school for which pupils were selected. The movement away from the 11+ examination gathered its own momentum despite the lack of research into exactly what was to replace it.

It is now widely accepted that re-organisation affected language teaching more directly than any other part of the curriculum. It was, of course, the slower learner's curriculum that was affected, for the faster learners had always been offered a foreign language in their grammar schools. In 1965, when Crosland issued his circular, only one in four pupils (those selected by a test of verbal ability) began a foreign language at 11+. By 1977, when the Inspectorate made its survey of 83 comprehensive schools, the percentages studying at least one language in each of the five secondary years were as follows:

| at 11+ | 89 per cent | at 14+ | 35 per cent | (when 'options' |
|--------|-------------|--------|-------------|-----------------|
| at 12+ | 85 per cent |        |             | are introduced) |
| at 13+ | 80 per cent | at 15+ | 33 per cent |                 |

Before we look more closely at the background to these tragically wasteful figures, there is one consequence of re-organisation to examine that has gone largely undiscussed. Re-organisation in most areas meant that co-education became the rule rather than the exception. The selective grammar schools had in the main been single-sex schools. Replacing them by co-educational comprehensives immediately affected those subjects which make demands on verbal 'awareness', and what psychologists call 'semantic memory'. It is known that, for reasons in some way connected with earlier physiological maturity (onset of puberty is some 18 months earlier in girls) girls score consistently higher than boys at 11+ on tests of semantic memory (while boys do better at spatial tasks and co-ordination tests).

Grouping boys and girls together for learning tasks, such as the attack on the foreign language, for which they are (at age 11+) so unequally equipped would seem, in any rationally researched and planned school system, to call for cogent justification overriding the evidence of its effect on performance. There is little doubt where this evidence points. To quote the NFER study, *Primary French in the Balance*:

> In the development of a pupil's attitude towards learning, the concept which he forms of his own aptitudes and abilities must undoubtedly play an influential role. Such a concept is thought to be formed through the pupil's interaction with 'significant others' in his environment . . . the child's notion of himself is dependent upon the approval of his teachers and upon how he compares himself with his fellows. (Burstall *et al.*, 1974, p. 227)

How does this show itself in the co-educational French classroom, where the verbal precocity of girls, increasingly marked as the two sexes progress through the primary stage, gives the girls an 18 months' head start at the beginning of the secondary course? Burstall's evidence is unequivocal:

With regard to achievement in French, the findings of the

secondary stage of the evaluation are clear-cut: both boys and girls in single-sex schools reached a higher level of achievement in French than did pupils of either sex in co-educational schools. [And as for attitudes:] Boys in single-sex schools had markedly more favourable attitudes towards learning French than had boys in co-educational schools (Burstall *et al.*, 1974, p. 240)

(It is right to add that Burstall also found that a 'significantly higher percentage of boys in co-educational than in single-sex schools enjoyed being at school'.)

Girls' verbal precocity is short-lived. When adolescence is complete for both sexes the difference between them, measured by tests of verbal memory, disappears. If anything, boys of 17 show greater verbal facility than girls of the same age. Unfortunately the short period when the difference in the verbal capacities of the two sexes is most pronounced (that is between the ages of 10 and 15) is precisely the period when curriculum, and career, choices are made. The effects of this for foreign language study are becoming clear, with the disappearance of boys from the faster streams in French, the increasing preponderance of girls scoring high grades in the 16+ examinations, the growing scarcity of boys in sixth-form foreign language sets and the growing disproportion between numbers of men and women graduating in foreign languages. Between 1969 and 1979 the number of men graduates in foreign languages applying to train as teachers on PGCE courses fell by one half (from 1,281 or 38.5 per cent of the total, to 616, or 29.9 per cent of the total: Hawkins, 1981, p. 17). Meanwhile precisely the opposite effect has been observed with regard to girls' achievement in mathematics, in co-educational classrooms. Academic observations of this kind, however, did not halt the drift away from selection at 11+ which, according to Crosland: 'was a product of fundamental value judgements about equity and equal opportunity and social division as well as about education' (Kogan, 1971, p. 190). By the end of the 1970s some 80 to 90 per cent of all state school pupils of secondary age were in schools that were comprehensive at least in name. How many of these schools have a truly comprehensive intake is uncertain; it must be very few, certainly, in the run-down urban areas where the social composition of the catchment area and the creaming-off of the few pupils fortunate enough to have encouraging homes leaves the so-called comprehensive heavily weighted with pupils suffering multiple disadvantage, who have enjoyed little quiet, unstressed, individual dialogue with a caring adult on which 'readiness to learn' can build, and whose reading ages on transfer to secondary school are well below the national average.

It was the ending of selection at 11+ that revealed the true nature of the inequality from which children suffer in our democracy. For a hundred years successive generations of devoted teachers and administrators had laboured to set children free from the limitations which denied them 'equality of opportunity' to develop into autonomous citizens and caring parents. It had seemed obvious that the chief restraint on freedom and equality of opportunity was *ignorance*. With ignorance went lack of the techniques to operate rewardingly in society, to earn a living and live a full life. It was ignorance and lack of skills that barred access to the stored expertise and discoveries of previous generations. This was, of course, true enough: and growing armies of children set free from such constraints by winning scarce places in state secondary schools of growing power, in the first half of this century, gave promise of what the democracy might achieve if all, or most, of our children could acquire the keys (especially the linguistic keys) to unlock the conceptual doors.

Sadly, just as the battle was being won, to bring knowledge and skills within reach of every child in the spirit of the schools dreamt of in the French Revolution in which all might find 'la carrière ouverte aux talents', it was revealed that 'ignorance' was not the main enemy. The map that the reformers had been following was incomplete. The road of free schooling, free books, subsidised transport, competitive open access to university with full maintenance grants for the successful, even 'positive discrimination' for priority areas, all of these, though *necessary*, were *insufficient* to help the children who most needed help. There was another restraint on children's ability to make use of any of these resources, a restraint that had been concealed by the selection process: it can be summarised as sheer 'parental inadequacy'.

It is now clear that adults differ very greatly in their capacity to be adequate parents. It is the most demanding role that adults are called on to act out in our complex society. It calls for qualities of character that many adults simply never develop. Being a good parent can best be learnt through the accident of growing up in a good home just as each generation of inadequate parents trains up a generation of inadequate parents in its own likeness. The real hazard, it is now clear, for any child, is to draw an unlucky ticket in the lottery of parental effectiveness. This has been amply shown by researches such as the Plowden (1967) survey of parental attitudes and by the work of Mia Kelmer Pringle (1980). In order to be able to profit from the education that the state provides, the child needs a parent who is willing to give *time* to being a parent and who can offer a *model* of responsible, mature, adult *will to learn*.

The implications of this for the comprehensive ideal have scarcely been discussed nationally in any depth. It seems certain that 'education for parenthood' must become one of the central themes challenging educators in the eighties and nineties. Equally urgent will be the search for ways of giving back to the generation of children who have been deprived of it, the precious gift of 'adult time' (dialogue, shared activities with an adult, learning curiosity by reliving the adult's curiosity and by having one's questions *listened to*). 'Adult time' on this scale cannot be given to children within the normal school pattern. The critical age for it is between two and five years. Where are we to find the caring adults in sufficient numbers for this dialogue and sharing of individual curiosities and discoveries about the world (and especially about the matching of language with concepts) on which school learning has to build?

'Adult time' for young children in the critical pre-school period is hardest to find when parents are under strain, in ill health, poorly housed and when families are large, when there is only one parent who must be both bread-winner and mother, and when, in consequence, babies are boarded out during the day with untrained and often unregistered child-minders. It is not surprising that researchers (for example Burstall *et al.*, 1974) have found a linear correlation between progress at foreign language learning and the status of the parental occupation.

A decade ago the Schools Council Working Paper No. 28 (Schools Council, 1970) warned that foreign language study was rapidly becoming a middle-class prerogative. Ironically enough this tendency was accelerated by the well-meant pressures from teachers to give more credit to oral skills and put less emphasis on writing. Oral skills thrive on travel, on home-to-home exchanges. These are ruled out for many children by parental circumstances. It is easier for the child from the disadvantaged home to make headway in school in subjects (such as the natural sciences) for which the school can provide the laboratory and the exciting discoveries within its own walls. The language teacher's 'laboratory' is the foreign country, the foreign family. Home background pressures keep the door to this laboratory closed to very many children who, at least, in the days when the spoken language counted for little, and the written test was all important, could defend themselves with their pen in competition with their rivals from middle-class homes.

It was necessary to spend some time on these preliminaries in order to establish who these slower learners are whose foreign language study we are to examine. It must be clear that they are not simply 'less able'. Talk of teaching 'across the ability range' is misleading. The statistics show that they are for the most part *boys* and that they are overwhelmingly drawn from one disadvantaged social background. The curriculum, so far as languages are concerned, in the fourth year of the comprehensive school, by the time that children have made their subject choices, based on success or failure in the first three years, is a curriculum clearly differentiated by these two factors of sex and social background. To speak of our slower learners as 'below average' is even more misleading. This might imply that about half the school population falls into the category. In fact the 'slower learners' whose case we have to examine are far more numerous. As we have seen earlier, the HMI survey of 83 comprehensive schools (HMI, 1977) showed that some *two-thirds* of pupils who begin a foreign language at 11 + drop it by the fourth year. The survey showed further that only *one in ten* of 11 + beginners attains the modest goal of a pass in GCE (or CSE equivalent) at 16 +. The *nine out of ten* who fall by the wayside would certainly not have dropped out if their progress had been rewarding. It is these tragic figures that give us some idea of the dimensions of our problem.

If we are to do justice to the great majority of our children who at present make such slow going of their foreign language, it seems that we have three questions to answer:

(i)   what exactly are their learning problems?
(ii)  what would a coherent linguistic education to meet their needs look like?
(iii) within such a coherent linguistic education what would be the place of foreign language study and what objectives, teaching methods and assessment techniques would this imply?

## Learning Problems

*Aptitude or Attitude?*

One would expect aptitude for foreign language learning and a positive attitude to it to go together. In fact it is a consistent finding of research that the two are not positively correlated. S. Krashen (1981) has speculated that 'aspects of aptitude relate directly to conscious language learning' (what Krashen calls the operation of the 'monitor') 'while attitudinal factors generally relate to sub-conscious language acquisition' (p. 24). In a study conducted at the Language Teaching Centre, York University, and reported by M. Buckby (1981), two carefully constructed and validated tests of aptitude and attitude were given to over 2,000 pupils in their third year in comprehensive schools. Buckby reports (p. 19):

> It might be supposed that the attitude of pupils towards learning a foreign language would be strongly influenced by their aptitude for learning it. That this did not seem to be the case for the project pupils is shown by the very low correlations for both the control and the experimental groups between their scores on the 'Attitude to French' factor (whether administered before or after the experimental year of 'graded objectives' work which the project was evaluating) and on the aptitude test.

What is meant by *aptitude* for foreign language learning? A central component, revealed by all the work on aptitude testing in the USA by P. Pimsleur (1966) and J.B. Carroll (1973), and in the UK by P.S. Green (1975), is what Carroll has called 'the individual's ability to demonstrate his awareness of the syntactical patterning of sentences in a language' (Carroll, 1973, p. 7). He suggests:

> linguistic 'competence' in the sense defined by Chomsky (1965) involves some kind of 'knowledge' of the grammatical rules of a language, this 'knowledge' is ordinarily out of conscious awareness . . . nevertheless, some adolescents and adults (and even some children) can be made to demonstrate an awareness of the syntactical structure of the sentences they speak . . . even among adults there are large individual differences in this ability, and these individual differences are related to success in learning foreign languages. (ibid.)

Beginning with the York Study (Green, 1975) and continuing with prolonged trials with learners of all ages, P.S. Green has found that language learning correlates consistently with the capacity quickly to accomplish two learning steps:

(i)   to spot the pattern in new language presented;
(ii)  to invent a new, analogous, item to fit the pattern.

For Pimsleur one of the key components of foreign language aptitude is 'the ability to reason analytically about verbal materials' (Pimsleur, 1966, p. 182). The central importance of this ability to analyse pattern in language has been shown by work on the short-term memory (STM). G. Olson (Olson, 1973) has shown that it is his ability to spot the pattern quickly and so to 'process' the message that enables the learner to overcome the constraints of short-term memory. Olson's experiments show little correlation between scores on tests of STM of the traditional kind (that is, tests of the ability to hold in STM strings of meaningless random digits) and language retention. Olson explains that this is because the learner with the capacity to identify pattern and to 'process' incoming messages overcomes STM restraints by concentrating more meaning into each 'bit' of information received. (For fuller discussion see Hawkins, 1981, p. 226.) A most interesting light has been thrown on this research in foreign language 'processing' by recent work on the difficulties many children face when learning to read. The move from what I.G. Mattingley (Kavanagh and Mattingley, 1972) has called 'primary language activity' (listening and speaking) to 'secondary activity' (reading and writing) poses special problems for those children who, owing to lack of appropriate dialogue at home, come to the challenge of reading and writing unprepared. As Margaret Donaldson has put it, in *Children's Minds* (1978), reading requires that the purely linguistic elements of the utterance (its syntax, semantics, the segments of which it is composed) must be 'disembedded' from the complex of signals of a non-linguistic kind and the often confusing expectations that accompany the message, and indeed *are* the message so far as the child is concerned. This process calls for 'awareness' of language which children have to learn:

the first step is the step of conceptualizing language – becoming aware of it as a separate structure, freeing it from its embeddedness in events . . . Some children come to school with this step already taken, or at least with the movement already begun. They come with an enormous initial advantage . . . in some homes awareness of the spoken word is greatly encouraged. Some parents talk about words to their children, play word games with them and so on. But most talk only *with* words. Indeed a great many children come to school not even aware that separate words exist – that the flow of speech can be broken up into these units. (Donaldson, 1978, p. 88)

It seems that as children move out of the familiar world of concrete objects, the 'enactive' universe of babyhood, into the symbolic world of language, everything turns on the hazard of how much opportunity they enjoy for patient, exploratory, corrective dialogue with a caring adult whom they can call their own, and who has herself (himself) mastered the processing strategies. The number of children who fall at this first hurdle is far greater than is commonly imagined. The National Child Development Study (Davie, Butler and Goldstein, 1972) showed that 48 per cent of the children in social class V were *poor readers* at 7 compared with only 8 per cent in social class I.

There is no evidence that the primary school helps these children significantly. Indeed if we examine an extreme case, the West Indian child, whose home background usually epitomises the problems discussed above, we find that his reading, well below average at age 8, falls steadily further below the average the longer he remains at school. For most such children life-chances are closed by the end of infant school, with the failure to read confidently and with relish (see evidence summarised in Taylor, 1981, p. 85). Conversely, as research at the Thomas Coram Research Unit, London Institute of Education, shows (Tizard *et al.*, 1981), when the school can help parents, even semi-literate parents, to *talk* to children regularly about their reading, the children's progress improves dramatically. The Thomas Coram findings receive strong support from research at Manchester University by Beveridge and Jerrams (1981). Clearly something happens during this precious individual dialogue with a caring adult which makes possible the difficult transition from 'primary' to 'secondary' language activity. I.G. Mattingley (in Kavanagh and Mattingley, 1972) has suggested that the key factor is 'awareness' of language. He points out that 'primary' language activity (spoken) is largely innate, whereas 'secondary' activity (written) has to be learnt. Primary activity seems to be 'pre-programmed' in the infant. It is fairly evenly distributed across the population in consequence, while standards of secondary activity, for which there is less evidence of pre-programming, differ enormously, from the widely read and subtly literate few to the functionally illiterate majority.

J.S. Bruner makes a similar distinction when he contrasts 'communicative competence', possessed by nearly all children, with 'analytic competence', the ability to 'turn language in upon itself'. He points out that one of the chief effects of schooling is that 'language context comes more and more to take the place of perceptual context' (Bruner, 1975, p.69). Somehow, then, in the course of individual dialogue with an adult who has made the journey before, the fortunate child begins to grasp the elements of 'awareness' of language, or of 'analytic competence' that will be needed to make the breakthrough to literacy. The less fortunate majority become ineffective readers. The relevance of this for the foreign language teacher is that, as the researches of Olson and Carroll and others have shown, precisely the same 'awareness' is called on at the age of 11+, when the adventure into the foreign language begins. Mattingley, in the essay quoted above, has suggested that the skill of reading is 'parasitic' upon the degree of awareness achieved in the 'primary' stage of listening/speaking. In the same way, progress into the foreign language, under classroom conditions in an English language environment, is a 'parasitic' activity. It may not be the same when the child learns the foreign language by 'immersion', as, say, an immigrant child does, but in the brief lesson, buffeted by the 'gale of English', learning a foreign language is 'parasitic' upon the 'awareness' of language already achieved, *largely outside of school*.

We have a situation, then, in which teachers of the foreign language and teachers of the mother tongue face a common problem: namely lack of 'awareness' of language among *most* of the pupils they meet. One might expect them to make common cause, to discuss their shared problems, to collaborate in programmes designed to restore to children deprived of it this precious linguistic awareness which opens the door to reading in English and a confident attack on the foreign language and lack of which denies access to the whole field of verbal learning in the curriculum. Instead we find these two groups of teachers too often working in sealed-off compartments. Never having been brought together during their university degree course, and having scant contact during their training year, they are unaware of the nature of the problem they both face. It is rare even to find them taking steps to agree a common vocabulary to use when discussing language with the pupils whom they teach in adjacent classrooms and in consecutive lessons.

## Attitude: the Role of 'Empathy'

If we are right in identifying 'awareness' of language, or of 'analytic competence', as the chief factor in aptitude (both for reading and for getting a foreign language under school conditions) we can cling to the hope of being able to do something about it. The researches at the Thomas Coram Institute challenge teachers of reading to experiment with a radical re-appraisal of traditional notions of co-operation with parents. The new approach calls rather for teaching *through* parents. Similarly, in many areas teachers of foreign languages and teachers of English are coming together to devise common programmes in 'awareness of language', of 'education of the ear', in short of 'secondary language activities' designed to help pupils who are slow at 'processing' messages (to use Olson's term) both in the mother tongue and the foreign language.

Problems rooted in 'attitudes', however, are much harder to solve. As we have seen, research shows little positive correlation between aptitude and attitude. Why this might be becomes clear when we examine one specific aspect of attitude towards foreign language learning, namely 'empathy' (the capacity to see the world from another person's point of view). It is a commonplace that children between the ages of six and nine show marked capacity for empathy. They readily sympathise with, indeed identify with, classmates who are in trouble, just as they put themselves in the skin of the characters in the stories that they never tire of hearing. This capacity to see the world through another's eyes declines catastrophically, however, with the approach of adolescence, and especially among boys. The reason seems to be that capacity for empathy is eroded by insecurity. To be outgoing towards what is different, and so challenging, whether it be the colour of skin one has not yet grown used to, or food whose taste or smell is unfamiliar etc., requires, above all, a basis of confidence about one's own values. Insecurity about how one is oneself regarded by society, and so about one's own 'self-image', undermines tolerance of other, different, ways of life. It is no accident that the most virulent bigots in the tribal rioting that has disfigured our cities are the adolescents and immediate post-adolescents. Adolescence, especially for boys, is traumatic because of the distorted picture most boys form of what 'manhood' calls for in our culture. It is a role for which most boys instinctively know they are ill-suited. In their doubt and insecurity they 'whistle in the dark' to keep their spirits up in the protective company of the gang whose shared talk, interests and uniform give an illusion of acceptance and a brittle confidence. The commitment to peer-group values is strongest when the ties with the home are tenuous and when the young learner has not been given, in the home, models of mature adult behaviour, or shared activities and dialogue with a caring adult. If his only adult models have been immature, insecure and so prone to reject as threatening everything that is different, the implications for foreign language learning are clear. No subject in the timetable challenges 'capacity for empathy' so directly. History and geography may challenge pupils to cross the frontiers of time and space in imagination, and envisage social and geographical climates very different from their own. The foreign language classroom challenges the pupil not simply to *discuss* differences but to *behave* in new ways. Emphasis on oral skills becomes doubly threatening to the adolescent (shy, voice breaking, clumsy) who is called on to make the ridiculous noises out loud for his mates to hear.

## The Role of Expectation

The pooling of insecurity and of prejudice against the unfamiliar which the peer–group epitomises clearly sets up expectations inimical to those school subjects which challenge parochialism. Other effects of expectation on learning, however, are more subtle. Consider how the eyes and ears work as channels of information. We do not see or hear the messages that come our way. We see and hear only those parts of the messages that we *expect* to receive. Our expectations act as a filter through which the messages must pass. This can be demonstrated by experiments with 'eye-teaser' pictures in which the hidden image (in, for example, an array of dots) at first impossible to identify, becomes obvious once its outline has been shown.

The role of expectation in hearing is even more marked, and in language learning, which has been described as 'a dialogue between the ear and the eye', knowing what to listen for becomes all important. The ear is a restricted channel of information compared with the eye. Consider its limitations:

(1) spoken messages fade within seconds; unless retained in the short-term memory long enough to be 'processed' (that is, their constituents identified and their role in the syntax taken in) they are lost, whereas the eye can simply take another look;

(2) the ears cannot swivel, as the eyes can, to follow the image;

(3) the ears cannot focus, still less, by parallax, measure distance and speed of approach, with the accuracy required, for example, to catch a fast-moving ball;

(4) most important of all, the ears, unlike the eyes, are not equipped with lids to cut out unwanted messages. From an early age we learn the trick of switching off hearing internally, in self-defence. But defensive habits of non-listening must be painfully unlearned and nowhere more so than in the foreign language lesson.

We plunge our slower learners at 11 + into the attack on the new language ill-equipped with the expectations or the listening tools for verbal learning much as the raw infantry recruits were launched at Passchendaele. It should not surprise us that so many of them are mown down or emerge from the battle vowing, as adults, 'Never again!'

It will be clear from our brief discussion of 'empathy' and of 'expectations' in learning (especially in knowing what to listen for) that 'motivation' or Bruner's 'will to learn' is largely conditioned by the environment and not a product of innate ability, or aptitude. This is not, of course, to deny the vast differences between children in innate capacity. A great deal of harm has been done, both to exceptionally gifted children and to children of limited gifts, by muddled thinking about 'streaming' in the comprehensive school. So-called 'mixed-ability teaching' is generally nothing of the kind, but teaching which goes at a pace suitable for those in the middle, to the neglect of the needs of the slower and of the faster learners (see evidence in Reid, 1981). Mixed-ability classes for language teaching are not favoured by Her Majesty's Inspectors. HMI are sound, common-sense judges of what they see happening in classrooms. In their survey of language teaching in 83 comprehensive schools (HMI, 1977) they describe as 'more fortunate' the schools in which the timetable is flexible enough 'to permit the modern language department to adopt a form of setting at the moment when it becomes necessary'. The tragedy of the muddled debate about 'mixed-ability teaching', particularly when conducted by those who do not actually do the teaching, is that it has distracted attention from the real needs of the slower learner.

## A Coherent Linguistic Education for the Slower Learner

Most discussion of the school curriculum assumes what we may call a 'horizontal' model. It considers the curriculum as an array of activities offered to the pupil at any one period in time as in expressions like: the 'secondary school curriculum' or the 'sixth-form curriculum'. This is the model that is assumed in the phrase 'language across the curriclum' as advocated in the Bullock Report, *A Language for Life* (Bullock, 1975).

The horizontal model is useful. It enables judgements to be made about the balance of activities in the school day or the school year, and about the extent to which the various school 'subjects' cohere (or more probably fail to cohere) to form a suitable programme. To revert to the Bullock Report, it very usefully showed, using the horizontal model, how unsatisfactory it is that responsibility for teaching 'language' should be confined to specialist 'English' teachers, rather than spread 'across the curriculum' into the science labs, the art rooms, the geography lesson, etc. Indeed the one major omission in an otherwise most useful report, which left foreign language teachers bewildered and discouraged, was the failure to make any reference to the role that the foreign language might play. 'Language across the curriculum' stopped, apparently, outside the foreign language teacher's door. It is this inexplicable omission from Bullock that we must try to repair, if we are to do justice to the slower learner. It will be even more important, however, to take a fresh look at the slower learner's problems, by adopting a 'vertical' model for the curriculum. By this we mean thinking of the child growing up and of the curriculum as offering a *succession* of learning experiences in the various stages of schooling: pre-school readiness for reading, breakthrough to literacy, getting the tools for learning in the junior stage, moving into the areas of the great mental disciplines in the secondary school, apprenticeship in school for the challenges of citizenship, of parenthood, of earning a living, specialisation in training for vocation post 16 + etc. Although each of these stages in learning has value of itself, and should rightly be judged for the richness and the coherence of the experience offered, the 'vertical' model serves to remind us that the child can only build learning at any one stage on the *expectations* set up previously. It is a recurrent criticism of the present curriculum that is lacking in continuity. Teachers at each stage do little or nothing to acquaint themselves with what experience their pupils have had before or to concert their methods or their objectives.

This is especially true of language experience. Just as on our horizontal perspective the foreign language teacher and the English teacher at present beaver away in adjacent classrooms without ever listening to each other, still less asking whether they might help each other, so if we look at the curriculum 'vertically' the foreign language teacher tries to present a new subject at 11 + for which no expectations have been set up earlier and for which pupils are not given the verbal learning tools in the primary school.

If we are to help the slower learner we must tackle the curriculum both horizontally and vertically. What such a rationally planned curriculum might look like I have tried to describe in detail elsewhere (Hawkins, 1981). It can be described here only in outline.

Considered vertically, the curriculum must attempt more systematically to give the tools for verbal learning. This means, first, helping the slower readers. They must be given back the individual dialogue with an adult of which they have been deprived. Ideally this adult should be the parent and many schools are now experimenting, in line with the researches at the Thomas Coram Institute, London, and the University of Manchester, in finding ways of prompting parents to set aside time daily to hear children read and to talk about their reading afterwards. It seems that it is this short time spent talking about the reading that is most important. There will, of course, be some children from backgrounds where the problems are such that intimate school and home co-operation is not possible. Here some substitute 'adult time' must be found. In the London experiments the children who enjoyed the regular reading and talk at home were compared with a control group of equally backward readers who were given teaching in school in small groups under optimum conditions by teachers specially trained for the work. Compared with the children in the experimental group, whose parents were prompted by the school and given materials and guidance for the nightly 'read and talk', the control pupils, given the best instruction that the classroom could provide, made little or no progress. It is 'adult time' for dialogue that the slower reader needs. Unless this can be provided the primary school cannot claim to be making a serious professional attack on the reading problems of its slower learners.

Second, the slower learner must be taught to listen much more systematically, which means 'education of the ear'. On the need to teach deliberately what Furth and Wachs (1974) have called 'thinking with the ears' the Bullock committee was divided. On the whole they preferred to hope that the ability to listen could be developed as part of the normal work of the classroom in association with other learning experiences, but they made the important reservation: 'deliberate strategies may be required, for it cannot be assumed that the improvement will take place automatically' (Bullock, 1975, p. 151, paragraph 10.21). 'Thinking with the ears' in the terms of Furth and Wachs does not come naturally to many children as part of their normal experience, as the majority on the Bullock committee hoped it might. Expectations, knowing what to listen *for*, have to be awakened.

Nowhere is this more true than in the approach to foreign language learning. It is not simply that many learners have never mastered the basic skills of keeping still, observing absolute silence and listening with complete attention for specific signals. They are simply not aware of the new signals of meaning that they have to attend to, such as strange stress patterns, unfamiliar intonation tunes, vowel or consonant differences that are phonemic in the foreign language if not in English.

More fundamentally the slower learner is insecure, as a listener. He lacks the confident approach of the sophisticated, practised listener who *expects* to hear new and interesting sounds and relishes the challenge to his ears. The slower 'thinker with the ears' is defensive, even suspicious, taking little relish from new listening challenges because some of his classmates clearly 'hear' what he cannot hear. New and unfamiliar sounds are now threatening, the classroom which specialises in them is unattractive. Our programme of 'education of the ear' will therefore try, as the pupil nears the end of the primary stage, to lead him towards this confident relish for new listening, and taste for adventure in thinking with the ears. It is only on a set of expectations emancipated from the habitual rhythms and vowels of his own dialect that an enjoyable attack on an entirely new language can build.

Education in listening, in our vertical curriculum, is a necessary preliminary to the development of 'awareness of language'. As we have seen, researchers in the area of primary school learning (for example Donaldson, 1978) and of foreign language acquisition (for example Olson, 1973) have identified lack of linguistic awareness as the common learning difficulty. A most encouraging development in language teaching has been the recent explosive growth of interest and experiment in 'awareness' courses. Over 50 schools are developing courses of this kind. Their progress is being monitored by the Centre for Information in Language Teaching (CILT), London. A working group on linguistic awareness has been set up under the National Congress of Language in Education based on CILT and convened by its director, John Trim.

Approaches to the planning of 'awareness of language' courses vary. The most successful are the result of co-operation between teachers of English and of foreign languages. In many cases it is the foreign language teachers who have taken the initiative, simply because in trying to meet the slower learner's problems in the foreign language they have realised the need for an apprenticeship in awareness of language. A typical syllabus in such a course, jointly planned and taught by the English and foreign language staffs, might include the following six broad topics (each one studied, perhaps for one term, in the first two years of the secondary school):

(1) communication without language (what it means to be an 'articulate mammal');

(2) how language works (including an experimental approach to learning the basic grammatical 'constituents', and their conventional names, challenging pupils to examine why some of these names may be misleading and inappropriate, and to invent better names for the grammar);

(3) written and spoken language (where did our writing come from; what other kinds of writing are used in the great language families of the world; how do spoken and written languages compare?);

(4) uses of language (a study of the many different uses to which language is put in our society, by different people, in different vocations; how we are manipulated by users of language etc.);

(5) varieties of language (the multi-lingual and multi-dialectal

nature of British society; the linguistic implications of membership of groups to which we are bound by treaty, such as the Council of Europe, EEC, NATO, the UN, the Commonwealth, etc.; the realities behind linguistic prejudice, etc.);

(6) acquisition of language (comparison of the two processes of acquisition of the mother tongue and learning of a second language, under different conditions, for example in school and, as immigrant child or adult, by 'immersion'; introduction to discussion of the role and responsibility of the parent as the child's sole linguistic 'informant' during the first critical five years of language learning, in preparation for a fuller discussion of the importance of 'adult time' in the home; project work and films etc. as part of the 'preparation for parenthood' course that must follow in the fourth and fifth years of the secondary course).

There will be many possible variations on this outline (some involving 'taster' introductions to several languages), but most of the courses at present being developed include these elements. All of them share one objective: to provide a forum in the school timetable where pupils from different linguistic backgrounds can pool their experience of language and where it is not assumed that one particular mother tongue or mother dialect is 'received' or 'normal' and others are aberrant. The course thus becomes a 'bridge' across the space between each child's own linguistic prejudices (for further discussion of this aspect of the course see Hawkins, 1974, p. 47; 1979, p. 61). It is seen also as a more practical way of promoting co-operation between teachers of English, teachers of the foreign language and teachers of, for example, the science subjects, who have an important contribution to make to 'awareness courses', than the Bullock committee's unfocused pleas for 'language across the curriculum' to which the response has been disappointing, for the predictable reason that it was never clear whose responsibility it was to take the initiative.

Pursuing our vertical model of the curriculum, the experience of foreign language learning offered in school, necessarily limited, must be seen as an apprenticeship for further study, of the *language of adult choice*, when adult career or leisure interests take shape after the trauma of adolescence. This view of the role of the secondary course has many implications, some of which we try to examine in our final section. One implication is that the secondary course must whet appetites, if our school leavers are to follow up their 'apprenticeship' in foreign language learning by continuing study as young adults of an ancillary language. It must be said, too, that the small fires of curiosity about language that we hope our awareness of language course will light in our pupils' minds will burn brightly throughout adult life in continuing interest in and respect for their mother tongue and a growing sophistication in distinguishing between what is discriminating and imitable in language use and what is tawdry and thoughtless.

If we now turn to consider briefly the 'horizontal' model of the linguistic curriculum, we find ourselves on fairly well trodden ground. As we have seen, the Bullock committee reviewed some of the shortcomings of the curriculum from this perspective, but failed to see that the foreign language teacher might have a contribution to make, 'across the curriculum', to 'a language for life'. While welcoming the well documented Bullock plea for a new approach to linguistic education, and especially the proposal that *all* teachers, regardless of their specialism, should have, in their training course, an introduction to linguistics, it is necessary to look more closely than Bullock did at the sheer lack of coherence in the linguistic menu we offer in the secondary school. In any one comprehensive school we may find *five* different kinds of language teacher operating, all trained in entirely different traditions and methods, and none having more than the vaguest idea of what goes on in the others' classrooms. The five kinds are:

> teachers of English (mother tongue);
> foreign language teachers;
> teachers of English (as second language);
> teachers of mother tongues of minorities ('mother tongue maintenance');
> teachers of the classics (Latin predominantly).

If we look at this situation from the pupil's point of view, he meets two kinds of experience of language: (1) further exploration of his mother tongue, of which he has a good 'primary mastery' (in listening/speaking) but which the secondary school must develop into command of the 'secondary' skills of reading/writing, and (2) the adventure into a second or foreign language (which for some pupils may be English).

The situation is complicated for some pupils (many West Indian pupils would come into this category) whose home dialect of English differs quite markedly from the dialect of English met in the school classroom and textbooks. It is true that many children seem to be well equipped to 'switch' what are sometimes called their 'repertoires' as they move from home, to school playground, to classroom, to interview for job, to peer group. Surely some attempt should be made, however, to help the child to make some coherent sense of the different experiences of language that come his way? It is unlikely that teachers of language will be able to do this so long as they continue to work in complete isolation from each other. It is for this reason that we have suggested (see, *inter alia*, Hawkins, 1981) a more coherent language curriculum for the 1980s. Just as, in the Middle Ages, the 'grammar school' pupil was offered a coherent 'trivium' of subjects, planned as a whole, and supporting each other: *grammar*, *logic* and *rhetoric* which equipped him to go on to the further study of the mediaeval 'quadrivium' at university, so we suggest a new 'trivium': (1) the mother tongue, (2) experience of a language other than the mother tongue and (3) the linking subject 'awareness of language'. The 'awareness' course would be jointly taught by *all* language teachers, pooling their specialist interests. They would seek help from their science colleagues and others for appropriate parts of the course. The biologist would help on the biological aspects of perception and speech, the historian would discuss the history of writing, printing, spelling, etc. The physics underlying simple introductions to phonetics would be studied in the lab.; geographical aspects of linguistic variety in the geography room. We have tried to suggest how language education might be given some coherence, both 'vertically' and 'horizontally', in the curriculum. It is time to turn to the crucial part of our problem: what exactly would be the role of foreign language learning in such a reformed curriculum?

## The Role of the Foreign Language

The reader who accepts our argument so far, and is prepared to support our plea for a coherently planned linguistic curriculum, which tries to make sense of the array of language experiences presented to the child, both successively or vertically as he moves from stage to stage, and simultaneously or horizontally as he follows his weekly timetable from one classroom to the other, may still wish to ask the question: but why must the slower learner actually learn to *perform* in a foreign language? If your course of 'thinking with the ears' followed by 'language awareness' achieves what you claim for it, will this not be apprenticeship enough? How do you justify the time and effort spent on trying to give the slower learner speaking and listening (even reading/writing?) skills in the foreign language?

Our sceptical reader may point out fairly that the *vocational* arguments for offering a foreign language to all pupils are extremely weak, so obviously weak that the slower learner sees through them. Most slower learning pupils cannot look forward to vocations that require foreign language skills. Parents, elder brothers and sisters, above all peer groups, are there to testify that the worker on the assembly line, the building worker, the nurse or clerk, the shop assistant or garage mechanic, do not need an ancillary language skill, in the way that (say) the future sales manager, or the accountant in the company with branches overseas, or the typist in the travel agency is going to need such a skill. And what of the young black in Brixton or Toxteth facing probable unemployment? Is the foreign language teacher to hold out the prospect that the skills he offers to teach will be 'needed' vocationally by the disadvantaged child from that background?

Of course there is the possibility that the slower learner may become a bricklayer or a lorry driver, and decide, as many skilled labourers are doing, to seek employment within the countries of the European Community. Will a language not be needed then? This is Catch 22, for who is to say which language it is to be? How can future adult language needs be predicted when the child is 11+? The teacher of the slower learner in, say, Holland or Sweden, even in France or Germany, can safely make such a prediction. English is the world vehicle language certain to be needed at all levels. This message is carried daily on the radio, in films, pop songs, air-traffic control. But for the pupil who already has English, which of the dozen or so possible languages that he may meet as an adult ought the school to offer if the justification for teaching it is purely vocational? Our answer is that we fully accept that the case for the foreign language in the core curriculum for the slower learner ought not to be based on vocational arguments. They are best frankly swept aside. The apprenticeship for which we are pleading, to prepare pupils to make sense of the multi-lingual (and multi-dialectal) society they must serve as adults, is part of *education* rather than of *instruction*. There seem to be three compelling *educational* reasons for making a foreign language part of the apprenticeship.

First we want to combat the kind of linguistic parochialism against which the young Russian genius L.S. Vygotsky warned in his seminal *Thought and Language* (Vygotsky, 1962), the manuscript of which was suppressed as too dangerous under Stalin in the 1930s. He pointed to the need to break out of the linguistic prison which he called 'primitive linguistic consciousness'. He told the story of the rustic who said he wasn't surprised that savants with all their instruments could figure out the size of the stars and their courses – *what baffled him was how they found out their names*! We are reminded of the now well known story told by the American linguist Yuan Ren Chao of the woman who could not understand how foreigners could use words like 'l'eau' and 'das Wasser' to describe what was obviously water. 'We English', she said, 'we don't just call it water. You see it *is* water, isn't it?' (Yuan Ren Chao, 1968, p. 2).

Our proposed 'awareness of language' course will be an important part of the attack on the parochialism that Vygotsky and Ren Chao describe. But an extra element is needed: the experience of making another language work for you. It is here that the foreign language is essential to our 'trivium'. It is necessary to get outside one's mother tongue, if only momentarily, to be able to look at it objectively.

Equally important as an educational reason for including a foreign language in the timetable is that it gives slower learners the chance to 're-categorise' (re-conceptualise) areas of experience that primary schooling leaves imprecise for many children. Typical examples are: the calendar (sheer uncertainty as to which month follows which, how many days are in each month etc.); mental arithmetic; telling the time; precise meanings of prepositions, colours, etc. Many more pupils than we might expect come to the secondary school with such gaps in their 'conceptual map' of how the world works, that it is impossible for the secondary stage to mean very much. Sensitive teachers of slower learners report from many different schools the marked improvement in reading skills in the mother tongue and in the whole attack on learning that follow from the introduction of suitable courses in a foreign language. A particularly interesting aspect of this interplay between the foreign

language and learning in the mother tongue is that in the foreign
language classroom the pupil goes through a progressive course in
(1) disciplined listening and (2) matching sounds to written
symbols. When this matching is logical and consistent (as notably in
Spanish, but also in German and Russian and even in French,
where the match is more consistent than in English), the
apprenticeship builds confidence, after a history of failure in the
primary school. This requires, of course, a carefully planned
introduction to the 'dialogue between ear and eye' which underlies
all language learning. It requires, also, the use of aids to perception
and retention, such as the use of colour-coding and of 'spatial
memory' to supplement the vagaries of verbal memory, especially
in boys. (For detailed suggestions see Hawkins, 1981, p. 250). This
approach also has obvious implications for the initial *choice* of the
language to be offered to the slower learner.

Here the claims of Spanish are strong, first because, as we have
said, the match between speech and the written form in Spanish is
so consistent and logical. (One consequence of this, incidentally, is
that learning to read their mother tongue presents few of the
traumas to Spanish children that English-speaking pupils face.
Spanish linguists comment on the frequency with which English
speakers spell out words to each other in conversation, and how
rarely one hears this in Spain.) Another advantage of Spanish for
the slower learner is that the Spanish tenses match English tenses,
unlike the French tenses, which work in disconcertingly contrasting
ways. Spanish and English are especially close in the so-called
'progressive' tenses ('I am eating', 'I was eating', etc.). As has been
shown elsewhere (Hawkins, 1981) these should be seen as
'perfective' tenses, since they imply (as the corresponding 'simple'
forms, 'I eat', 'I ate' do not imply) that the action described is
temporary, and *will come to an end.* Understanding these forms in
this way explains why, in both Spanish and English, it is impossible
to use certain verbs in these 'perfective' tenses. In Spanish, as in
English (but quite unlike French) verbs fall into two categories:
verbs of 'perfective meaning' (which make no sense unless the
action they describe is understood as being complete – example: to
shoot/tirar) and verbs of 'imperfective meaning' (which carry no
such implication – example: to know/saber). The simple rule is:
verbs of 'imperfective meaning' such as know/saber cannot be used
in 'perfective' tenses (*I am knowing/*estoy sabiendo). It is
interesting that in Spanish this division of the commonly used verbs

into these two categories goes further than in English in one particular: there are even two verbs 'to be', one (estar) which is 'perfective' in meaning and one (ser) which is imperfective. We may contrast this exact matching of 'I am eating' and 'estoy comiendo', with the problems and misunderstandings for the slower learner produced by the economy of the French 'je mange' covering both of these meanings, and the consequent errors (*je suis mangeant, etc.) that it gives rise to.

A much more fundamental linguistic contrast, however, is presented by grammatical gender. English is unique among the languages of Europe in having got rid of grammatical gender, by a fortunate accident, in the 200 years following the Norman conquest. (Prior to that date, of course, Old English had possessed the three genders of the Germanic family.) This undoubtedly makes it easier for the foreigner to enter English, especially to construct simple phrases in the early stages without gross error, with all that this means for motivation and encouragement for the young learner. For the English speaker, the first steps into any of the European languages are correspondingly hard. He cannot frame the simplest sentence with any certainty of avoiding a gross error of gender, and unless the gender is accurate a cascade of errors of 'concord' (adjectives, articles, pronouns) follows the initial mistake. It is not an exaggeration to suggest that grammatical gender may be the single biggest hurdle for our slower foreign language learner. If the journey into the new territory of grammatical gender is obviously easier in one language than in the others, this should surely count as a most telling reason for choosing that language, for slower learners to begin their apprenticeship? Gender in Spanish is much less fraught with problems for the English speaker than (say) French, for the simple reason that the two genders, masculine and feminine, are much more clearly signalled by the spelling (that is by endings in 'o' and 'a' respectively) in Spanish than in French, where the word endings have in so many cases changed to the neutral ending 'e' regardless of gender. The doubts about gender that beset the young learner trying to construct the simplest phrases (is it *le* or *la silence*? *le signe* or *la signe*? *un empire* or *une empire*? etc.) trouble the Spanish student much less frequently. *Silencio/signo/imperio* etc., and a host of other nouns cognate with French, signal their gender unmistakably by their spelling. The learner who tackles French *after* an apprenticeship in Spanish soon realises his good fortune, compared with someone who encounters French first!

Having chosen our language with the learner's problems in mind, we must be prepared to teach it in such a way that it offers an enjoyable apprenticeship. Motivation is all. The slower learner is by definition insecure. He does not enjoy the resilience and mental toughness of the faster intellect, confident that the task will yield to concentration and effort, and relishing the challenge the harder it is. Insecurity makes for a short wind, intellectually. The slower learner needs objectives that are set over a shorter term, with rewards for each lap of the track accomplished.

It is here that the work on 'graded objectives' is so significant. The explosive interest in 'grades' in foreign language learning (on the model of the eight musical grades found so successful in motivating young learners along the hard road towards mastery of difficult instruments) has been monitored expertly by the Centre for Information in Language Teaching. Interest in the new developments was greatly stimulated by the publication of the evaluation report by Buckby (1981), referred to earlier (p. 105). This reported the large-scale project centred on York and Leeds in which some 2,000 pupils in their third year at comprehensive school were involved. The project was carried through by teams of teachers in collaboration with university tutors in French teaching and in psychology. It is unnecessary to do more than refer the reader to Buckby's fascinating account of the experiment. He shows convincingly that the results 'strongly support the hypothesis . . . that the experimental pupils [that is those offered the graded objective course] would show significantly more positive attitudes to learning French than the control pupils' (that is those taught by traditional methods without the stimulus, to pupils and their parents, of the 'grade' concept).

One caveat only should be entered. It is one that has been recognised by some of the proponents of 'graded objectives'. It concerns the danger of losing sight of the educational aims of our course. Our purpose is not *simply* to equip our slower learners with 'survival skills', in the shape of a few mechanical phrases. Performance in the language, we readily accept, is essential. Without it the course loses appeal and the apprenticeship is second-hand. But we are aiming at education, not instruction. We want to make a contribution to insight into language itself, its place in our lives, its variety and richness, its fascination and the dangers of linguistic parochialism. We should, therefore, take care, as already some of the perceptive groups working on 'graded objectives' are doing, to include in the syllabus at each 'grade' not simply *performance* tasks but questions calling for insight into the structure of the foreign language, its contrasts with English at the phonological, the semantic and the structural level. A notable example of imaginative work in this area is the 'graded objective' project worked out by the West Sussex team led by Eric Garner.

Setting this dual objective for our graded programme for the slower learner (combining 'insight into pattern' with 'doing things with words') is completely in line with theoretical lessons concerning language acquisition that have gained significant ground in the past five years. It is now widely accepted that language learning is most effective when it combines the two 'levels' of activity: (1) concentrating on study of the *form* of the message (the 'medium') and (2) concentrating on achieving some purpose *other than* getting the form correct (that is concentrating on the 'message' itself). This has been most interestingly set out by Professor C.J. Dodson (Dodson, 1978), based on his observations in the bilingual schools of Wales. Parallels between his theory and the work of S.D. Krashen and E.W. Stevick are developed in Hawkins (1981). It is along these lines that we may look to see the most fruitful developments for slower language learners in the 1980s.

The implications for teachers and for those who prepare materials are clear. The teacher will need to be able to recognise when pupils are being asked to operate at Dodson's 'level one' and when at 'level two'. Too often hitherto school courses have concentrated exclusively on the first level which Dodson calls 'medium-orientated'. The whole of the GCE O-level course, except parts of the 'oral', remains at this level for most pupils. In fact the picture may be more complicated. Stevick (1976) suggests that rather than think of two levels we ought to think of a range of levels of *depth of meaning* at which classroom activities may be pitched. 'Other things being equal', he claims, 'the *deeper* the source of a sentence within the student's personality, the more lasting *value* it has for learning the language' (Stevick, 1976, p. 109). Why this is so was made clear as long ago as 1923 by Otto Tacke in his paper (published under the title that Viëtor had used forty years before) *Der Sprachunterricht muss umkehren*: 'A will to mean must always underlie the learning of expressions in the foreign language, otherwise the foreign expressions *do not stick*' (quoted in Butzkamm and Dodson, 1981). That this same equation holds for the acquisition of the mother tongue is shown by the experiments of Lois Bloom (Bloom, 1974) and Dan Slobin (Slobin and Welsh, 1973).

They found that in spontaneous speech, when children have an 'intention to mean' something that matters to them, they can utter complex speech patterns which they are incapable of repeating later when asked merely to imitate a recording (that is, concentrating on the 'medium' not the 'message', in Dodson's terms).

Otto Tacke's insight may be traced back (Hawkins, 1981) to earlier studies such as those of Felix Franke (1884) and Harold Palmer (1917). In Palmer's monumental, and too long neglected, work he argues that 95 per cent of all the vocabulary learnt in the foreign language is got subconsciously and only 5 per cent by 'conscious study' (that is by what Krashen calls the application of the 'monitor'). The process may be more complex than Palmer supposed, but the interest of his, and of Tacke's, insights for the teacher of the slower learner is clear. Hitherto many faster learners had access to 'message-orientated' activities in two ways: (1) by going abroad on educational visits, and (2) by reading for meaning in texts that genuinely interested them. Our slower learners have usually dropped their language before the fourth and fifth years, and so missed both of these activities, in too many schools.

The challenge is clear. We have to devise ways of allowing slower learners to make use of the foreign language to serve *their* purposes. This will mean encouraging oral work, especially oral comprehension activities, in which pupils transact meanings that are personal to them. It will involve also providing reading materials *from a very early stage* which are within the grasp of the slower learner and which are intrinsically interesting. That this can be done the pioneers of the 'graded objectives' are showing.

Professor Dodson and his German colleague offer further excellent examples in their paper referred to above of dialogues recorded in the classroom which involve pupils in genuine 'message-orientated' activities while detailed descriptions, at four suggested levels of 'depth of meaning', of both 'productive' and 'receptive' language work, are described in Hawkins (1981). Our argument, set out in necessarily condensed form in this chapter, has obvious implications for teacher training. First, it follows from what was said in the early part of the chapter that young language teachers must be sent into schools *expecting* to co-operate with colleagues 'across the curriculum' in making pupils more critically 'aware of language' as the essentially human characteristic. The best preparation will be experience of such co-operation while at university or on the training course. This means that tutors must themselves practise such co-operation, constantly giving their students examples of it during training. Second, language teachers (like all other teachers – as the Bullock committee recommended) must be given a basic introduction to 'language awareness.' This must include an understanding of language variety and language change and some insight into the nature of the dialects likely to be met in school, especially the dialects spoken by socially disadvantaged groups such as West Indian children. An essential aspect of this training (and one which would usefully bring together teachers of foreign languages and teachers of English) would be a study of the ways in which *learning to read at 5 +* (in a school dialect which may not be used in the children's home) and *learning a foreign language at 11 +*, pose similar problems to slower learners, and precisely how the learning problems differ. Third, the 'method element' of the training course must take account of recent work on levels of depth of meaning in classroom dialogue. It might start from the discussion of the 'speech act' as described by the philosopher John Searle and his just dismissal of 'foreign language teaching' as 'non-serious language', meaning language in which the speaker is not intending some purpose that matters to him (Searle, 1969, p.57). As we suggested above, more fortunate, faster learners compensate to some extent for the personal meaning-lessness of the textbook by *reading* for their own meanings, at least in schools where *choice* in reading is encouraged from an early stage. The challenge, if we are to be fair to the slower learner, is to bring to the analysis of classroom activities a much higher degree of professionalism, equipping teachers to distinguish with precision the levels of depth of meaning which different classroom activities evoke.

Finally, teacher training courses must face the problem of motivation. Work on short-term, graded objectives has pointed the way forward. Not the least interesting of the effects of this approach has been the awakening of interest among parents. Motivation begins at home. Teachers are learning how to arouse and sustain interest *through* parents. Here the foreign language teacher can learn from the Thomas Coram Institute and Manchester experiments described earlier. The notion of a school curriculum that is 'autonomous' and independent of home background is an illusion. Foreign language study for the slower learner must involve co-operation with parents as partners before the course begins, in the preparatory stages of getting the tools for verbal learning, and at every graded step along the way. The whole adventure into the foreign language will be as challenging for the families of many slower learners as for the pupils themselves. Only by working with and through the parents, in foreign languages, as in teaching written skills in the mother tongue, can we help to motivate slower learners.

# References

Beveridge, M. and Jerrams, A. (1981) 'Parental Involvement in Language Development: an Evaluation of a School-Based Parental Assistance Plan', *British Journal of Educational Psychology*, 51 (3) (November), 259–69

Bloom, L. (1974) 'Talking, Understanding and Thinking' in R.L. Schliefelbusch and L.L. Lloyd (eds.) *Language Perspectives – Acquisition, Retardation and Intervention*, Macmillan, New York

Bruner, J.S. (1975) 'Language as an Instrument of Thought' in A. Davies (ed.), *Problems of Language and Learning*, Heinemann, London

Buckby, M. (1981) *Graded Objectives and Tests for Modern Languages*, Schools Council, London

Bullock, A. (Lord Bullock) (Chairman) (1975) *A Language for Life*, Report of Committee of Enquiry appointed by the Secretary of State for Education, HMSO, London

Burstall, C., Jamieson, M., Cohen, S. and Hargreaves, M. (1974) *Primary French in the Balance*, NFER, London

Butzkamm, W. and Dodson, C.J. (1981) *Communicative Competence*, IRAL, Julius Groos Verlag, Heidelberg

Carroll, J.B. (1973) 'Implications of Aptitude Test Research and Psycholinguistic Theory for Foreign Language Teaching', *Linguistics*, 122, 5–13

Chomsky, N. (1965) *Aspects of the Theory of Syntax*, MIT Press, Cambridge, Mass.

Davie, R., Butler, N. and Goldstein, H. (1972) *From Birth to Seven, National Child Development Study (1958 Cohort)*, Longman, London

Dodson, C.J. (1978) *Bilingual Education in Wales*, Schools Council for Wales, Evans/Methuen Educational, London

Donaldson, M. (1978) *Children's Minds*, Fontana/Collins, Glasgow

Franke, F. (1884) *Die Praktische Spracherlernung auf Grund der Psychologie und der Physiologie der Sprache dargestellt*, Altenburg, Heilbronn

Further, H. and Wachs, H. (1974) *Thinking goes to School*, Oxford University Press, New York

Green, P.S (ed.) (1975) *The Language Laboratory in School: Performance and Prediction: the York Study*, Oliver and Boyd, Edinburgh

Hawkins, E.W. (1974) 'Modern Languages in the Curriculum' in *The Space Between*, CILT Reports and Papers 10, CILT, London

———— (1979) 'A Possible Way Forward', Appendix to *The Early Teaching of Modern Languages*, Nuffield Foundation, London

———— (1981) *Modern Languages in the Curriculum*, Cambridge University Press, London

Her Majesty's Inspectorate (1977) *Matters for Discussion 3: Modern Languages in Comprehensive Schools*, HMSO, London

Kavanagh, J.F. and Mattingley, I.G. (1972) *Language by Ear and Eye*, Massachusetts Institute of Technology, Cambridge, Mass.

Kogan, M. (1971) *The Politics of Education*, Penguin Education Special, Harmondsworth

Krashen, S.D. (1981) *Second Language Acquisition and Second Language Learning*, Pergamon, Oxford

Olsen, G.M. (1973) 'Developmental Changes in Memory and the Acquisition of Language' in T.E. Moore (ed.), *Cognitive Development and the Acquisition of Language*, Academic Press, New York

Palmer, H.E. (1917) *The Scientific Study and Teaching of Languages*, Harrap, London, re-issued D. Harper (ed.) (1968) Oxford University Press, Oxford

Pimsleur, P. (1966) 'Testing Foreign Language Learning' in A. Valdman, *Trends in Language Teaching*, McGraw-Hill, New York

Plowden, B. (Lady Plowden) (Chairman) (1967) *Children and Their Primary Schools*, Report of the Central Advisory Council for Education, England, HMSO, London

Pringle, M.L.K. (1980) *A Fairer Future for Children*, Macmillan, London

Rampton, A. (Chairman) (1981) *West Indian Children in Our Schools*, Report of a Committee of Enquiry appointed by the Secretary of State for Education, HMSO, London

Reid, M., Clunies-Ross, L., Goacher, B. and Vile, C. (1981) *Mixed Ability Teaching; Problems and Possibilities*, NFER-Nelson, London

Schools Council (1970) *New Patterns in Sixth Form Modern Language Studies*, Working Paper No. 28 (out of print), Schools Council/Evans Methuen, London

Searle, J. (1969) *Speech Acts*, Cambridge University Press, London

Slobin, D.I. and Welsh, C.A. (1973) 'Elicited Imitation as a Research Tool in Developmental Psycholinguistics' in C.A. Ferguson and D.I. Slobin (eds.), *Studies in Child Language Development*, Holt, Rinehart and Winston, New York

Stevick, E.W. (1976) *Memory, Meaning and Method*, Newbury House, Rowley, Mass.

Tacke, O. (1923) *Der Sprachunterricht muss umkehren*, Oldenburg, Leipzig

Taylor, M. (1981) *Caught Between*, Review of Research into the Education of Pupils of West Indian Origin, NFEW/Nelson, London

Tizard, J., Scholfield, W.N. and Hewison, J. (1981) 'Collaboration between Teachers and Parents in Assisting Children's Reading', *Br. J. Educ. Psychol.*, 52, 1–15

Vygotsky, L.S. (1962) *Thought and Language*, Massachusetts Institute of Technology, Cambridge, Mass.

Yuen Ren Chao (1968) *Language and Symbolic Systems*, Cambridge University Press, New York

# 7 THE LEARNER OF ABOVE-AVERAGE ABILITY

## D. Nott

A foreign language teacher in a comprehensive school soon realises that the methods and objectives that were used and set for 'grammar school' pupils are not appropriate for the average pupil in the comprehensive school. My thesis, in this chapter, is that these methods and objectives are not appropriate for the above-average foreign language learner either, whether in a comprehensive or in a selective school. For as I said to my first PGCE student to get a job in a selective school: 'Don't forget *any* of the methods and techniques you've acquired here and used on teaching practice (in a comprehensive school) – they can *all* be used with above-average pupils, *and* to better effect!' That is not the whole story, however: able pupils can assimilate new language more speedily and efficiently, and therefore appropriate materials and methods must be chosen with their particular needs in mind.

This chapter is entitled 'The Learner of Above-average Ability' because any reference to 'gifted children' would have been misleading and restrictive. My concern here is with the pupils who would have been O-level candidates, or who are aiming at the top three grades in the new 16+ examination system. In selective schools, these pupils are in the majority of classes; in comprehensive schools, they are in the top set(s) or band after the first year, which is generally mixed-ability.

Many of these pupils are subjected to a diet which is heavily loaded with grammar, vocabulary lists, translation and writing. Because they are more able, they tend to do relatively well in end-of-year assessment tests, on work which has not really stretched them. Although some selective schools – and a few comprehensives – rightly insist that all their pupils should study a foreign language until 16+, in the majority of comprehensive schools up to half the number of pupils who could reach one of the top three O-level grades, or their equivalent, are not even entered for the examination. This massive drop-out of able pupils takes place alongside a national shortage of able and competent linguists as future teachers, and as future users of foreign languages in their working life.

**The Potential of the Able Pupil**

Able foreign language learners' needs can be expressed very simply: (1) to have their ability and potential recognised by their teachers; (2) to be stretched to the fullest possible extent of their capabilities, through appropriate learning activities; (3) to practise co-operation with less able contemporaries; (4) to work in a spirit of emulation of other able pupils, instead of competition.

The following points could serve as guidelines for the foreign language teacher in helping able pupils achieve their potential:

(1) The able pupil learns faster than the others, so a sense of achievement and self-confidence in using the foreign language can be instilled from an early stage, for example, by learning dialogues and short sketches, and acting them out.

(2) The able pupil can generalise more rapidly from material and examples which have been studied and practised, and can adapt and apply them in new situations, with new meanings. A minor example: two third-year pupils, composing a dialogue in which a spy attempts to phone someone in the Kremlin, recalled *Cochon de rosbif!* from a play previously read in class, and made their frustrated spy shout down the phone *Cochon de russebif!* A more substantial example: another third-year pupil, after various classroom activities on the theme of supersonic travel, was writing about this. Having read, with the class, an article on Concorde which began:

> Quitter Paris à 7 heures du matin, prendre le café à Dakar, arriver à Rio pour déjeuner, retrouver Dakar avant la fin de l'après-midi, atterrir à Paris à 22 heures très exactement: seul Concorde pouvait permettre cet exploit . . .

he wrote a piece which began:

> Rendre sourds tous ceux qui l'entend(ent), détruire l'atmosphère, démolir les fenêtres, causer le cancer, tuer tous ses passagers: seul Concorde peut faire tout cela . . .

and another fifty words in similar vein.

(3) The able pupil can be taken more quickly to the stage where the foreign language is a means to other, non-linguistic ends:

appreciating humour, discovering points of view, being gripped by stories, expressing himself and his opinions, entertaining and instructing fellow pupils (not to mention the teacher) by what he says or writes in the foreign language (see below, pp. 152–3, 162–3, for example). It is a restrictive, even a fallacious idea, in teaching able pupils, to see foreign language study as (1) sufficient motivation in its own right and (2) as an autonomous intellectual discipline.

(4) The able pupil can be trained to use the foreign language creatively, giving rein to his own imagination and need for independent thought and action. Examples of this include the O-level candidate who, during the oral test which was being recorded for moderation by the Board, proceeded to ask the examiner (his teacher) what his own views were on the topic being discussed; or the results achieved in group work related to *Le petit Nicolas* (see below, pp. 148–53).

(5) Last, but not least, the teacher should be aware of, and welcome, his able pupils' capacity to take ideas further than he intended: the door to this *dépassement* should always be open. How does one react, for example, when a sixth-former, after his oral test with the French assistant (during which each pupil had to talk about a book he had read), returns to his classmates announcing triumphantly 'I did it!' and when the French assistant in question hesitantly says to the teacher, 'One of your boys talked about an unusual book: *Alphonse chez le coiffeur . . .*'? Suffice to say that the whole class subsequently found themselves each writing a chapter of the 'book' in question, under the direction of the inventive miscreant. The end-product was magnificent: a racy cops-and-diamonds story set in *Le coiffeur*, a night-club of ill-repute . . .

## Motivation and Reward

The foreign language teacher in a comprehensive school, wishing to identify and 'feed' his able pupils (while attempting to lead *all* pupils away from 'I can't', through 'I can' to 'I did') is faced with massive obstacles, not the least of which is the nervous exhaustion produced by teaching seven lessons a day, with breaks lost to, or interrupted by, disciplinary or pastoral matters. The necessary intellectual adaptation, when going from the dreaded 'French Studies' set to the docile top set, becomes instead heart-felt relief at the prospect of

Figure 7.1

*Québec Français* (October 1981), C.P. 9185, Québec, G1V 4B1, Canada

peace and quiet. Result: able pupils are not stretched by appropriate materials, activities and attention.

For these pupils, 'motivation' and 'reward' then come down to one thing: passing examinations which, at both 16+ and 18+, still bear the imprint of the traditional degree course in modern languages: each level is a pale imitation of the one above, and stifles teaching methods at the level below.

The tragedy is that teachers believe that present examination syllabuses *require* them to discourage linguistic adventurousness in their pupils, and to stick closely to the exercises set by the boards. As a result, the foreign language course follows a downward spiral: teachers become more and more obsessed with a list of vocabulary and grammar that must be 'known', and pupils retain less and less of this 'knowledge' because they have had no opportunity to *do* anything with it. The language-learning process is sacrificed to assessment techniques, so that at A-level, for example, 72 per cent of the candidates in French with one major board failed to achieve half marks in the prose translation, in both 1980 and 1981. How many wearying 'proses' had these hapless candidates 'done', for two years or more?

Three ways in which pupils' motivation can be increased, and their efforts rewarded, are discussed briefly here.

*Accuracy or Fluency?*

Showing an obsession with accurate pronunciation is a sure way of inhibiting pupils of all abilities, many of whom are still shy about speaking to secondary school teachers in their own tongue; in the foreign language class, these pupils are easily frightened into silence, or retreat into inaudible murmurings.

Pupils must feel, from their very first lesson, that *any* utterance in the foreign language is welcome: 'Say what you like, as long as it's in French.'

The criterion by which pupils' 'accuracy' in spoken language should be assessed, is whether the listener can catch the correct *meaning* of what is being said. This meaning is conveyed less by the pronunciation of any one sound, than by the overall intonation (along with a host of non-linguistic signals, which pupils should be encouraged to identify and use).

Due attention should, of course, be given to pupils' pronunciation difficulties: sounds which are completely new, such as the French [r], [y] and the nasal vowels, need immediate and special attention, but in a relaxed atmosphere (how amusing, to produce these odd noises), with firm guidance (teacher and pupils co-operate in tackling the sounds).

Knowing when and how to correct and drill pupils' pronunciation is an essential skill for the successful foreign language teacher – a skill more easily applied if the pupils have been used to speaking the foreign language to one another in communicative contexts, where they will have discovered for themselves the vital importance of distinguishing between *le* and *les*, for example. They will then accept more readily being drilled in recognising and producing certain sounds. If this drilling is done in whole phrases, which the pupils need to say during pairwork, they can derive an immense sense of achievement from discovering that they can say some phrases quite fast, with appropriate intonation: they look surprised at themselves, but very gratified!

*Bringing in Outsiders*

The foreign language teacher should be constantly on the look-out for allies in the task of creating situations in which his pupils can, and want to, speak the foreign language: not teachers, but classroom helpers. Three possible sources of help are discussed below.

(1) *Older pupils* Help from this source is available to any foreign language class (in the case of an 11–16 school, by inviting ex-pupils following a post O-level foreign language course locally). Up to four fifth-formers at a time could be released from their foreign language lesson to work with younger classes; similarly, individual sixth-formers, or the whole group, could take part in lessons lower down the school. They could help with pairwork, or work with a selected group of younger pupils; sixth-formers could provide the focus for group work.

(2) *The foreign language assistant* While the DES doctors confer in hushed tones about the possibility of centralised feeding, the body of the foreign language assistant scheme grows steadily more emaciated. In schools which do have or share the services of an assistant, care needs to be taken to ensure that these encounters are structured and conducted in such a way as to make the most of them. Each class in a school should have an opportunity to meet and question the assistant, to ask him about himself, and to talk to him about themselves. Up to the fifth year, the assistant can help with

the demonstration and practice of all forms of pairwork. If sixth-formers are used to speaking the foreign language with their teacher and among themselves in pairs and groups, the assistant's work can be integrated with the current week's or fortnight's activities round a theme or topic: situations can be devised where, for example, members of the class have to ask him questions, or introduce a discussion in front of him.

(3) *PGCE students* For schools within a minibus ride of a centre training PGCE students, a number of alternatives to the 'one teacher, one class' straitjacket are opened up. Pairs of students could visit a class, perhaps once a week, for language activities involving dialogues, role-play, drama, etc. With the sixth form, groups of PGCE students could come in to work on a one-to-one basis, giving sixth-formers the opportunity to introduce and talk about themselves in the foreign language. Brief 'talk-sheets' can be given out; if these are soon discarded, the session is working! Conversely, teachers can be invited to meet PGCE students in their department, to give an account of how they tackle a particular age-group, or part of the syllabus, or type of activity.

## Visits and Exchanges

First-hand contact with the foreign country, if it is carefully prepared, conducted and followed up, is a major motivating factor for foreign language learners of all abilities; by definition, the above-average pupil is able to make more of the experience than others.

*Years 1–2* A (long) day trip to France is feasible from anywhere in Lancashire/Yorkshire southwards, and gives experience of sights, sounds and smells difficult, if not impossible, to re-create in the classroom. Carrot: lunch in a French restaurant; stick: a workbook.

*Years 2–3* A class link with a school abroad can be established, with the help of the CBEVE. An excellent description of such a link is given in Jones (1979). Elements of the scheme include: exchange of display material (for example on the home town), exchange of letters between individual pupils, exchange of cassettes (content structured in advance by collaboration between the foreign language teachers on each side for individual listening (introducing oneself, etc.) and class listening (for example interviews with local people).

Several possibilities exist for a class or group of pupils to stay abroad (for 5–8 days, usually) in a residential centre or hotel, with lessons in the morning and excursions in the afternoon.

*Years 3–4* The class link can develop into a home-to-home exchange, during school or holiday time or both, and on a simultaneous or, preferably, consecutive basis.

*Years 4–5* The class link can be continued, with activities and materials becoming more topic-based, with a view to the oral and other tests at 16 +.

*Years 6–7* Individual sixth-formers should be allowed to stay for up to a term in the foreign country, preferably on a reciprocal basis; they can carry out History/Geography/Economics assignments, help with English lessons in the foreign school, etc.

Individual home-to-home exchanges (minimum three weeks) should be regarded by foreign language teachers as an integral part of the A-level course, on the same basis as, for example, field-work in Geography. Sixth-formers should be given a project to carry out, for example, making recordings of local people; follow-up for these exchanges should be systematic, so that those returning can give some account of their experiences and reactions to those who have not yet gone.

'Talk-sheets' are essential here, as a stimulus and a framework for discussion (for example *Vivre en France: appartements, maisons individuelles*; *La télévision, en France et en Grande-Bretagne*). These sessions could involve both the lower and the upper sixth; each small group could appoint a *rapporteur*, who makes notes for the discussion among the whole group.

### Coursebooks, Syllabuses and Methods

'Get out your *Sprich mal français*. Turn to page 27. Start reading, Sarah/Smith. Now translate that sentence. What does *ohne méthode* mean, anybody? Not seen it before? Right, put it in your vocabulary books. Stop chattering, get on with it. Now where were we? Carry on reading, David/Davies. No, the *second* sentence. Stop sniggering, over there. Right, if everyone's listening. No, *der Lehrer EST paresseux*. Say it again. Now translate it. (Half an hour later.) Right. Look at page 78. Question one, *Warum machen wir cet exercice?* Who can answer that?

A coursebook is a trap for the inexperienced teacher. It generally exists independently of the accompanying recorded or visual material, contains masses of words, sentences, grammar and exercises, set out in a way that invites reading aloud, translation, a few desultory questions in the foreign language, and then the rest of the 'work' in English. From the outset, the learner is invited to read (and hear) about *other* people using the foreign language. The usual idiom is descriptive, and the usual person is the third, whereas the order of priorities in real life is more likely to be that one needs to speak to someone else about *oneself*.

The very existence of the coursebook, with one identical copy for each pupil, suggests, if it does not impose, the same pace and style of working for the whole class. *No* coursebook, used on its own, can be suitable for the whole class (whether mixed-ability or streamed); *any* coursebook can and has to be adapted by the teacher to suit the needs of each individual pupil.

Most coursebooks appear to cover a definite syllabus, giving teacher and class a sense of progression, but in practice, this tends to mean that the language itself (above all its grammar) is the main focus for teaching and learning. The ideal syllabus for language learning up to 16+ would put the focus on situations, and gradually supply the learner with the language he needs, to cope in those situations. Progression would not be linear, but along an ascending spiral, where the learner keeps returning, but at a higher functional level, to situations previously encountered.

Now that educationalists of all colours are calling for greater attention to be paid to the teaching of life-related skills, it is high time for methods of teaching, learning and assessing, which have been successfully practised by teachers of English as a foreign language, to be looked at, adapted and adopted for foreign language teaching in this country. At the moment, the two worlds seem to be blissfully unaware of each other's existence, like Britain and Athens in the fifth century BC.

In order to teach almost any language material, whether from the most old-fashioned textbook imaginable, or the latest action-packed set of comic strips, or a set of readers, or teacher-produced materials, certain steps have to be followed, even with able pupils, if they are to assimilate and retain the material. The basic sequence should move from listening to speaking, followed by reading and, finally, writing. The pupils should at all times understand the meaning (overall or precise, depending on circumstances) of what they are listening to or reading: if any translation into English is necessary, it should be supplied by the teacher, as a kind of footnote. The pupils should be given the opportunity to approach this material from a number of directions and through a variety of activities. They should be enabled to say the new words and structures for themselves, in a context which is meaningful to them, as soon as possible in the teaching sequence. They should be given a clear model to imitate, for any spoken or written activities.

In almost any teaching sequence, pupils can be given the opportunity to use the foreign language instrumentally, that is, in such a way that the words they utter are followed by some event. Repeated experience of this 'power of words' can have a lasting and beneficial effect on pupils' motivation and self-confidence. For example, if the coursebook requires the teacher to 'do' the words for the parts of the body, he can give commands to a 'robot' pupil, or pupils (*Lève la main! Ferme les yeux!* etc.) then other pupils can give the commands; later, simple pairwork activities can be devised on the same lines.

A more complex sequence, involving commands, is given below (note: an 'auxiliary' is required: a pre-rehearsed member of the class, a sixth-former, an assistant or a PGCE student):

(1) The teacher plays the part of a Hollywood film director (lounging on a chair with feet on the table, using a cardboard megaphone, etc.); two pupils are volunteered to be cameramen; the 'auxiliary' comes into the classroom and proceeds to mime the actions of Rudolf, who has just received a farewell letter from Juliet (this letter: *Rudi, Unsere Liebe ist aus, J.*, is a vital 'prop'); in despair, he shoots himself.

(2) The teacher-director intervenes (in the foreign language) at this point, tells the 'actor' how bad his performance was, and orders him to go through it again. This time the director calls out an order before each action. Sometimes the actor is slow, or hesitates, enabling the director to repeat the order.

(3) Now it is the class's turn, cued by the teacher (flashcards?) to call out the orders. The basic pantomime principle must be observed, that is no action takes place until the order has been called out loudly and clearly enough.

(4) The class, working in pairs, writes down a complete list of orders. Some pairs (perhaps the weakest ones) will do this for the scene they have just watched; the rest will work out a list for other,

related, scenes, for example Juliet deciding to write the farewell letter; the postman delivering the fateful missive; Rudolf telephoning Juliet from a call-box in a desperate attempt to get her to change her mind.

The point about such activities, quite apart from their intrinsic merit in involving the pupils in the language-learning process, is that they can be devised for most of the grammar points served up in the coursebook (for example for the past tense, a detective interrogating a suspect about his movements on the day of the crime).

## Learning by Heart

'Learning by heart' conjures up pictures of dull English poems, listlessly recited, or lists of dates, rivers, formulae, etc. Such practices are of no help to the teacher of foreign languages, for whose pupils 'learning by heart' should not be an end in itself, but a means to (1) recalling and re-creating a pleasant experience (for example singing a lively song, first with, then without, the recording) or (2) assimilating basic speech patterns: phrases produced automatically in a given context by native speakers, the small change of everyday personal and social life – in short, what to say and how to say it.

'Learning by heart' begins in the first year with simple, one-sentence pairwork exchanges (which the pupils may not have even seen written down), from which able pupils can soon progress to short dialogues, practised until the pupils no longer need the text, and presented in front of the class (and a microphone). If pupils are trained to use the foreign language in this way, the range of situations in which they can be persuaded to speak from memory can be steadily extended. Indeed, this range *must* be extended, as there is a limit to the number of times a fourteen-year-old will want to 'play shops', for example.

*Teaching Sequence – 'Pourquoi tu pleures?'*

All that is needed for this work are some copies of the text (see Figure 7.2) and a tape/cassette-recorder with microphone. Although it is a made-up text, it is close enough to authentic speech patterns to be highly suitable for imitation, from the third year upwards.

## Figure 7.2

### *Promenade*      **Pourquoi tu pleures?**

METS ton manteau! Où sont tes bottes? Va chercher tes bottes! Si tu ne trouves pas tes bottes, tu auras une baffe! Et on restera à la maison! Tu veux qu'on reste à la maison? Tu sais, moi, je n'ai aucune envie de sortir, surtout par ce temps. Et j'ai plein de choses à faire à la maison, plein.

Non, bien sûr, tu ne veux pas rester à la maison . . Alors, va chercher tes bottes! Bon, ça y est? Tu es prêt? Je vais mettre mon manteau et on part. N'ouvre pas la porte! Tu vois bien que je ne suis pas prête, non? Bon, allons-y. Où sont mes clés? Tu ne les as pas vues, par hasard? Elles étaient sur la table, j'en suis sûre. Ah non! je les ai. Allons-y. Donne-moi la main.

Quel temps! Ne parle pas sinon tu vas prendre froid à la gorge et on appellera le docteur. Tu n'as pas envie qu'on appelle le docteur, n'est-ce pas? Alors, tais-toi. Et marche plus vite! On n'a pas beaucoup de temps. Laisse cette ficelle! Je t'ai dit cinquante fois de ne rien ramasser par terre. C'est plein de microbes. Tu tomberas malade et on appellera le docteur. Je te donnerai un bout de ficelle à la maison, si tu es gentil, bien sûr.

Ne traîne pas les pieds comme ca! Tu es fatigué ou quoi? Quand on est fatigué, on reste à la maison. Tu n'avais qu'à ne pas me demander de sortir. J'ai plein de choses à faire à la maison, plein! Qu'est-ce que tu veux encore? Un pain au chocolat? Je t'en achèterai un au retour, si tu es sage. Et ne marche pas dans les flaques d'eau! On dirait que tu le fais exprès ma parole!

Allez, va jouer maintenant. Moi, je reste ici. Ne va pas trop loin, hein! Je veux te voir. Ne te roule pas comme ça dans le sable! Tu vas te faire mal. Et puis je n'ai pas envie de passer ma vie à nettoyer tes vêtements. J'ai assez de travail comme ça. Où tu as touvé ce ballon? Rends-le au petit garçon! Rends-lui son ballon tout de suite!

Excusez-le, madame, il ne s'amuse qu'avec les jouets des autres. Joue un peu avec ta pelle et ton seau. Tu as perdu ta pelle? Elle doit être dans le sable, cherche. Une pelle, ça ne disparaît pas comme ça. Mais cherche! Comment veux-tu la trouver si tu ne cherches pas? Tu n'as pas besoin de te coucher par terre pour chercher! Qu'est-ce que tu as trouvé là? Montre! C'est dégoûtant, dégoûtant. Jette-le tout de suite! Il n'y a rien de plus dégoûtant qu'un ver de terre.

Allez, joue un peu avec ta pelle et ton seau, car on va bientôt partir. Ton père ne va pas tarder à rentrer. Et puis j'ai plein de choses à faire à la maison. Ne mets pas tes doigts dans le nez! Si tu veux te moucher, prends ton mouchoir.

Allez, allons-y. Tu vois, le petit garçon s'en va aussi avec sa maman. Au revoir, madame. Viens je te dis! Tu n'entends pas? Eh bien, tu ne l'auras pas ton pain au chocolat! Regarde dans quel état tu as mis tes vêtements! Allez, donne-moi la main. Et tiens-toi droit! Marche plus vite, on n'a pas de temps à perdre. Qu'est-ce que tu as à pleurnicher encore? Bon, je te l'achèterai ton pain au chocolat.

Un pain au chocolat, s'il vous plaît, madame. Merci, madame. Ne le tiens pas comme ça, tu salis ton manteau, tu auras une baffe! Et je le dirai à ton père! Il ne va pas être content du tout. Et tu sais comment il est, quand il se met en colère.

Je t'ai déjà dit de ne jamais appuyer sur le bouton de l'ascenseur! Bon, enlève tes bottes, je ne veux pas que tu mettes du sable dans toute la maison. Enlève-les immédiatement! Pourquoi tu pleures? Qu'est-ce que tu as? On a été se promener, comme tu voulais, je t'ai acheté ton pain au chocolat et au lieu d'être content tu pleures! Il va me rendre folle cet enfant.

VASSILIS ALEXAKIS

*Le Monde* 11–12 April 1976

*Preparation* A few words (for example *une baffe*) or constructions (for example *Tu n'avais qu'à ne pas*) need to be explained or translated, as soon as copies of the text have been given out. The teacher then briefly sets the scene: Mother and small child, about to go out for a pleasant (?) walk . . .

*First reading* This is a key stage in the process: the teacher reads the whole text aloud, in a lively manner, miming the gestures (looking for keys, opening door, smiling ingratiatingly at other child's mother, etc.) wherever possible. The teacher can then ask a series of very simple, rapid-fire questions: *Qui parle ici? A qui? Quel âge a-t-il? Où vont-ils?* etc. More searching questions could then be asked in English, for example 'Do you know anyone like this? Tell us about it. How did it make you feel?' Make sure that the 'point' of the last line has been understood and, if possible, appreciated.

*Second reading* Ask if anyone would like to have a go at saying one or two sentences for themselves. Say that they are to try hard to imitate you, and to pretend to be the nagging mother. Read a paragraph, or less, aloud: volunteers read it immediately after you.

*Third reading* (If time is short, combine this with the second reading.) Tell the class that they must choose one paragraph and learn it by heart (the long middle paragraph falls naturally into two parts). Guide their choices so that the ablest pupils take on the longest paragraphs. Say that you are now going to help them prepare their piece. Go through the passage, inviting pupils to ask for help with their paragraph. Drill phrases as necessary, then read a whole paragraph for the chosen pupils to imitate. (Meanwhile the rest of the class rehearse their paragraph in pairs.) Maintain an attitude of helpfulness and support for each pupil's efforts to play the part.

*Recording pupils' performance* Ensure before the lesson that the recorder and microphone are in working order and that the recording level is right. The pupils come out one by one to record their piece; be ready to prompt with whisper or gesture, and to stop the tape and start again if a pupil dries up completely. The pupils are not required to be word-perfect, but to be faithful to the sense: one *bon* or *alors* more or less, words left out, or even added, show that the pupil has entered into the spirit of the exercise.

*Marking the performances* In a subsequent lesson, announce that you and the class are now going to mark each performance, under two broad headings: accuracy of pronunciation and fluency and expressiveness. They are to work in pairs for this, and are encouraged to justify their marking when it diverges from the teacher's estimation.

*Other activities*  Working in pairs, the pupils are set to make a list of the expressions that seem to them typical of *spoken* French. This list can cover (1) interjections (*allez*), (2) repetition (*dégoûtant. . .; il . . . cet enfant*), (3) vocabulary (*plein de choses*), (4) structures (*pourquoi tu pleures?*). Each pair might find only one or two examples, but taking the class as a whole, over a dozen items could be found. Here, as in other areas of foreign language learning, it is good motivation to focus occasionally on the results of collective effort, rather than on how much one individual knows.

Pairs of pupils can also work out, for one or two paragraphs each, what the child (1) was doing and (2) might have been thinking. The resultant narrative (1) and interior monologue (2) could be worked on collectively and written on the board or overhead projector: each pupil will have contributed to the final product.

Pupils could be set to compose (individually, in pairs or in groups) narratives, monologues or dialogues based on similar situations; these could be acted, read out, or simply handed in.

With encouragement, the pupils will re-use phrases from this text in spoken or written work done many months afterwards.


**Pairwork**

The idea that learners of a foreign language should practise speaking the language by talking to each other in pairs is taken for granted in the teaching of English as a foreign language, yet it is only beginning to appear in foreign language coursebooks in Britain (for example Rowlinson, 1979 and 1980) and it is still viewed with suspicion, even hostility, by many foreign language teachers in both Local Education Authority and independent schools. Objections seem to fall into two main categories: (1) 'They'll only mess about, or talk about football/boys/me, in English' (cf. the Guinness advertisement 'I don't like it because I've never tried it') and (2) 'They won't learn anything and their mistakes will go uncorrected,' showing the latent paranoia of some teachers who fear that revolution or, worse, self-sufficiency will break out if the teacher is not in rigid control of every syllable uttered in the foreign language classroom.

*Advantages* (1) Pairwork enables pupils to speak and listen to the foreign language in a less formal and intimidating context than the usual teacher-pupil exchange. (2) It demonstrates to the pupils that they can use the foreign language for face-to-face communication. (3) Each pupil speaks the foreign language far more than in the usual teacher-centred situation. (4) Each pupil is given much-needed practice in *initiating* conversational exchanges and in *asking* questions. (5) Pupils are co-operating with each other to improve their performance. (6) Unlike grammar sentences, drills and audio-visual responses, pairwork encourages pupils to use language in a constructive, even creative, manner. (7) Able pupils can add to the basic script, or invent new ones, without being held back by the slower pace of others in the class.

*Problems* Difficulties arising during pairwork can generally be traced to certain clearly defined causes. (1) Each class must be trained, carefully and gradually, to work in pairs, beginning with 'one-liners' (simple greetings, and everyday enquiries), then moving on to very short dialogues (shopkeeper-customer, etc.), and so on. (2) the teacher must establish a good working relationship with the pupils, and create a pleasant, co-operative and supportive atmosphere in the classroom. (3) Instructions for pairwork must be simple and clear, and the activity must be capable of being demonstrated in front of the class by the teacher and a helper (visitor, student, language assistant, sixth-former or pupil from the class itself). (4) Pairwork must not have the false status of an 'extra', done very rarely; if it is a frequent and regular part of a language-teaching sequence, pupils will slip easily into their pairwork places, roles and frame of mind, instead of wasting time and losing concentration because of unnecessary movement and excitement.

*Materials* All that is needed is a card (or even a slip of paper) for each pupil, showing the necessary picture, dialogue or instructions, as appropriate; sometimes the necessary material will be on the board, or in the pupils' books, or in their heads. The meaning of what is to be said must be clear to everyone before pairwork starts.

To begin with, any text must be short, but even in the first year one should use only material that is genuinely 'communicative', i.e. capable of being acted by the pupils as themselves or in a role, and not just a lifeless code. As this way of working becomes established, variations can be introduced: (1) a dialogue script with gaps, to be filled in, during preliminary discussions in pairs, from a list of alternatives or words chosen by the pupils themselves; (2) a script with certain words or phrases underlined, to be replaced with others to create a 'new' dialogue; (3) more loosely structured scripts, for example a set of instructions (in English or in the foreign language) to each partner, from which the dialogue has to be made up. The different gradations of support given, and the possible permutations, are endless; the aim is to increase gradually the pupils' repertoire of pairwork activities, moving from exchanges based on a fixed script, towards an awareness of how linguistic structures can accommodate a variety of content.

*Method* Different combinations of pupils are possible (next-door neighbour; rows one and three turn round to face rows two and four; pupils choose their partners, etc.), and the formula should be varied to suit the type of work, the mood of the class, and so on.

Pairwork should not be used with new material, but for further practice and performance of material that has already been carefully taught and practised by other means.

If the dialogue contains difficult sounds or phrases, these should be drilled with the whole class, and with individuals, before pairwork starts.

The pupils must have a good, clear spoken model from which to work. This means that the teacher should act out the dialogue more than once, first taking both sides and speaking with the maximum of expression and gestures, and the minimum of reading from the script, and then with good pupils (or an outsider – see pp. 134–5), taking one side of the dialogue, then the other.

Left to their own devices at this point, the pupils will start reading their script as if from the coursebook, without looking at their partner, and rushing through it so they can say 'We've finished!' To avoid this, make clear to the class, if necessary by using one pair as a demonstration model, that they are to (1) look at each other, (2) try to act the part, if they are playing a role, (3) be expressive, in face, speech and even gesture, (4) use the script as a prompt, glancing at it only when they have to, and aiming to discard it as soon as they are able to, (5) help each other to play their part better.

During pairwork, the teacher must circulate as much as possible, and intervene, discreetly but firmly, with help and encouragement: ask to hear a couple of lines, respond positively to requests to add to, or alter, the script. The teacher's role here is akin to that of a producer during rehearsals.

Generally speaking, several pairs should be given the opportunity, when they are ready, to 'say their piece' in front of the class. Depending on the time of day or month, they will be eager or reluctant to do this, but the teacher should not take no for an answer if he has overheard good work during 'rehearsal' – overcoming the show of reluctance put up at this point by some pupils, particularly girls, is part of the teacher's job, and a vivid illustration of what is meant by 'giving the foreign language learner a sense of achievement'. Finally, the teacher should lead the applause for a particularly good performance.

A few suggestions for, and examples of, pairwork suitable for the three main stages of the secondary school course are given below.

*Years 1–3* Pairwork can begin almost immediately in the first year with the exchange of simple greetings. This basic routine can then be built up week by week with the addition of simple enquiries and exchanges of views on name, age, health, date, weather, daily routine, likes and dislikes, etc.

Dialogues suitable for pairwork should be devised for each new unit of the course being followed. Preferably, these will be situation-based, involving personal enquiries and simple role-playing exchanges about home, school, holidays, shopping, travel, town and country, etc.

Some dialogues should be memorised and performed in front of the class. Some of these should be gone over again from time to time (more interesting and useful as revision than merely going over lists of words and verbs!), for example when the topic comes up again.

*Second-year class* (wide ability range, comprehensive school): a sequence of lessons involving pairwork.

(1) Classwork: listen to a tape of a conversation between a waiter and a customer; look at photos of a restaurant, a menu and a bill.

(2) Individual work: compose one's own menu, under various headings (Potages, Desserts, etc.); write each item down, with its price.

(3) Work with the teacher: the teacher plays the part of the waiter, goes round the class greeting the 'customers' and taking their orders, following a set pattern (*Bonjour monsieur. Vous désirez? Et avec ça? Voulez-vous un dessert? Qu'est-ce que vous voulez boire?*).

(4) Individual work: copy from the board the waiter's questions

and write down also one's own version of the customer's replies.

(5) Pairwork: (a) Using these notes, act the scene between waiter and customer, then change roles; (b) try to act the same scene without looking at the notes; (c) act the same scene, but using one's *partner's* 'menu' – the waiter should note down the orders as he hears them.

(6) If desired, a similar sequence of work can be followed for the bill, using a set dialogue model (*C'est combien? – Ça fait 'x' francs, monsieur – Voilà 'y' francs. Gardez la monnaie!* etc.).

*Years 4–5* By the fourth year, pairwork should occur regularly as one stage in the sequence of work from the coursebook (for example if the current unit tells of a day in the life of a taxi-driver, pairwork sequences could involve the driver and a variety of passengers, or an interview with the driver). Similarly, dialogues can be made up, based on scenes from readers (see also *Group work*, below).

Pairwork can form one stage of the work on all new grammar and structures, and for revision. For example, outline 'talksheets' can be devised to prompt questions and answers around the subject of *Samedi dernier*, *Ce matin* or *Pendant les vacances*, to give practice in using the perfect and imperfect tenses correctly. Some dialogues should still be memorised; pupils will do this more readily, if they have been trained to do so from the early years.

Lessons devoted to examination preparation need not be labelled 'the oral', 'guided composition' and so on: pairwork, particularly involving situations and role-play, can draw on 'input' material for listening and reading comprehension, be related to one of the oral topics, and form part of the preparation for a piece of guided composition. In other words: a sequence of activities centred around a particular topic or situation, giving practice in using language that will be needed in more than one part of the examination.

*Fourth-year class* (top set, comprehensive school): a lesson involving pairwork.

(1) Materials: a large photo, or OHP transparency, or drawing on the board, of a public telephone coinbox in France; a cardboard cut-out telephone receiver; copies of the script; French coins?

(2) Situation: a French boy or girl helps an English guest to

make a phone call in France.

(3) Model dialogue, to be varied or simplified as required (note that *all* the movements and actions should be clearly mimed!):

F: Tiens! voilà la cabine. Allons-y! (. . .) Bon, décroche le récepteur.

E: Je décroche le recepteur . . . Et maintenant, qu'est-ce que je fais?

F: Tu mets une pièce.

E: Je mets une pièce . . . Ça y est. Et maintenant?

F: Tu fais le numéro.

E: Bon. Je fais le numéro . . . Ça sonne! . . . Allô . . .

(4) Teaching sequence: the class should be made familiar with aspects of the French telephone system, including personal reminiscences on the part of the teacher; in a subsequent lesson, pupils could be helped to compose and enact a telephone conversation; for another suggestion, see pp. 157–8 (*Comic monologues and sketches*).

*Years 6–7* In the sixth form, working with small numbers, pairwork will take place in a different atmosphere, with a freer framework of instructions, a greater range of subject-matter and fitting into different sequences of activities.

Certainly, every cycle of language work should include stages of pair and group work, ranging from closely scripted practice of new structures and role-play with script or instructions, to discussion of a topic with perhaps a few questions or notes as a guide, leading to the pooling of ideas in group discussion.

In the sixth form, as elsewhere, one learns by doing: it is therefore essential not to bewilder the class by a sudden increase in the amount of 'input' material, but instead to ensure that there are ample, and carefully structured, opportunities for sorting, assimilating, practising and producing new language.

## Group Work

In the sixth form, group work can be seen as a natural extension of pairwork, but with younger pupils, it is more convenient – and prudent – to see them as two distinct types of activity. The main advantage of group work is that it can reproduce in the classroom a real-life situation, where 3–4 people together discuss, plan, prepare and carry out a particular activity. Such a sequence of work normally takes longer than any pairwork activity, and may indeed extend over more than one lesson.

For group work to succeed, the teacher must have established a good working relationship with the class, otherwise concentration and momentum will soon be lost, and time wasted. Guidelines and objectives for the group activity must be clearly set out: there is generally no mysterious 'group dynamic' at work to provide the necessary impetus and purpose.

## Examples of Group Work Practised Successfully with Able Pupils

*Year 1* (grammar school). Simple shopping scenes, worked out by each group of pupils using the basic structures already taught, acted out in front of the class and recorded.

*Year 2* (older pupils learning English, in Spain). Class divided into 3–4 groups; each group carries out a different activity using appropriate materials and practising different skills: a 'colour-coded' dialogue pasted onto card and cut up (the group have to put the dialogue in its correct order and then act it out); a crossword with clues in the form of a gapped dialogue (solve the crossword, then act out the dialogue); pictures and sentences as stimulus material for a series of dialogues in a shop, etc. After about ten minutes, each group moves on to a new activity.

*Year 3* (pupils from independent schools in Paris and Manchester). Group and pairwork sessions involving approximately 50 pupils, half of them French and half English, structured so that all communication is across the language gap: teaching each other descriptions and stories based on objects and pictures, interviews following a joint visit to York, games of twenty questions and alibis, etc. An admirably clear outline of these sessions is given by Race and Thorpe (1980). A further example of group work using a class 'reader' is given below.

## Teaching Sequence Using 'Le petit Nicolas'

*Level* Year 3 to year 4 (even year 5, if they can spare the time) or, more properly: as young as the pupils' experience of French will allow.

*Materials:* 'Le petit Nicolas' or 'Les vacances du petit Nicolas' (Longman). These stories, adapted from the ones now published in

France in the Gallimard Folio Junior series, offer countless possibilities for use in the French language classroom, but their successful exploitation depends on careful and imaginative preparation and presentation. (Two further titles in the Nicolas series can be kept as additional reading for addicts.)

*Preparation* Drop everything else for about two weeks' French lessons. Announce this to the class, so as to generate a sense of anticipation, not about the contents of the stories themselves (these may disappoint some pupils), but about what the class will be *doing* with them . . .

*First stages* The pupils' first encounter with Nicolas and his friends must be a lively, entertaining experience. The teacher could place the Nicolas books in their context (French primary schools of thirty years ago, but with characters and situations not so far removed from French – or British – school life today). If it is feared that some new words and phases will get in the way of overall understanding, translations of these should be given in advance.

The teacher now reads the first chapter to the class, with the maximum of expression and dramatisation. By making remarks and asides at appropriate moments, the teacher can foster in the pupils the attitudes that will be a help with later stages of the work: awareness that this is everyday language, much of it in dialogue that can be imitated (even – especially! – the insults); at all times the class should be encouraged to see themselves as future authors of, and actors in, Nicolas-type sketches. If there is time left at the end of this lesson, some of the main phrases used in the first chapter could be reviewed orally by the teacher: rapidly, snappily, using English or French equivalents as the cue, with class repetition in chorus (spoken at proper speed, with full expression).

For the first homework, the class could be set to prepare the next one or two chapters, using the vocabulary lists and the comprehension questions for help and to check understanding. The next lesson, after a rapid recall of some phrases from the first chapter, should be an accelerated version of lesson one, covering one of the two chapters studied for homework.

*First writing* At this stage, the class could be set to do, in pairs, some simple writing based on what has been covered so far: brief notes on some of the characters (for example *Alceste: Mange tout le temps*; *Agnan: Premier de la classe, chouchou de la maîtresse*), or very short dialogues involving any two characters. These activities make the class used to the idea that what is in the book can be worked on, rewritten, assimilated, etc. by the pupils themselves. (It is a sad fact that many able learners never reach this stage, so that when they cease to study a foreign language, they still feel 'outside' it, unable to tune in to a simple conversation or a magazine article.)

If the class have previously had sufficient practice in writing French, the next homework could be to write a résumé of one chapter, or even to rewrite one chapter from the standpoint of one of the characters.

In subsequent lessons, the course of events must be varied, so that it never feels as if the class is simply 'doing the next chapter', until the bitter end! Indeed, little or no attention need be paid in class to about half the remaining chapters; for the others, the emphasis will have gradually shifted from the teacher reading aloud to the pupils working on the material, with the teacher's help, for example by composing short dialogues between Le Bouillon and Alceste, or the teacher and Clotaire.

*Work in groups* When most of the class have read almost the whole of one book, the teacher can now outline the *next* stage of the work, presenting it as the main point of the whole sequence: the pupils, working in groups of two to four, are to compose a sketch, to be acted out in front of the whole class, and involving some of the characters from the book plus, if desired, one outsider. When they have formed their groups (allow for individual affinities, but look after 'loners'), and some of the implications and possibilities of the activity have begun to sink in, someone will probably ask, 'What can we write about?' The answer is that they can choose any situation they like, but that you will start the ball rolling with some suggestions, for example: (1) A dramatisation of part of any chapter from the book; (2) a dramatised version of an 'additional' chapter; (3) a scene set in an entirely different location, for example Nicolas' class on an outing to Paris, or a trip to England, or an exchange visit to your pupils' school.

Allow groups up to half a lesson for preliminary discussion: first ideas about choice of situation and characters (using individual pupils' personalities!), one or two scraps of dialogue. Circulate freely around the class, encouraging them to ask for help (at this stage, mainly with planning the sketch); be ready for the group that announces, defiantly or despondently, 'We don't know what to do' (alternative (1) is there as a rock-bottom choice for such groups . . .). Set a homework in which each pupil has |to produce a draft of part of a sketch (preferably under the group's orders);

encourage them to talk about their sketch during breaks and elsewhere.

For the following lesson, groups sit together again to compare notes and begin their full draft; the teacher now goes round giving detailed advice with vocabulary, etc. The criterion for this should be made clear to all: each sketch will have to be understood by the whole class, so that bizarre words or over-complex structures are to be avoided. Groups should be urged to draft clear, simple, comprehensible scripts, containing as many words and expressions from the book as possible. Clear advice and stern orders must be available now for any group who, even by this stage, has done very little work.

For the next homework, an agreed version of the script should be written up by each pupil in the group (each pupil in a group will be given the same mark). Collect, mark and give back this homework in the usual way. (At this stage, one or two lessons may be devoted to entirely different work.)

The groups now prepare their 'final acting script', including mention of props and stage directions, and rehearse it during a lesson. Go round the groups listening and advising on intonation, etc. For the following homework, each pupil studies and rehearses his part; if some can be persuaded to learn their part, so much the better, but this is not essential. Tell them that their performances will be recorded.

*Making the recordings* During the next two lessons, the sketches are performed; it is essential to check beforehand that microphone and recorder are in good working order, and that the recording level is right. Encourage audience interest, but ensure *silence* at the start of each performance and *attention* throughout. Discourage interjections (example, as one pupil misses his cue for a second time: 'How come they got 20?!'); be ready for the unscheduled entry of the headmaster/senior mistress, for whom top sets are meant to be seen, but not heard.

In the following lesson replay the recorded performances to the class, inviting them (in pairs or groups) to mark these, in terms of (1) quality of *script* (language used, appropriateness of material to character and situation) and (2) quality of *performance* (French intonation, etc.; good acting and directing). The pupils will listen to each other's performance with renewed interest and, without fully realising it, will be training their ear and exercising their judgement in very useful ways; to assist this, the teacher should be prepared to discuss his criteria in arriving at his own marks.

*Notes and questions* If a sequence of work of this kind is undertaken, some of the stages outlined above should be omitted: there would never be enough time to cover them all!

But can one afford the time, for example with a fourth- or fifth-year class, for work such as this? The answer is another question: can one afford *not* to do it? The immediate benefits are obvious: increased enjoyment, motivation and a sense of participation; there will also be dividends in the examination: confidence in handling dialogue will help with the various forms of structured composition and with the oral test, whether it consists of topics, general conversation, situations or role-play. Pupils are far more likely to remember French they have worked with and used in the classroom, in recognisable contexts, than the lists of words and phrases which are traditionally taught 'for the examination'.

The script that follows was produced by three members of a third-year class in November 1979. (Mistakes have not been corrected.)

### *Jouons au football avec le chiffon!*

*Personnages:* Alceste, Clotaire, Eudes, un surveillant.
*Histoire:* Après un peu de conversation générale ils commencent à jouer, et se battre. Mais un surveillant entre et les grondes.

| | |
|---|---|
| Alceste: | Bonjour, je suis Alceste, j'aime manger. |
| Clotaire: | Et je suis, er . . . Clotaire, je suis le dernier de la classe. |
| Eudes: | Et je m'appelle Eudes. Je suis très fort et hier j'ai donné un coup de poing à Agnan et maintenant il est mort. |
| C: | Où est Nicolas, Alceste? |
| A: | Il à la grippe, Hourah! |
| C: | Chouette! |
| E: | Nicolas est mon copain meilleur, voulez-vous des coups de poing? |
| C: | Un coup de quoi? |
| E: | Tu es sourd comme un pot! Un coup de poing, stupide! |
| C: | Qu'est-ce que c'est? |
| E: | Un de ces . . . |
| | (Ils commencent à se battre.) |
| A: | Taisez-vous, je désire manger avec du calme. |

| C: | Vilain cafard! Hé, j'ai une idée. |
|---|---|
| A. et E: | Mon dieu! |
| A: | Tu as une idée? (Il s'évanouit.) |
| E: | Ce n'était pas moi. Je ne lui ai pas donné un coup de poing. |
| C: | Est-ce qu'il est mort? |
| A: | Non! Mais où suis-je? |
| E: | Tais-toi car Clotaire a une idée. Quelle est ta idée? |
| C: | Jouons au football avec le chiffon! |
| A: | D'ac! |
| E: | Chic! |

(Ils commencent à jouer.)

| A: | J'ai marqué un but, hourah! |
|---|---|
| E: | Sale menteur! Ce n'est pas vrai! |
| A: | Mais si, c'est vrai, c'est vrai! Tu es un dingue. |
| E: | Tu me fais rire, c'est toi qui est le dingue. |

(Eudes donne un coup de poing sur le ventre d'Alceste qui commence à pleurer.)

| A: | Je ne pourai plus rien manger. |
|---|---|

(Il est sorti de la classe.)

| C: | Tu es un bébé Alceste. |
|---|---|

(Clotaire et Eudes commencent à jouer encore.)

| C: | J'ai marqué un but. Ça fait le score trois à un. |
|---|---|
| E: | Ce n'est pas vrai, il est trois à deux. |
| C: | Mais non, il est trois à un et si ça ne te plaît pas restes chez toi. |

(Ils commencent à se battre mais un suveillant entre.)

| S: | Interdiction de se battre à l'école. |
|---|---|
| C: | Mais le score est trois à un monsieur. |
| E: | Ce n'est pas vrai il est trois à deux. |
| C: | Sale menteur! |

(Ils commencent à se battre.)

| S: | Taisez-vous! |
|---|---|
| C: | De quoi te mêles-tu? |
| E: | Oui tu es un espèce d'idiot. |
| S: | Ça suffit! venez ici! |

(Ils sont sortis de la classe. Et on entends beaucoup de bruit.)

| S: | Vous aurez des gifles. |
|---|---|
| E., C. et S: | Aïe! Hou! Aïee! |

**Using Authentic Material**

The use of authentic material links the foreign language course with the real world, not in order to 'learn about' pollution or town planning in the foreign country, but to hear, read and imitate ways in which native speakers and writers express their reactions to life. Such material is not too difficult to use before 16: a second-year mixed-ability class can work profitably from a video of Télé-Journal, and a third-year class of average ability can listen without panic to a France-Inter news bulletin: it all depends on the objectives that are set for the pupils, and the help that they are given in attaining them.

The first encounter with authentic material can be in the first term of year 1: signs, notices, menus, etc. Able pupils are often starved, at this vital stage, of authentic material; in a mixed-ability class, additional material should always be available for those who are ready to tackle it (instead of the pointless 'start looking at the next unit'). Able pupils can be equally starved in a selective class, if learning the foreign language is presented merely as an uphill grammatical slog, with the teacher obstructing the view from the summit.

Recordings of songs (to be sung-along-with) and poems (to be declaimed and even learnt by heart) should be used frequently in the first two years. By the third year, able pupils should have the opportunity, at least once a week, to hear and read authentic texts on subjects of interest and entertainment for young people and others in the country concerned. The resultant sense of achievement, on the part of pupils who are able to say, to friends or family, 'I heard that on the French news/read it in a French magazine,' is a key element in the process of motivation and reward for the able pupil, which alone makes possible the survival and renewal of foreign language studies in this country.

*Teaching Sequence – 'La ville idéale'*

*Level* Year 3 to year 6, depending on pupils' previous experience of listening to authentic material. For younger pupils, more support could be given for vocabulary and structures; for older ones, further spoken and written tasks could be devised.

*Materials* A recording of a one-and-a-half-minute extract from France-Inter (*reportage dans la rue – quatre passants répondent à la question: 'Pour vous, la ville idéale, qu'est-ce que c'est?'*); full and/or gapped transcript of text; vocabulary sheet and work-sheets (see below). If so desired, instructions and listening/speaking tasks could be recorded as well, so that the cassette and work-sheets can be used by individual pupils during class or private study time.

*Vocabulary sheet*  A list of 10–20 words likely to be unfamiliar to the class, with their English translation; an English translation of 6–12 words and phrases from the text (for 'word-hunt'); a similar list, but in French, of equivalents for 6–12 words and phrases from the text (the drawback of this is that very often if the alternative French expression *were* more appropriate in that context, the speaker would have used it! This problem arises frequently with learning or testing tasks which are 'all in the foreign language': transformation/substitution drills where it is easy for the pupil to think that the synonyms are indistinguishable both in meaning and in use, multiple-choice answers where a synonym is given in place of the word or phrase used in the text in order to make the correct answer less obvious, etc. In such cases, careful presentation by the teacher is needed, to make the necessary distinctions); 'key words': the pupil is set to find 6–12 expressions of 2–6 words each which seem to contain the central ideas in the text, and to write these down with an English translation.

*Work-sheet (1): speaking.* Questions on the text: these must be simple, capable of being answered rapidly with phrases that occur in the text itself (there is in fact no need for these questions to appear on the work-sheet, unless the teacher wishes them to be studied beforehand. At all events, this sequence is there in order to make the pupils say for themselves some phrases in the text, and to make them familiar with the ideas expressed. It should not be used as an oral task if teacher and/or class are feeling sluggish!); sentence completion: a list of statements, taken or adapted from the text (for example *Il faudrait centraliser . . ., Ce que je crains le plus, c'est . . .*) to be spoken aloud, imitating as far as possible the speech patterns of the recording (here too, the teacher may prefer to conduct the task without reference to the work-sheet); oral composition: the pupil is asked to respond to the question *Pour vous, la ville idéale, qu'est-ce que c'est?* as if he were any one of the passers-by, or each of them in turn.

*Work-sheet (2): writing.* Transcription of an extract from the test; translation into English of this or another extract, presented by stopping the recording after each phrase; retranslation: from a printed translation of part of the text, the pupil is set to write down the original French, with or without the help of the recording, played in sections; essay: a description of the pupils' own *ville idéale*, composed as a statement, or as an interview with a questioner, or as a dialogue with someone with different views.

*Sequence of activities* Give out vocabulary sheet and go over the first list, pointing out difficult words and answering pupils' enquiries. Say briefly and in general terms what the text is about and for whom it was intended.

First hearing of recording: point out that this is so that the pupils can 'tune in' to the text, and perhaps pick out some ideas and phrases. (This stage can be omitted.) Look at the next list of words (English translations or French equivalents), pointing out that the 'original' phrases are all in the recorded text.

Second hearing, in sections: the pupils, working individually or in pairs, write down the original words for each phrase. When this is completed, a full transcript of the recording may be given out, so that the pupils can check their answers. Alternatively, the transcripts may be given out later, or at the end of the sequence of work, or not at all. Ask quick-fire comprehension questions on the text.

Give out the 'speaking' work-sheet. Go through the list of incomplete statements (referring to the transcript if necessary), asking pupils to volunteer one or more possible completions. Go through the list again, this time insisting on speed and intonation; cue each sentence by calling out the number and pointing to one pupil. Oral composition: explain to the pupils what they have to do, then encourage them to launch themselves into a reply even before they know how it will end; accept, encourage even, false starts, hesitations (*euh . . ., les . . ., les . . .*) etc. The aim here is to re-create as closely as possible for each pupil the way in which French people themselves speak. (With an experienced class, this stage could be tackled or repeated as pairwork.)

Give out the 'writing' work-sheet. The sequence in which these tasks are carried out will depend on various factors: the need to break up the previous sequences which involve intensive listening and speaking, the homework timetable, etc.

All that, from one-and-a-half minutes of text? In practice, there will not be time to cover every stage in the above sequence, and in any case, each text calls for a different approach. But the important point is that the emphasis throughout has been on varied activities centred on a relatively limited amount of language and ideas. (This contrasts starkly with traditional textbooks or audio-visual courses,

where far too much material is given, and far too little done with it.)
Able pupils who have been given the experience of work such as
that outlined above, even a few times in the two years to O-level/
16+, will derive a sense of achievement from their foreign language
studies, and may even be more interested in pursuing foreign study
beyond 16+, in which case they will have acquired a sounder basis
for A-level work.

## Comic Monologues and Sketches

Faced with the average coursebook or examination paper, a pupil
could be forgiven for concluding that the French are very good at
buying ice-creams or going for bicycle rides, but that they seldom, if
ever, laugh.

Comic material, if carefully selected and presented, can be used
to good effect in the classroom, to overcome this barrier to
communication. Recordings with audience laughter can have an
*effet d'entraînement* on a class, provided the pupils have been
enabled to understand what is meant to be so funny. Since laughter
is a serious and important matter, it can give a tremendous boost in
confidence to pupils who have been able to enjoy for themselves
something that makes the French laugh.

Recordings of several 'comedians' are easily available in France,
and in some cases collections of their sketches have been published
in paperback, for example Fernand Raynaud: 'Le 22 à Asnières',
'Les œufs cassés', 'Restons Français', 'Bourreau d'enfants' – nearly
a hundred of his sketches are printed in *Heureux!* (Gallimard Folio
No. 838); Raymond Devos: 'L'homme existe, je l'ai rencontré',
'Mon chien, c'est quelqu'un' – more than seventy of his sketches are
printed in *Sens dessus dessous* (Livre de poche No. 5102).

## Teaching Sequence – 'Le 22 à Asnières'

*Level*   Year 3 to year 7.

*Materials*   A recording of the sketch, transferred to tape or
cassette. A transcript of the sketch, presented in an 'annotated'
form, that is with asterisks by words and phrases in the text, and
English translations in the margin alongside.

*Introduction*   Ask which British comedians they like best, and
why; outline briefly the main differences and similarities between
laughter-makers in Britain and in France. Explain briefly how the
French telephone system operated before the introduction of STD
in the late 1970s, the frustrations experienced by users, and the

ridicule heaped on it by all and sundry, including Raynaud in this sketch, which became famous (people spoke of something as being *plus difficile à obtenir que le 22 à Asnières*, for example).

Give out copies of the script, and briefly outline the situation: the typical Parisian official, the timid provincial, the series of foreigners barging past him, etc.). Invite further queries on the language or the situation, but keep the class's attention away from the punch-line!

*First hearing*  Play the recording, either (1) straight through, to allow it to be appreciated as a whole, or (2) in sections, if it is feared that comprehension and concentration might sag. Ask if there are any further queries about words etc.; exchange ideas and reactions informally with the class; suggest, casually, that they might like to hear it again . . .

*Second hearing*  Play the recording again, straight through, or perhaps in sections if it was heard straight through first time. This second hearing should be quite fresh for the class, since much of the humour of the sketch lies in the manner (for example voices, timing) rather than in the content.

The aim is to enable a class to appreciate the sketch in conditions as nearly similar as possible to those of a French person listening to the record and/or reading the text. If that has been achieved, then the main purpose of the exercise has been fulfilled. However, some follow-up activities can be devised, with the aim of helping the pupils to assimilate and use for themselves some of the language of the sketch.

*Further activities*  Practise with the class a dozen or so phrases from the text, drilling expression and intonation, for example: *Comment vas-tu Christiane? . . . Je voudrais le 22 à Asnières . . . Vous pensez que ça va être long?*

Give out a gapped version of a passage from the sketch; the class try to fill in the blanks, with or without the help of the recording.

Give a lightning vocabulary/phrase test (to be done in pairs?): 20 items in English to elicit such phrases as *tant mieux, donner un coup de fil, faire attention*; help the class by giving them the context for each phrase, for example by reminding them what was said just before the phrase in question.

Set the class to compose, in pairs, short dialogues adapted from one part of the sketch; they then act these out in front of the class.

Group work: groups of 3–4 pupils each compose a sketch loosely inspired by the situation in Raynaud's sketch (see above, pp. 147–53, for details of group work).

*Teaching Sequence – 'Miss Solitude'*

If a class works regularly with authentic texts where the subject-matter is interesting and well presented, each pupil can be encouraged to treat these texts as a source of language and inspiration for personal writing. Below the sixth form, this approach can lead, as we have seen, to lively and entertaining writing in the foreign language. In the lower sixth, the teacher can offer his pupils what amounts to an 'unwritten contract': 'I expect above-average work from you, and in order to get this, I am prepared to give you above-average help and encouragement with language and content.' In the upper sixth, able pupils are ready to tackle a text such as 'Miss Solitude' (see Figure 7.3).

The essential point in working with a text such as this, which has a strong story line and human interest, is that it should make a vivid impact on the pupils *at the first reading*. This is impossible if the text is read unseen; preparation should be undertaken by the teacher with the class, rather than giving out the text and telling the pupils to look up all the words they don't know in a dictionary, which would be a depressing and time-wasting experience.

Instead, the teacher should give out the text and then, without revealing the story, explain or translate some 30–40 words and phrases, varying the length of explanation according to the interest or usefulness of the words. One can invite questions about further unknown phrases, but there is no question of putting together the story-line: we are still at the stage of sorting out pieces of the puzzle.

The scene can now be set briefly, in English: the Buttes-Chaumont park (near the 'East End' of Paris); Mlle S—; the unseen observer-narrator, through whose eyes we are invited to follow the scene. Having creating, in a modest way, an atmosphere of attention and expectancy, the teacher can then read the text through, without interruption, with maximum expression, particularly in the soft registers, and discreet pauses for effect. The pupils will probably prefer to be able to look at their copy of the text while it is being read.

After the reading, it is best to leave the pupils alone with their thoughts for a moment: certainly no further linguistic explanations should be given, unless requested; instead, the teacher should simply be receptive to any impressions or reactions that pupils care to express, in French or in English.

This text has been used successfully with both boys and girls, in

Figure 7.3

## PORTRAIT

# *Miss Solitude*

ELLE ne me voit pas. Je l'observe. La nature est très moqueuse. Dans le jardin des Buttes-Chaumont, elle est aussi perdue qu'un moineau égaré dans une chambre. Elle époussette enfin, une chaise de fer, s'assied. Frileusement. Sort un livre. Son après-midi commence.

Mlle S... est si triste qu'on ne voit même plus qu'elle est laide. Mais elle ne s'aime pas assez pour oublier qu'elle n'est pas belle. Je regarde son petit visage, pâle et contracté par la haine de cette vie. Je connais bien le thème de son histoire, le synopsis, comme on dit maintenant. Professeur dans un C.E.T. de banlieue lointaine, elle est, à trente-cinq ans, la femme la plus célibataire de Paris. Nous avons échangé quelques mots, quelquefois — des mots comme des couteaux dans une plaie fraîche.

### Une certaine laideur

Parce qu'il n'y a que les vieux à pouvoir vivre comme les vieux, elle m'a expliqué, non sans circonlocutions, le sentiment de solitude presque insoutenable qui l'accable. Autant qu'elle peut, elle fuit le studio que l'administration lui concède dans le périmètre du C.E.T. « Vous comprenez, ces logements, c'est conçu pour une vie de famille, avec un mari et des enfants. Autrement, ce n'est pas tolérable. »

C'est une curiosité, Mlle S... J'ai rarement vu quelqu'un d'aussi mal dans sa peau. Mais après tout, quelqu'un qui est bien dans sa peau n'est peut-être qu'un inconscient. Ou un salaud ? Elle n'est pas récréative. Mais elle est étrange. Ce qui est une manière d'être étrangère partout. Je l'aime bien. Une des raisons qui font que je l'aime, c'est que personne ne l'aime.

« Ils ont ri de ma solitude. » Elle m'a dit vivre entourée d'ennemis sans pour autant cesser d'être seule. Les gens ne peuvent comprendre combien une femme se sent seule quand, pendant des années, elle a dû étouf-

fer en elle tous ses sentiments. Ils ne lui pardonnent pas non plus un visage si ingrat. Et y a-t-il solitude plus profonde qu'une certaine laideur ? Qu'une certaine désolation de la laideur ?

Les Buttes-Chaumont, c'est plein d'amoureux. Quand ils passent, son cœur crève. Pour se protéger, il lui faudrait tuer délibérément sa sensibilité, tenter de se délivrer de la douleur par le non-désir. Facile à dire ! Je la verrai un soir pleurer presque après les avoir regardés s'embrasser.

« Personne ne m'a jamais dit : « Mon chéri », l'entendrai-je murmurer, pleine de la nostalgie d'un passé qui n'a jamais existé et peut-être ivre, aussi, de ressentir jusqu'à la douleur le désir d'être prise dans des bras.

C'est tout le drame de sa vie : elle n'a jamais été amoureuse. En amour, elle est comme un aveugle qui entend parler de couleurs et n'en a jamais vues. Et son malheur n'est pas qu'elle en souffre. Mais qu'elle souffre en vain. Il n'y a pas que les amoureux à être seuls au monde. Je ne crois pas qu'elle ait jamais tenté de se révolter. Contre qui ? Contre quoi ? C'est comme ça. Elle n'y peut rien.

### La fierté

Ce qui m'inquiète aujourd'hui est que l'arbre contre lequel elle s'est malencontreusement assise est celuimême où, quelques jours plus tôt, des enfants ont oublié un « message », comme disent les joueurs de rallye-papers. Ce message, il me déplaît beaucoup qu'elle en prenne connaissance, l'ayant moi-même lu avant de le remettre bêtement à sa place, une heure avant qu'elle n'arrive. Qu'elle se tourne, fatalement, le papier blanc coincé sous l'écorce entrera dans son champ visuel. Et alors...

Pour l'instant, elle feuillette son livre d'un air las. Parce que pas grand-chose suffit à vous faire plaisir lorsqu'on est bien résigné, lire lui permet, la plupart du temps, d'au moins oublier la dure et triste réalité. Cela endort son ennui total, c'est-à-dire son impossibilité de communiquer avec les êtres et les choses. Car si enfermée dans sa peau, elle ne s'aime pas, elle n'aime guère non plus les gens. Le ressort est bloqué. Elle ne peut se détendre. Elle n'est pas du même peuple. Pour échapper à sa détresse, elle n'a qu'une recette : la fierté. Ce qui la perd. On la croit poseuse alors qu'elle a une pudeur atroce qu'on prend pour du dédain.

## L'idée fixe

Encore que plus immergée de caractère qu'un iceberg, elle m'a exposé, un autre soir, sa « philosophie ».

*Plus je suis solitaire, plus je suis dépourvue d'amis et de défenseurs, plus je me dois de respect. Vous comprenez, on ne m'a pas accordé le droit d'être bonne. »*

Quand — Dieu sait pourquoi ! — elle éprouve en ma présence l'exceptionnel sentiment de confiance qui, chez les êtres apeurés, tient lieu d'amour, c'est toute son âme souterraine qu'elle dévoile, peut-être sans s'en apercevoir.

« *Il me semble qu'il n'y a rien pour moi sur la terre. Non, je ne connaîtrai jamais le bonheur. Je suis bien trop bête !* »

Elle m'avouera, une autre fois, lutter depuis plusieurs années contre l'idée fixe de son cerveau enténébré. « *A quoi bon continuer de vivre ? On est si seul... tout seul ! Pourquoi ne pas finir tout de suite ? Je n'ennuierais plus personne, même pas moi ! Dans la solitude, j'ai failli devenir folle.* »

Quand ses yeux gris sont sur moi, c'est le désespoir qui me regarde. On peut voir dans son cœur désert les araignées tisser leur toile. C'est le regard d'une âme inapte à vivre. Et c'est d'autant plus désolant que, godiche et mal attifée, il n'y en a pas moins sûrement de belles et bonnes choses en elle. Et finalement, le plus difficile n'est pas pour elle de vivre seule. C'est de souffrir seule.

Paraphrasant Valéry, j'ai failli lui dire un jour : les uns sont assez bêtes pour s'aimer. Les autres pour se haïr. Deux manières de se tromper. Peut-être avez-vous la meilleure part ? Mais je savais ce qu'elle aurait préféré : aimer — et — se tromper. La sachant également assez portée sur les choses de Dieu (le Christ n'est-il pas, dans bien des cas, le mari des femmes qui n'en ont pas ?), j'ai pensé lui parler de l'homme d'Assise. L'essentiel n'est pas qu'on me comprenne, mais que, moi, je comprenne les autres. Et non qu'on m'aime, mais que j'aime les autres, disait le Poverello. Mais à quoi bon les mots quand on est fixé ?

Sans cesse, elle interrompt sa lecture pour laisser errer ses yeux. Alors, à travers les branches, son visage glacé m'apparaît. Si la beauté peut servir de masque à la laideur, pourquoi l'inverse ne serait-il pas possible ? Comment peut-on être assez imbécile pour n'attacher de beaux sentiments qu'aux beaux visages ? J'essaie de l'imaginer avec d'autres traits. C'est difficile. Tout son corps n'est qu'une grosse misère. Et quelle physionomie ! Tout crie en elle : mon âme et mon corps sont en peine.

## Le message

Mais elle a fini par se tourner vers l'arbre. Et c'est alors que survient la chose inévitable. Elle tire, de sous l'écorce, le papier plié. Un message ! Depuis vingt ans, elle vit sans raison aucune. Sa vie s'écoule et se perd en néant. C'est dire si dans son existence tragiquement banale, tout fait événement ! Je la vois, anxieux, déplier la feuille quadrillée. Avec lenteur. Son visage prématurément fané — mais mieux vaut être fané que pourri ! — s'altère, s'éclaire, vire au rose. Tout cela très vite. Elle relit le message. Le relit encore. Elle le lisse. Elle le range avec beaucoup de soin dans son porte-cartes. Alors, enfin, elle sort de son sac à main un mouchoir petit, très fin, et le porte à ses yeux.

Ce que dit le message ? Peu de chose. De simples mots : « *Pour celui qui me lit : je vous aime.* »

**PIERRE LEULLIETTE.**

comprehensive and independent school sixth forms; the most gratifying part of the work, each time, has been the pieces of written French which some pupils have produced, inspired by the text. If the text has been read as part of the class's work on the topic of women in society, or human relationships, then one of the essay titles set (sixth-formers always appreciate being offered a choice of subjects for an essay: it encourages them to see it as a piece of *personal* writing) can be 'Miss . . .'. Point out that the designation has its origin in beauty contests (Miss France etc.), and means that the person concerned is the *epitome* of the particular category, the champion. Encourage them to choose a 'Miss . . .' that appeals to their own imagination, or reflects some of their own pre-occupations. One can expect offerings such as 'Miss Beauté', 'Miss Aujourd'hui' and once even, 'Miss Célimène', signé (rageusement) Alceste!

The pupils should be reminded of the set-up in the original text (an unseen observer who does not intervene), and encouraged to adapt some of the structures (for example *si triste qu'on ne voit même plus qu'elle est laide*) and, of course, the vocabulary, to their own purposes.

The piece that follows was written by a boy in the upper sixth in January 1980. (Mistakes have not been corrected.)

### Mme. Moyenne

Bonjour, je m'appelle le Dieu. Puisqu'il n'y a rien d'agréable à la télé, je regards la Terre pour m'amuser un peu. Il y a, là-bas, une maison toute brune avec des fenêtres carrées, derrière lesquelles les rideaux bruns sont tirés; on dirait peut-être un grand carton que quelqu'un a laissé tomber par hasard, et puis l'a oublié tout à fait. Qu'est-ce que qu'il contient alors, ce carton? – rien d'extraordinaire; c'est Madame Moyenne qui y habite.

Elle porte des vêtements bruns et un visage que l'on trouverait dans un dessin fait par un enfant de dix ou onze ans; il n'y a aucune tache de rousseur, aucune chose qui la rendrait ou laide ou belle – elle est si moyenne qu'elle est unique.

Elle regarde sa montre qui s'est arrêtée il y a trois jours, mais à quoi bon savoir quelle heure il est? – ça fait peu de différence dans sa vie. Il est resté six heures et demi pendant trois jours qui auraient pu être trois secondes – rien n'a bougé, rien ne s'est changé.

Sa journée est comme un train – sa routine la porte partout, et il lui faut seulement monter et descendre, sans effort, et sans se servir de son esprit parce qu'elle a besoin seulement de deux pieds et de deux mains, ou même une suffirait!

Même ses pensées suivent une routine; à huit heures, quand elle boit du café au lait (elle le préfère, car il est brun), elle se dit qu'elle est libre et sans responsabilité. A midi, en mettant la table pour le dîner, elle commence à ésperer que l'après-midi soit passé, sans admettre qu'elle s'ennuie. A trois heures, elle décide de ne pas se tuer aujourd'hui, en remettant le couteau dans le tiroir. A quatre heures et demie elle se regarde dans le miroir et elle se pose des questions auxquelles sa réflexion ne peut pas répondre. Pourquoi doit-elle rester ici dans la maison, toute seule, pendant que son mari fait un métier intéressant, entouré de camarades et de confrères? Pourquoi est-elle obligée de s'ennuyer chaque jour à faire le ménage et la vaisselle avec le même balai et les mêmes assiettes? Et pourquoi est-elle si différente de ces jolies filles dans les chansons que l'on écoutes sans cesse à la radio?

J'ouvre mon registre de créations pour chercher son nom, mais je ne le trouve pas; donc ce n'est pas moi qui a créé cette Madame Moyenne; elle ne peut pas être un vrai être humain. Je réalise, alors, que cette femme n'est que la création des hommes et des femmes qui veulent discuter le rôle de 'la femme' dans la société. Ils veulent savoir exactement ce qu'une femme est, afin d'avoir de telles discussions. Ils peuvent donc regarder leur Madame Moyenne, et dire que la femme (chaque femme) devrait faire un métier ou bien qu'elle est trop faible pour le faire. Mais la vérité, c'est que chaque femme est différente; une femme pourrait ressembler plus à son mari qu'à sa voisine, par exemple. Toutes les femmes ne devraient pas se trouver dans la même catégorie; elles devraient faire la chose la plus convenable à leur propre situation, à leur personalité. Madame Moyenne n'existe pas.

## References

Jones, B.L. (1979) 'Le jeu des colis – an exercise in foreign language communication', *Audio-Visual Language Journal*, *17* (3), 159–167

Race, A.T. and Thorpe, I. (1980) 'Exchange groups and pair work' in *The Teaching of Modern Languages: a View for the 1980's*, Headmasters' Conference, London, pp.5–8

Rowlinson, W. (1979 and 1980) *Tout compris*, Parts 1 and 2, Oxford University Press, Oxford

# 8 THE LANGUAGE TEACHER AS A 'SNAPPER-UP OF UNCONSIDERED TRIFLES'[1]

N.K. Cammish

The language teacher who picks up a tea-towel on which are depicted Goldilock's Three Bears, each in an appropriately sized bed with appropriately sized boots lined up at the foot, and who thinks of drying the cutlery, is no Autolycus. He should have realised, of course, that the tea-towel makes a perfect visual aid for practising the comparative and superlative structures! –

ce lit-ci est plus grand que ce lit-là
ces bottes-ci sont moins grandes que ces bottes-là
le plus grand ours se trouve à droite
le Père est plus gros que la Mère
le petit lit est plus confortable que les grands lits . . .

It is rare to find a foreign language course or textbook tailored exactly to the needs of a particular class or particular teacher: supplementary materials are always needed to provide variety, extra practice and motivation. New and different materials, snapped up from other sources, can help to practise and consolidate teaching points in an interesting way when a return to the course materials for 'revision' would produce only groans from one's pupils. Courses which make unrealistic demands on the pupils, expecting important and difficult new structures to be absorbed and activated for use on the basis of a few examples and minimal practice, need extra materials so that the structure can be manipulated, re-used and re-worked, and exploited creatively. Where is one to find these materials? A teacher with the instincts of Autolycus and some pedagogical insight knows there are many useful resources which can be developed into teaching aids for foreign language learning.

Frances Hodgson (1961) in her exposition of how to use Cuisenaire rods to teach most of the basic structures of French, shows how much can be done with equipment originally intended for the teaching of mathematics. Tapes of sound-effects which tell a

164

story, intended as a stimulus for L1 language development in slow learners (LDA, Sound Stories), can be used to stimulate narrative work in the foreign language:

| Tape sounds | Teacher's questions |
|---|---|
| (alarm clock rings) | Qu'est-ce qui s'est passé? |
| (movement and yawn) | Et Pierre, qu'est-ce qu'il a fait? |
| (footsteps) | Où est-il allé? |
| (water running, splashes) | Qu'est-ce qu'il a fait? |
| (razor) | Et ensuite? |
| etc. | |

A picture of a contemplative face, cut out from a magazine or colour supplement and mounted as a flash card, could be used as a stimulus for an open-ended, creative exercise practising 'penser à quelque chose':

| T: A quoi pense-t-elle? | P1: Elle pense à son ami |
|---|---|
| | P2: Elle pense au futur, au mariage |
| | P3: Non, elle pense au déjeuner! |
| T: Comme toi, Pierre! | P4: Elle pense à la discothèque |
| | P5: Elle pense à la robe qu'elle va acheter |
| T: Bonne idée! Oui, Pierre? | P3: Elle pense au gâteau qu'elle va manger! |

A song, a poem, an advertisement, a timetable, an empty cheese box, a photograph, a doll, a visitor, all can be resources for the resourceful language teacher, and if he can learn to do simple drawings on the blackboard or for the spirit duplicator, and use the paraphernalia of life as stimuli for lessons, his resources are infinite. The only problems are those of storage and retrieval.

Most of these materials cost nothing: they would normally be ignored or thrown away if the teacher did not spot their potential as teaching aids. Let us take for example the advertisement in Figure 8.1 which appears on wrapping-paper used by a *fromagerie* in Boulogne. How could this be useful in the classroom?

Advertisements like this lend themselves to question-and-answer work in the foreign language and also to information retrieval exercises where pupils could be asked such questions as:

Figure 8.1

*La Fromagerie*

*de Philippe Olivier*

*Maître fromager*
*Diplômé*

*Affineur*

*43 - 45, Rue Thiers*
*Boulogne-sur-Mer*

*Membre de la*
*Guilde des Fromagers*

- *20 Variétés de Fromages de tradition*
  *Nord-Picardie (voir notre dépliant)*
- *Livraison Possible sur Hardelot et*
  *Le Touquet - Paris - Plage*
- *Organisation Complète*
  *Buffets, Repas fromage,*
  *Soirée raclette,*
  *Fondue de 50 à 500 personnes*
- *Vous retrouverez nos fromages à Londres*
  *Restaurants : Waterside Inn - Gavroche*
  *Le Gamin - Poulbo - Interlude*
  *Tante Claire etc...*

- *La Fromagerie est ouverte de*
  *7 h 30 à 12 h 30*
  *14 h 30 à 19 h 30*
  *Fermeture Dimanche et Lundi*
  ☎ *31.94.74*

What is the address of the cheese–shop? What is the owner's name? Of what guild is he a member? What area do the traditional cheeses come from? How many people can the shop cater for at 'fondue' parties? Name two restaurants in London which serve these cheeses. What time does the shop open? For how long does it close for lunch? What days is the shop closed? What is the telephone number of the shop?

It could also be used for games of the type – 'My grandmother went to market and she bought . . .' Taking the role of *le fromager*, each pupil would have to say something about himself using information in the advertisement, after first repeating what preceding pupils had said:

P1: Je m'appelle Philippe Olivier.
P2: Je m'appelle Philippe Olivier et j'ai une fromagerie.
P3: Je m'appelle Philippe Olivier, j'ai une fromagerie et je suis maître fromager.
P4: Je m'appelle Philippe Olivier, j'ai une fromagerie et je suis maître fromager et ma fromagerie s'ouvre à 7h.30 du matin.
P5: Je m'appelle . . . etc.

On a more macabre note, even an epitaph can be used for teaching. A quick sketch of a gravestone (see Figure 8.2) could be used to practise the structure *ne . . . plus*.

The information board of a large store (Figure 8.3) could be reproduced to practise a variety of structures and dialogues.

Despite the books and articles which have appeared over the years with their ideas on how to produce and exploit materials for language teaching (see, for example, Wilson, 1979; Jones, 1979; Hornsey, 1975), too many modern language classes are restricted to the basic textbook and the great wealth of material which could enrich and enliven their lessons is ignored. It is fortunate that some textbooks published more recently (for example, Rowlinson, 1979; Asher and Webb, 1982) do in fact make considerable use of posters, notices and advertisements.

One of the main sources of material for the snapper-up of unconsidered trifles is the magazine, the colour supplement and the catalogue. A library of flash cards built up from such sources can enrich teaching by providing variety, colour and pace in the consolidation of vocabulary and the practising of structures (see

Figure 8.2

T:    Pauvre Jean Duclos! Il ne chante plus.
P1:  Il ne rit plus
P2:  Il ne court plus
P3:  Il ne danse plus
P4:  Il ne boit plus
P5:  Il ne mange plus
       etc . . .
T:    Et sa femme Guillemette, elle aussi, elle ne peut plus chanter!
P1:  Elle ne peut plus boire
P2:  Elle ne peut plus tricoter
P3:  Elle ne peut plus écouter la radio
P4:  Elle ne peut plus travailler
P5:  Elle ne peut plus regarder la télévision
       etc . . .

Figure 8.3

| HYPERMARCHÉ SOLEIL | |
|---|---|
| *Sixième étage:* | Jouets<br>Radio, télévision, disques<br>Restaurant |
| *Cinquième étage:* | Chaussures<br>Chapeaux |
| *Quatrième étage:* | Vêtements (femmes)<br>Vêtements (hommes)<br>Bijouterie |
| *Troisième étage:* | Rayon de sports, Vélos |
| *Deuxième étage:* | Mobilier<br>Articles de cuisine<br>Tapis et rideaux |
| *Premier étage:* | Agence de voyages<br>Librairie, Coiffeur |
| *Rez-de-chaussée:* | Comestibles<br>Vins, Liqueurs, Tabac |

Nous sommes au 3$^e$ étage.
Pour acheter . . ., où faut-il aller?
Il faut monter/descendre au ——$^e$ étage/au rez-de-chaussée.

McAlpin, 1980). Collected under such headings as Animals, Birds, Buildings, Transport, People, Food and Drink, Clothing and Verbs, sets of flash cards make flexible teaching materials which can be used for a variety of teaching points in a wide range of teaching situations. A basic collection of twenty different faces, for instance, a sort of portrait gallery of various ages and types, could serve as stimulus for the following elementary language work:

(1) Description
Comment s'appelle-t-il/elle?    Il/elle s'appelle . . .
Quel âge a-t-il/elle?    Il/elle a . . . ans.
Comment est-il/elle?    Il/elle a les cheveux —— et les yeux ——.

Comment est-il/elle? – (Il/elle est + (adj.)?)    Il/elle est + (adj.).
(2) Contrasts in Meaning
Il est heureux/beau/vieux/riche/etc.?    Non, il est malheureux/laid/jeune/pauvre/etc.

(3) <u>Agreeing and Disagreeing</u>

| Il est beau/ | Mais non, il n'est pas beau. |
| | Oui, bien sûr, il est beau. |
| Il n'est pas beau? | Mais si, il est beau. |

(4) <u>Stating Preferences</u>

| Tu préfères cet homme-ci ou cet homme-là? | Je préfère cet homme-là. |
| Pourquoi? | Parce qu'il a les yeux bleus. |
| etc. | etc. |

(5) <u>Comparing</u>

| Le garçon est plus gros que la fille? | Non, la fille est plus grosse que le garçon. |
| etc. | etc. |

(6) <u>Selection</u> (from several *portraits* displayed at once)

| Qui est-ce qui + (verb)? | C'est (la fille) qui (sourit). |
| | (le bébé) (dort) |
| | (l'homme) (chante) |
| | etc. |
| Qui est-ce qui est + (adj.)? | C'est (la femme) qui est (riche). |
| | (l'homme) (triste) |
| | (le petit garçon) (bête) |
| | etc. |

Follow-up exploitation could include designing 'Wanted!' posters, with portraits and descriptions; role-playing dialogues describing a missing person to the police; and a variety of games of the '*Il ou elle*' type.

At a higher level, the same set of 'portraits' can be used for lively oral interrogations: a pupil selects a 'portrait' and, taking the role of the person portrayed, has to answer questions fired at him by the rest of the group. The questions can start off simply enough but soon challenge even the most quick–witted *personnage*: *Où habitez-vous?* is no problem, but *Qu'est-ce que vous avez enterré dans le jardin à minuit?* demands more imagination and ingenuity.

It cannot be over-emphasised that a single set of flash cards, as in the 'portraits' example, can be used for practising a great variety of structures. Their use for presenting concrete vocabulary – *C'est un homme* – *C'est une petite fille* – *C'est un bébé* – is only the beginning: they can serve as a stimulus to a wide range of structures at different levels, and hence unquestionably justify the time and effort spent in preparing them.

Another useful category of flash card which can be made from magazine pictures is that of verbs. In teaching French, a set on the topic *'On fait sa toilette . . .'*, for practising reflexive verbs, could be used as follows –

(1) Que fait-il? Que font-ils?      Il se rase/se douche/se lave
                                                 Ils se brossent les dents
                                                 Ils s'habillent
(2) Qu'est-ce qu'il a fait hier?    Il s'est lavé
     Qu'est-ce qu'il fera
     demain?                                 Il se lavera
(3) Que dit-il? Que disent-ils?    'Je me lave'   'Je me rase'
                                                 'Nous nous baignons'

Asking what the character is saying is particularly effective when confirmatory cardboard speech bubbles are used in conjunction with the flash cards (Figure 8.4). This technique, of course, makes the cards effective for the practice of the first persons singular and plural of the verb, as well as the third persons.

Figure 8.4: Cardboard Speech 'Bubbles' Used in Conjunction with Flash Cards

Figure 8.5:  La Famille Bilimbi et la Famille Patapon

Source: Ministry of Education and Culture, Seychelles.

Another familiar but indispensable teaching aid which can be made with magazine or catalogue pictures is the family group. Suitable figures are cut out and either mounted together to form a wall picture or separately to make flannel-graph figurines. The Bilimbi and Patapon families (Figure 8.5), drawn by Paul Yerbic for the Seychelles French course *'PAF!'* (1976), show the type of pictures that should be chosen: forethought and planning can produce a set of visuals which can serve to practise asking and answering the following questions:

Comment s'appelle-t-il/elle?
Quel âge a-t-il/elle?
Comment s'appelle (la mère) de . . . ?
Qui est (le fils) de . . . ?
Qu'est-ce qu'il/elle porte?
De quelle couleur est (sa jupe)?
Comment est (Madame Bilimbi)?
(Monique) est plus (petite) que (Gaston)?
Qui est le plus (gros/vieux/petit)?
Où est (Gaston)? Il est (à côté de/à droite de/à gauche de . . . /
   entre . . . et . . .)
Que fait (Madame Patapon) tous les jours? Imagine-toi! . . .
Qu'est-ce qu'elle a fait hier?
Que fera-t-elle demain?

In developing one's own materials it is important to plan so that the possibilities for exploitation are not limited to only one or two structures. The rows of people in Figure 8.6, for instance, originally designed for practice of ordinal numbers, lend themselves to a variety of oral and written work. It is well worth the time spent in preparing aids of this type when the amount and diversity of practice is so large:

(1)   Comment s'appelle la première/la deuxième/la troisième
      fille?
      Comment s'appelle le premier/le deuxième/le troisième
      garçon?
      (Questions asked first in numerical then random order)
(2)   Le (troisième) garçon – quel âge a-t-il? et la (cinquième)
      fille? etc.
(3)   Qui s'appelle ——? Qui a —— ans?

Figure 8.6:  Ordinal Numbers

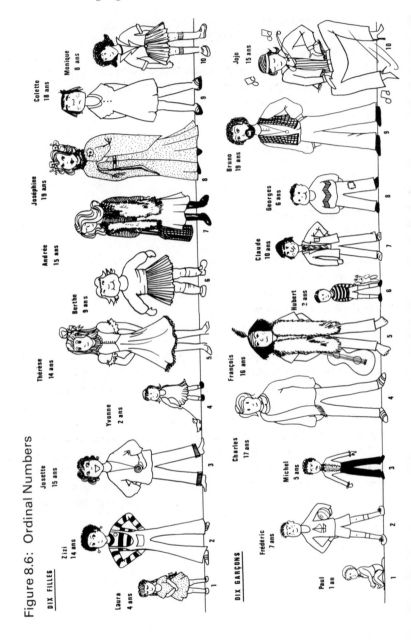

La sixième fille? Le dixième garçon?
(4)  Qui est-ce qui est + (adj)?
(5)  Qui est-ce qui + (verb)?
(6)  Comment est la (neuvième) fille/le (septième) garçon?
(7)  Tu préfères (Charles) ou (François)? Pourquoi?
     (Josette) ou (Zaza)? Pourquoi?
(8)  Où est ——? Il/elle est + (prepositional phrase) + (Name)
(9)  Qui est le plus gros/heureux/petit/bizarre/jeune, etc.?
(10) Comparez la quatrième fille et le quatrième garçon.
     Comparez la septième fille et le cinquième garçon. Etc.

For the practice of a particular structure such as *avoir mal à* there are many materials which can be collected or made. 'Blood-stained' bandages are particularly successful! Pieces of bandage with 'blood-stains' made with a red felt-tip pen, placed on various parts of pupils' bodies, make for humorous and lively practice of:

Où est-ce que tu as mal?
J'ai mal au/à la/à l'/aux ——.

Magazine pictures of various parts of the body make useful flash cards for quick revision of the necessary vocabulary before starting work on the structure. Magazines published for doctors and other members of the health services are an excellent source of advertisement pictures of sutured hands, reddened eyes, bandaged legs and other injuries and illnesses and make realistic if gory flash cards for practising *Il/elle a mal à* . . . A current colourful advertisement depicting a covered body being carried away on a stretcher makes a fine conclusion to the oral practice, acting as a stimulus to produce a dozen different proposals from the class as to what is the matter:

Il a mal à la poitrine.
Il a mal au ventre, etc.,

or, in the case of the writer's class, the statements:

Il a mal partout!
Il est mort!

A large magazine picture or poster of a person, overlaid with white card 'bandages' in appropriate places makes a useful wall-picture for either oral or written practice, whilst a simple drawing of a bandaged person duplicated for pupils (see Figure 8.7) is useful material for the transfer from oral to written work. The blood-stained bandages used earlier in the learning process can be re-used effectively later at the exploitation stage when role-playing at the doctor's surgery or at the hospital is done.

The time and trouble taken in snapping up unconsidered trifles, developing them as teaching aids and incorporating them into one's lessons is well re-paid by the variety, liveliness and flexibility which result. As we have seen, magazine pictures in particular, used as

Figure 8.7

Pauvre   Jean—Paul!

Où est-ce qu'il a mal?

Il a mal à la tête

flash cards, are a rich and never-ending source of materials for practice. Where objects in a magazine picture can be isolated and cut out, they can be mounted on card as flannel-graph figurines and used in the same way as those produced commercially – small squares of sand-paper stuck to the back will make them stick well to felt-boards. Flannel-graph materials, with their infinite possibilities for practice (see, for example, Romary, 1969), are well worth developing as an adjunct to any course.

Another source of materials, often neglected but worth exploration, is that of songs and poems, not only for their own sakes but because they can be exploited for the learning of vocabulary and structures. The songs and poems traditionally included in textbooks are often merely for decoration, too difficult and not those most exploitable in the languages classroom. Although the poems discussed below are far from being 'unconsidered trifles', some of the songs are of the ephemeral, popular type, useful for pedagogical rather than aesthetic reasons.

Some of the poems of Jacques Prévert might almost have been written with the modern languages teacher in mind. In 'Le Bouquet', for instance (Prévert, 1949, p. 198), the little girl, the young woman, the mature woman and the old lady (easily illustrated by some of the *portraits* discussed earlier) are presented one by one with the freshly cut flowers of the first fading to the dying ones of the *vieille femme*. In nine simple, repetitive lines, Prévert sums up the human condition in language which pupils can tackle at quite an early stage in their learning of French and yet feel that something adult and worthwhile is being said.

*Le Bouquet*

Que faites-vous la petite fille
Avec ces fleurs fraîchement coupées?
Que faites-vous la jeune fille
Avec ces fleurs, ces fleurs séchées?
Que faites-vous la jolie femme
Avec ces fleurs qui se fanent?
Que faites-vous la vieille femme
Avec ces fleurs qui meurent?

J'attends le vainqueur.

(Jacques Prévert, 'Le Bouquet', from *Paroles*,
©Editions Gallimard)

The fourfold repetition of the question addressed to each person in the poem produces a sort of mini pattern-drill, pedagogically useful and yet aesthetically pleasing in a way no pattern-drill could ever be. A fourth-year class of average and below-average girls with whom this poem was used coped well with the simple symbolism and managed the following type of question and answer sequence:

> T:   Qui est la première/seconde/troisième/quatrième personne?
> Comment sont les fleurs de la petite fille/de la jeune fille/de la jolie femme/de la vieille femme?
> Comment est la petite fille?
> Oui, elle est jeune. Alors, elle ressemble à . . .
> Oui, à des fleurs fraîchement coupées . . .

and later on:

> Pourquoi la vieille femme ressemble-t-elle à des fleurs qui meurent?
> Oui, c'est ça, elle aussi, elle meurt.
> Et qui est le vainqueur?
> Oui, c'est ça. C'est la mort.

*Le Message*

La porte que quelqu'un a ouverte
La porte que quelqu'un a refermée
La chaise où quelqu'un s'est assis
Le chat que quelqu'un a caressé
Le fruit que quelqu'un a mordu
La lettre que quelqu'un a lue
La chaise que quelqu'un a renversée
La porte que quelqu'un a ouverte
La route où quelqu'un court encore
Le bois que quelqu'un traverse
La rivière où quelqu'un se jette
L'hôpital où quelqu'un est mort.

(Jacques Prévert, 'Le Message', from *Paroles*,
©Editions Gallimard)

Similarly, the poem 'Le Message' (Prévert, 1949, p. 184) might almost have been written for pupils to study the construction of subordinate clauses and the agreement of the past participle with the preceding direct object. Prévert is playing a linguistic game, using an almost identical grammatical structure in each of the twelve lines of the poem; from the language teacher's point of view, the form resembles that of a pattern-drill. Attention is focused on simple objects – *la porte, la chaise, le chat, le fruit, la lettre,* and on the places – *la route, le bois, la rivière* et *l'hôpital.* The person about whom the story is told, never anything more than '*quelqu'un*', appears always in a secondary position in the sentence, in the subordinate clause, so that he or she appears to exist only in relation to the objects and places, almost as though human existence has reality only to the extent that it impinges on the objective world of chairs, doors, roads and rivers. If the lines were written down in any other order, they might be a list of examples from a grammar book. Rather than present his fourth- and fifth-year pupils with disconnected examples of the grammatical points, by using this poem the teacher can give them the delight of discovering the story which lies behind the simple lines. Reconstitution of the story by means of simple question and answer can lead to a useful L2 narrative exercise:

Qui est arrivé chez lui?
Qu'a-t-il fait d'abord?
Une fois entré dans la mansion, qu'est-ce qu'il y a fait?
Où s'est-il assis?
Qui est venu dire bonjour?
Qu'est-ce qu'il a fait?
Qu'est-ce qu'il a pris sur la table?
Qu'est-ce qu'il a fait?
Il a continué à manger?
Pourquoi pas?
Oui, il a vu une lettre. Qu'a-t-il fait donc?
Il est resté assis?
Qu'est-ce qu'il a fait en se relevant?
Comment s'est-il relevé?
Il est resté dans la maison?
Il a refermé la porte?
Quelle route a-t-il prise?
Comment?
Il s'est arrêté près du bois?

Où s'est-il dirigé?
Qu'est-ce qu'il y a fait?
Qu'est-ce qu'il a voulu faire?
Où l'a-t-on emporté?

Further exploitation could lie in open-ended questioning on the identity of the writer of the letter and what he or she had said in it. The oral reconstitution could lead to written composition and better pupils might practise the grammatical points in the poem by attempting to write their own original stories in a similar way.

'Déjeuner du Matin' is another poem by Prévert (1949, pp. 144–5) much appreciated by modern language teachers not only for its own sake but also as a tool for the practising of the *passé composé* (see, for example, Levy, 1970/71).

### Déjeuner du Matin

Il a mis le café
Dans la tasse
Il a mis le lait
Dans la tasse de café
Il a mis le sucre
Dans le café au lait
Avec la petite cuiller
Il a tourné
Il a bu le café au lait
Et il a reposé la tasse
Sans me parler
Il a allumé
Une cigarette
Il a fait des ronds
Avec la fumée
Il a mis les cendres
Dans le cendrier
Sans me parler
Sans me regarder
Il s'est levé
Il a mis
Son chapeau sur sa tête
Il a mis
Son manteau de pluie

Parcequ'il pleuvait
Et il est parti
Sous la pluie
Sans une parole
Sans me regarder
Et moi j'ai pris
Ma tête dans ma main
Et j'ai pleuré.

(Jacques Prévert, 'Déjeuner du matin', from *Paroles*,
©Editions Gallimard)

Once again, the stark simplicity of the language makes it possible for the pupil to tackle an adult poem without encountering the linguistic difficulties that such poems usually present. In order to depict the character's desperate, obsessive concentration on each tiny movement of her companion, on each everyday action he performs, Prévert's sentences are not only short but stripped of everything but the essential. Each action, unimportant in itself, takes on significance and an air of tragic finality. Intensive question and answer work to reconstitute the story gives pupils excellent practice in manipulating the *passé composé*, and the lines

Il a mis
Son manteau de pluie
Parce qu'il pleuvait

serve as an example of perfect/imperfect tense usage. It is interesting to note W. Rowlinson's exploitation of the idea of the poem in a passage in his *Tout Compris* textbook (1979, p. 183) where although the relationship between the characters is different and the story humorous, the same pedagogical advantage is taken of the minutiae of daily actions and the repetition of verb forms.

Finally, in *Le Retour au pays*, the teacher of a class approaching O-level is provided by Prévert with material macabre enough to motivate gruesome-minded adolescents and containing a range of grammatical points, structures and expressions which might almost be a summary of an examination syllabus. Poems like those of Prévert, exploited in oral and written work, can add new dimensions to lessons and yet at the same time provide the language practice needed by the learners.

Songs can be used in the same sort of way, not only for singing and enjoyment but as a tool for practice and consolidation. For instance, 'Je n'attends plus personne', sung by Françoise Hardy, is an excellent source of material for expressions with *ne . . . plus, ne . . . personne, ne . . . rien*, whilst the traditional 'Sur le pont de Nantes' can serve as an amusing and lively stimulus for free composition.

Pop songs can of course be depended upon to appeal to pupils and from the teacher's point of view, can be exploited in a variety of ways. For instance, Sheila's 'Pendant les vacances' and 'Première Surprise-Partie', dealing as they do with adolescent attitudes and problems, could prove a good stimulus to both oral and written work. In 'Pendant les vacances', the theme is separation from one's boyfriend during the long summer holidays.

Some classes today might find this theme a little dated, but this is easily remedied by the teacher's treatment of it (see below). Older pop songs such as this often have the essential characteristic of being well sung, clearly enunciated and immediately comprehensible – an important consideration from the teacher's point of view.

> Demain je pars
> Et tout l'été
> Il va falloir
> Nous séparer.
> Pendant les vacances,
> Essaie de ne pas m'oublier. . . .

This could serve as a basis for letter-writing: the girl writes to her boyfriend about what she is doing on her holidays and how she misses him; two versions of the boyfriend's replies could be written – one honestly describing how he has been enjoying himself without her and the other recounting the same incidents but giving the impression that he is having a miserable time. Another useful exercise which would practise the future tense would be for pupils to imagine how the boy and girl will pass the summer:

> T:   Comment Pierre passera-t-il l'été?
> P1:  Il s'amusera
> P2:  Il sortira avec d'autres filles
> P3:  Il ira danser avec Thérèse

P4:   Il se promènera avec Zaza
P5:   Il passera l'après-midi au café avec Marie
P6:   Il ira au cinéma avec Colette
P7:   Il achètera un cadeau pour Claire
P8:   Il téléphonera à Simone
etc.
T:   Et la jeune fille?
P4:   Elle ne s'amusera pas
P1:   Elle se promènera lentement et tristement
P9:   Elle pensera à lui
P10:   Elle rêvera de lui
P11:   Elle achètera un cadeau pour lui
T:   Mais non! Elle n'est pas bête! Elle s'amusera sans lui. Que fera-t-elle?
P12:   Elle sortira avec Louis
P13:   Elle ira danser tous les soirs
P14:   Elle se baignera dans la mer avec Charles
P15:   Elle jouera au tennis avec Philippe
T:   Oui, c'est ça. D'autres garçons lui plairont.

Similarly, in 'Première Surprise-Partie', the teenage theme is that of getting permission from parents to have a party:

Ce soir, pour la première fois,
Mes parents m'ont enfin permis
D'inviter des amis chez moi.
C'est ma première surprise-partie.

The girl's mother thinks she is too young but finally the parents agree:

Ils se sont quand même mis d'accord
Après des heures de discussion.
Sans reconnaître qu'ils avaient tort,
Ils m'ont donné la permission.

The shouted refrain of 'Premi*è*re surprise-partie! Premi*è*re surprise-partie!' is so repetitive that no pupil will ever forget the gender of *surprise-partie!* and useful constructions such as *permettre à quelqu'un*, *se mettre d'accord*, *donner la permission à* and *se reconnaître que* can be exploited by the teacher:

| Vos parents vous permettent d'aller | chez vos ami(e)s? |
|---|---|
| | à la discothèque? |
| | au cinéma? |
| | à l'étranger? |
| | aux concerts de (. . .)? |
| Ils vous permettent | de vous coucher à minuit? |
| | de vous lever très tard? |
| | de ne pas venir à l'école? |

Oral and written composition on the theme of 'Une surprise-partie désastreuse' could follow.

At a higher level, with fifth- and sixth-form pupils, the song 'Ça je n'ai jamais vu!', sung by Graeme Allwright, not only contains a rich variety of vocabulary and structure, but can introduce a popular theme of folklore and folk literature, the comic husband of the unfaithful wife.

The contrasts in tense such as 'J'ai vu un cheval dans l'écurie où je mettais le mien', 'J'ai vu un chapeau accroché où j'accrochais le mien', 'Sur une chaise j'ai vu un pantalon où je posais le mien' and 'J'ai vu une tête sur l'oreiller qui (ne) me ressemblait pas', make excellent examples for revising the use of the imperfect tense. There is a whole series of lines using the *ne . . . que* construction, and even more interestingly, illustrating the agreement of the preceding direct object: 'Ce n'est rien qu'une vache à lait, que ta mère m'a donnée', 'Ce n'est rien qu'une vieille casserole que grand'mère m'a donnée', 'Ce n'est rien qu'un vieux chiffon que Maman m'a donné, and 'Ce n'est rien qu'un vieux melon que grand-père m'a donné'.

The story can be re-told in the third person and in indirect speech or from the point of view of the wife, or the class could be asked to explain away various peculiar objects ostensibly found in the classroom. Songs can be sung and enjoyed in their own right of course but, pedagogically, their worth is doubled if they are exploited in both oral and written exercises.

Songs, poems, realia, flash cards and other aids prepared by the teacher are not decorative non-essentials in the language classroom. They are tools by which the teacher can provide stimulation, liveliness and interest in his lessons, and properly exploited, give the practice and consolidation of structures his pupils need.

The committed teacher of modern languages views the world

around him like Autolycus, seeing in objects, pictures, songs, poems, newspapers, labels and tea-towels possible materials for use in the classroom, just waiting to be snapped up.


## Note

1. Autolycus in *Winter's Tale*, Act IV, Scene ii.


## References

Asher, C. and Webb, D. (1982) *French for You*, Hutchinson, London

Hodgson, F.M. (1961) *Language Learning Material*, Educational Explorers, Reading

Hornsey, A.W. (ed.) (1975) *Handbook for Modern Language Teachers* (Part 4: 'Using Documentary Data'), Methuen, London

Jones, B.L. (1979) 'Le jeu des colis – an Exercise in Foreign Language Communication', *Audio-Visual Language Journal, 17* (3), 159–67

LDA (n.d.) *Sound Stories* (LDA materials for children with learning difficulties), Wisbech, Cambs.

Levy, H. (1970/1) 'French in the Middle School – Post AV French', *Audio-Visual Language Journal, 8* (3), 135 *et seq.*

McAlpin, J. (1980) *The Magazine Picture Library*, Allen and Unwin, London

Ministry of Education and Culture, Seychelles (1976) *PAF!* (Première année de français) – polycopié, Ministry of Education, Seychelles

Ministry of Education and Culture, Seychelles (1977) *La famille Colibri* (Deuxième année de français) polycopié – Ministry of Education, Seychelles

Prévert, J. (1949) *Paroles*, Gallimard, Paris

Romary, G. (1969) *L'utilisation du tableau de feutre dans l'enseignement des langues vivantes*, Hachette, Partis

Rowlinson, W. (1979) *Tout Compris*, Book 1, Unit 59, Oxford University Press, Oxford, p. 183

Wilson, G. (1979) 'The Use of "Small-Ads" in Language Teaching' (German examples), *Audio-Visual Language Journal, 17* (1), 46 *et seq.*

## Recordings

Allwright, G. 'Ça je n'ai jamais vu', *Les petites boîtes*, 63 25 604, Mercury, Paris

Hardy, F. (1964) 'Je n'attends plus personne', *Françoise Hardy*, Disques Vogue VRL 3000, Villetaneuse (Seine)

Sheila 'Pendant les vacances' and 'Première Surprise-Partie', *Sheila Troisième Disque*, 432 931 BE, Philips, Paris

# 9 ASSESSMENT AND TESTING

## G.H. Soles

The aim of this account is to discuss and evaluate the types of testing and assessment appropriate to foreign language learning and the various reasons why assessments need to be made. The principles of testing and examining procedures will be considered and related to the practical situation.

There are various reasons why the teacher needs to make assessments of his pupils. He needs the information acquired through testing in order to help him teach more efficiently; he needs feedback (Castigliano, 1971). It is essential to know whether or not the pupils have understood the work properly, so that misconceptions may be corrected. If one particular notion is a necessary stage before a second can be learned and understood, then the teacher must make sure that each pupil has acquired it before moving on. The teacher must also have a means of discovering whether his approach to a particular topic was successful or whether he has to try again with a different strategy. He must be able to grasp his pupils' level of attainment and ability if they are to be directed on to the next phase of learning. He must, therefore, have feed back to enable him to adjust the pace of his course; not so fast that the learning is left in confusion, not so slow that one topic is over-emphasised, resulting in restlessness and boredom.

The teacher needs to monitor the progress of individuals and classes. Pupils may have to be allocated to different streams or sets and their levels of attainment in the foreign language are usually important factors in these decisions. Progress of parallel sets under different teachers may need to be compared and checks must be made on the progress of individual pupils in a class (particularly in mixed-ability groups) if the teacher is to ascertain who may need extra help. A teacher new to a school or to a particular group may find records of previous attainments helpful to him. Parents and pupils will want to know what progress is being made from year to year and what standards have been reached.

Testing and assessment are important factors in the evaluation of materials. Departments can be involved in substantial expenses for textbooks and sundry materials. The test is an important guide in judging if children learn more, or more quickly, or like learning more than with the former method or the old book. It is necessary to have something to base judgements on, to make comparisons with the previous performances.

The decisions on which pupils ought to be entered for public examinations will, to a large extent, depend on the teacher's own evaluation of the pupils' capabilities. Education is concerned with the development of children's personalities, skills and abilities and if the teacher is taking his job seriously, he ought to know the current state of development of the pupils in his charge. In order to do this, he needs to be equipped with a variety of techniques to make his assessments and to record and interpret the results.

Ideally the assessment should be made in relation to each pupil's potential, how far each has made use of his ability, rather than in competition with other pupils. However, the measurement of potential is an area where techniques are even less accurate than in the measurement of attainment. It can be misleading to both pupils and parents if they are told that the child has worked well and to the best of his ability throughout the school, only to find at the end of the course that he has attained no more than a very modest level indeed.

The limitations of assessment techniques should be realised. They provided no more than a basis on which judgements can be made. Much still depends on the teacher in the interpretation of the results.

The testing situation can also be an aid to learning, as an incentive to pupils, a goal to aim for and a focus for a course of study. Many linguists and educationalists concur that tests must reflect the teaching process (Davies, 1968: Rivers, 1969: Rowe, 1969; Valette, 1967). Thus, much as the teacher may emphasise oral fluency in the classroom, if all the tests are written ones, pupils will soon concentrate on perfecting skills of reading and writing. If pupils are expected to develop primarily the skills of listening and speaking, then listening and speaking skills must be given in proportion to the relative importance of that objective. Valette (1967) maintains that time allocated to testing should provide a rewarding experience and that the test should furnish an opportunity for a pupil to show how well he can handle specific elements of the foreign language. She asserts that the teacher must not design a test to indicate his pupils' ignorance or lack of application.

If a pupil is expected to demonstrate his abilities, it is necessary that he should learn as soon as possible after the test how well he has performed. The test fulfils its function as a part of the learning process if correct performance is immediately confirmed and errors pointed out. Rowe (1969) links the testing and learning processes, contending that specific aspects to be tested should be assessed as separate items, although ability in isolated areas does not indicate overall ability to handle the language.

Page (in CILT 4, 1970) warns that examinations should not influence teaching methods. Teachers should aim at teaching their subject to the highest level of competence that pupils can attain and tests and examinations should arrive as an incidental, objective assessment of that attainment. There are obvious dangers in teaching towards the examination, for using the latter as the only objective can lead to the worst kind of practice, neglecting those facets of the course which are not tested or not testable and it can stimulate an unhealthy competitiveness in the class (Ingram in Davies, 1968).

Before proceeding into the elements, it is necessary to define what is meant by the word 'test' and the closely related terms 'assessment' and 'examination'.

Assessment is an all-embracing term covering any of the situations in which some aspect of a pupil's education is, in some sense, measured by the teacher or another person (Lawton, 1978). Thus a comment on a child's general attitude to his work for the purpose of an end-of-term report is based on an assessment.

A test refers to a particular situation set up for the purpose of making an assessment, of whch the pencil-and-paper test in the classroom is an obvious example.

An examination is concerned with a larger-scale test, or more commonly, a combination of several tests and perhaps other assessment procedures, whether within the school or conducted by an external examining board. An examination in a foreign language, for example, may include a test of creative writing in the form of a narrative and letter written to an imaginary person abroad, an oral test and perhaps an objective test of comprehension, thus attempting to measure attainment in several different aspects of the subject.

There would not, therefore, seem to be any sharp distinction between the three terms, but a considerable overlap. Continuous assessment, for example, of the type generally required by the CSE boards, may be based on a series of tests at the end of each phase of learning or be a succession of periodical reviews of work accomplished in class or at home, taking into account oral contributions. It could be argued that all these are variations on the same theme and that the same principles should underlie the construction of a standardised test, an examination or a classroom test, although there will be important differences in degree and detail.

The most important factors in the choice of assessment would appear to be the type of test to use and what language items it should contain. The questions depend entirely on the purpose of the test, the material known and the kind of pupils whose ability is being measured.

Many theorists (Davies, 1968; Huebener, 1965; Mackey, 1965; Rivers, 1969; Robinson, 1970) agree on four different categories of language tests: achievement, proficiency, aptitude and diagnosis.

Achievement tests measure a pupil's control of language and are used to assess what has actually been learned in relation to what is supposed to have been learned (Rivers, 1969).

Proficiency tests determine the present level of language skill. Davies (1968) proposes the use of proficiency tests to predict skill in language for a future task or vocation but Lawton (1978) argues that no matter how carefully it is devised for predictive purposes, if the prediction is to cover too long a period, many other factors such as good or bad teaching, continued good or poor motivation and unusual personal circumstances may mean that the subsequent performance does not necessarily match the initial suggested potential or lack of it.

By means of an aptitude test, it is possible to assess a person's capacity for further language study. Robinson (1970) suggests that this type of test can be of great help in giving the teacher some indication of how fast a certain pupil may progress and from what type of teaching procedure he may profit. Carroll (in Davies, 1968) points out from his data that foreign language aptitude is not specific to particular languages or particular groups of languages.

Lawton (1978) outlines the increased usage of diagnostic tests to indicate points at which a pupil has failed to learn something. They usually diagnose difficulties which a pupil is experiencing and teachers can use their results to indicate where to apply remedial measures.

In any consideration of assessment in schools, the link between testing, evaluating and curriculum development must be established. Suggestions for changing the curriculum in foreign languages have been gathering momentum in recent years. Many teachers are finding difficulty in keeping pace with innovation. Perhaps the greatest problem in curriculum development is ensuring that teachers become fully cognisant of it and can consider its adoption on a permanent basis. It is necessary to have something on which a decision can be based and the teacher as an evaluator has a role to play. At this level, the evaluation will be essentially a personal concern; whether the course or syllabus will suit his style as a teacher, his pupils, his school. In addition to the assessment which may be made for a public examination under the auspices of an examining board, the teacher will need to devise his own scheme for the new course in order to provide himself and others with information on his pupils' progress and attainment at various stages. He must also be able to interpret the results of these assessments and to supplement them with information from other sources and with his own professional opinion, where necessary, in order to make a judgement of the success of the method in the context of his own particular situation.

At this stage the relationships between assessment and evaluation need to be defined. Assessment implies a measurement of children's educational attainment, whereas evaluation is a much broader concept and is concerned not only with attainment but also with many less definable but equally important factors such as children's attitudes to learning and the impact of the new curriculum. It could be said that assessment is concerned with how well the child has done, but evaluation with whether it was worth doing in the first place (Kelly, 1977).

In the light of changes in the aims and methods of language teaching that have come about recently, it is necessary to decide, first, what is to be tested. Having defined clearly what knowledge and what skills are to be assessed, reliable tests must be devised to measure this knowledge and these skills. Huebener (1965), Harding (1967), Lado (1961), Davies (1968), Rivers (1969) and Valette (1967) advocate the testing of the four language skills of aural comprehension, oral expression, reading comprehension and written expression.

Huebener (1965) maintains that it is more scientific to test the four skills separately, but the majority of linguists agree that these skills are combined in various ways in different language activities, for example aural comprehension and oral expression are needed for conversation.

In considering the criteria for the marking of tests, Huebener (1965) proposes the adoption of a positive scheme where marks are given for what is correct, therefore the pupil is gaining credit for what he can produce, as opposed to a deductive scheme where marks are taken away for everything wrong and then deducted from the total possible.

There would appear to be general agreement among theorists that the concepts of validity and reliability are essential in the production of a good test (Carroll in Davies, 1968; Harding, 1967; Lado, 1961; Otter, 1968; Rivers, 1969; Truchot, 1971; Valette, 1967). If a test measures what it is intended to measure then it is a valid test. The validity depends not only upon its relevance to the group for which it was designed but also on the purpose of the test. If a test were to yield the same scores one day and the next with exactly similar populations, under the same conditions with no intervening instruction, then it can be said to be reliable.

If the number of pupils taking the test is too great for all the scripts to be marked by a single teacher, some form of standardisation will be necessary. Otherwise, if one marker is severe and the other lenient, the children who have given good answers to the question marked by the lenient marker will score better than those marked by the more severe marker. If one teacher gives consistently higher or lower marks than another, a difference of standards is the result. It can be detected by comparing the average marks given to the same set of scripts by the two teachers and can be corrected by a straightforward scaling of marks. However, the range of marks used may be different, with one teacher using the whole of the mark range, thus implying that he can detect considerable differences between the pupils, while another bunches the marks together. This produces a difference of discrimination.

Teaching language as communication has become an accepted and popular aim of the foreign language teacher. To most this entails producing a curriculum whereby the pupil must be taught to speak the language with some fluency and authentic idiom. The ability to speak and understand a language necessitates a generalised use of highly complex skills, but is probably the most highly respected and useful aspect of language proficiency.

Although there may be four aspects of the use of language, commonly referred to as the four language skills, they overlap, are often integrated and are certainly not specific to any one aspect. For some restricted purposes, it may be useful to separate language abilities into those concerned primarily with the written medium and those associated basically with the spoken medium.

In testing spoken language Rivers (1969), Perren (in Davies, 1968), Lado (1961) and Valette (1967) maintain that auditory and oral abilities are often so closely involved with each other that they cannot be separated. Testing oral ability is relatively easy in the early stages, but it becomes increasingly difficult as competence increases. As soon as original communication (as opposed to imitation) begins, the real difficulties arise. Often one can only judge what the pupil wants to say by what he does say, which makes it extremely difficult to determine extraneous criteria of good performance. The real test of whether the candidate can speak the language is whether he can say something which is understood by the listener as relevant to a particular situation. Robinson (1971) contends that the test situation must be motivating and real, so that the pupil speaks freely and so that his production is representative of his capacity to speak in most contexts. The most effective means of discovering how much a pupil has benefited from an oral language curriculum is to place him in a sitution where he has to communicate.

Many of the problems of oral marking can be overcome if the material is recorded. The teacher or examiner does not have to contend with conducting the test and simultaneously assessing it. Difficult interviews can be listened to again at leisure, a second opinion asked for and sample material is available for departmental discussion. Indeed many GCE and CSE boards have adopted this method for the conduct of some of their oral tests. Dyson (1972) found that even experienced examiners were liable to sudden inconsistencies and he concluded that more reliable results would be obtained by multiple marking from tapes.

Objective tests (usually multiple choice) have become an established feature of both courses and examinations in foreign languages. An objective test is one in which questions are set in such a way as to have only one correct answer. The term 'objective' refers to the marking procedure only, since devising the test remains subjective (Prescott in CILT 4, 1970). The characteristic contribution of objective testing has been that it has made possible rapid, reliable marking, regardless of numbers.

Before appraising the limitations and strengths of these tests, it is necessary to define an objective item. This is an entire question, although the word 'item' is preferred because it does not necessarily take the form of the interrogative and is not restricted to grammatical questions. In a multiple choice item the stem is the initial part, either a partial sentence to be completed, a question or several statements leading to a question or incomplete phrase. The choices from which a pupil must select his answers are known as options, responses or alternatives. One response is distinctly correct or more suitable than the others. Incorrect responses are called distractors and should be so worded that they seem attractive to the uninformed pupil. If a distractor is so obviously wrong that it is never selected, it plays no useful role in the item and should be eliminated or replaced by a new alternative.

The teacher must decide carefully which skills he wants to test, whether there should be a time limit for any individual test items and what types of question he should use. The instructions should contain nothing that is irrelevant or misleading to confuse the pupil and questions should deal with one language problem at a time. The incorrect choices must be definitely incorrect, yet appear attractive to the pupil. However, deliberate setting of traps should be avoided (Brings, 1970; Hutchings, 1970).

In order to find out in detail how the individual parts which make up a whole test have been operating, it is helpful to calculate two indices, those for facility and discrimination. The facility index is defined as the percentage of pupils who answer a particular question correctly. Satisfactory items are usually those with a facility value of approximately 50 per cent, ranging perhaps from 30 per cent to 70 per cent. This does not mean, however, that all the pupils will obtain fifty marks out of a hundred, because although 50 per cent will have answered each individual question correctly, it will not be the same 50 per cent each time.

The discrimination index is a measure of the extent to which a particular item can distinguish between the most proficient and least proficient candidates. The discrimination value is usually expressed as a decimal number between $-1.00$ and $+1.00$. Normally discrimination values of $+0.3$ or higher would be considered acceptable by test constructors.

Objective tests have their obvious advantages. They can pose a series of precise problems which can be clearly stated and quickly responded to. They can provide a wide content coverage. Moreover, because of the comparative precision of each item, the danger of overlap is reduced. An objective test can be quickly and accurately marked as well as being tried out in advance by means of pre-testing and, on the basis of the evidence obtained, papers of differing levels of difficulty can be set.

The disadvantages of these tests are that they cannot measure written or oral ability; they can all too easily test only factual recall or simple understanding of facts; they may encourage pupils to guess the answers and are difficult and expensive to construct. Objective tests in modern languages have become synonymous with tests of reading and listening comprehension and are popular with most GCE and CSE boards for their public examinations.

The most widely used type of objective reading comprehension consists of a reading selection, followed by a series of items in statement or question form with four or five completions, one of which the pupil has to choose. The completion statements should not repeat the exact words, but rather reproduce the idea. The obvious and the absurd must be avoided, for the reader could eliminate them without actual comprehension. In addition to testing pupils' ability to grasp basic ideas and details of a reading passage, this type of format may be used to test vocabulary, idiom and structures. The pupil may be required to choose appropriate synonyms and antonyms, related words, definitions or the word that describes a particular situation or person. Moys *et al.* (1980) criticise the latter type of item, arguing that it is unrealistic and would be self-evident in a real-life situation.

The greatest difficulty for a traveller to a foreign country is not primarily that he cannot make himself understood. This he can frequently do by gesture and limited oral expression. His first problem is that he cannot understand what is being said to and around him. Consequently there is no communication and the visitor's speaking skills cannot be exercised to great advantage. Teaching comprehension of speech is therefore of primary importance if the communication aim is to be achieved (Rivers, 1969).

Listening comprehension can be tested as an individual skill or in connection with other skills. The major aim is to ascertain the pupil's facility to understand a foreign language at normal speed as spoken by a native speaker. The types of listening comprehension tests are:

majority of foreign language learners and find it surprising that compulsory writing forms a major part of most public examinations at 16+. They argue that this component reflects and reinforces the artificiality of foreign language learning in schools and imply that many people write very rarely nowadays to any great extent. The type of writing produced tends to be concerned with compiling lists and filling in forms, neither of which is represented in the written papers of public examinations.

The use of translation is an integral aspect of many of the traditional GCE examinations, for example in JMB O-level syllabus A. The use of this device in testing during the formative development of language learning in pupils is controversial (Hodgson, 1956; Calvert, 1965). It is argued that translation is an art quite distinct from the ability to use a foreign language. It presupposes the knowledge of a language in addition to the mother tongue, but it is additional to this and is not a valid test of ability to use the language productively. It can only be accepted at a very advanced level with students who already have a good, practical mastery of the language. The use of translation in foreign language learning and testing dates back to the last century when modern languages had to be found a place in the school curriculum. The grammar-translation method is and was taught following the principles of the classics as a means, so it was claimed, of training logical facilities. Its formal approach is detached from actual language and depends on the memorisation of rules explained at length, with groups of words. The words are then put together according to the rule, thereby giving practice in the application of the rule (Mackey, 1965). The teaching begins with rules, isolated vocabulary items, paradigms and translation. Easy classics are then translated with the teacher and his class moving from one half-digested item to another. The manner in which the vocabulary is taught usually presents special difficulty to the learner. No scientific choice of words is made, based on frequency counts or practical utility. The words are usually listed and supposed to be memorised as individual units. Consequently, they are not usually retained in the memory on account of their excessive number. It is in the washback effect on teaching that translation is at its most harmful, for the teaching procedure is inadequate, with no attempt made to drill and recall words in subsequent lessons and teaching them out of context makes meaningful retention almost impossible. The grammar is traditional, derived from Latin and based on artificial rules and classifications. It is taught abstractly, analytically and deductively, even to young pupils who are still insecure in the logical processes of abstraction and deduction. As a result, very little transfer of learning occurs between theory and practice, with very little opportunity for manipulation of the foreign language. Translation is the device by which meaning is conveyed in the grammar-translation method. However, according to recent research in language psychology and neuro-psychology, learning any language results in active, productive memory-traces being formed in the brain. Learning a foreign language leads to the formation of a new and totally separate system of traces upon which an existing system should not encroach (Appelt, 1968). This would suggest that translating, which is a special skill in itself, should no longer be the chief means nor the principal goal of foreign language instruction, because it confuses the different systems of memory traces, this inhibiting the pupils from thinking originally in the foreign language. There would appear to be no justification, whether theoretical or practical, for adopting a translation approach. The formal methods allied to this skill do not teach the language but about the language, and suggest that learning a language is purely an intellectual exercise without any other function or value.

Dictation is also a common feature of the more traditional Ordinary-level examinations but Prescott (in CILT, 1970) contends that it measures very little of language. Word order, words and aural perception cannot be tested by this design. Spelling, inflection and punctuation can be tested in this way, but he maintains that the complicated apparatus of dictation is not necessary.

Teachers of modern languages are currently involved with a re-appraisal of the aims and objectives both of learning and examining. The most significant move towards modifying the curriculum has been the replacement of the separate GCE and CSE examinations by a common system of examing at 16+. In July 1976 the Schools Council recommended that the two examinations should be replaced, and the eight GCE boards and fourteen CSE boards divided into consortia for 16+. This recommendation followed a sustained period of feasibility studies and experimental joint examinations by consortia of GCE and CSE boards, although as early as 1975 the Modern Languages Association was expressing disquiet at the speed at which the feasibility studies were being judged and cast doubts on the appropriateness of some of the evaluations, contending that they did not reflect the opinions and experience of the 'ordinary teacher' (MLA, 1975, p. 98). The Schools Council's proposals were that a common system of examining should be designed for the 40 to 100 percentile range of ability; that examinations under three modes should be available, and to guarantee a reasonable degree of comparability, criteria should be discussed for the syllabuses and schemes of assessment. The results should be stated by means of seven grades on a single scale, which should be linked to the existing Ordinary-level and CSE grades for an introductory period. They recommended that the examinations should be teacher-controlled and regionally based, with schools having a choice of board (that is, the best of both GCE and CSE worlds) and that the Schools Council should have a co-ordinating role (Waddell, 1978, p. 5).

Opinions tended to differ on the proposal that only 60 per cent of the ability range should be provided for in the new examination system. The Joint Council of Language Associations (Wright, Ramsay and Richards, 1974, p. 85) agreed with the Schools Council, although Davidson (1973, p. 16) argued that 'perhaps the most disappointing feature of the proposals [was] the restriction of the target users to the 40–100 percentile range of ability'. The MLA (1975), however, contended that the examinations in the feasibility studies did not cater for the wide strata of ability.

The Schools Council and HMIs would appear to concur on the advantages to be gained from a common system, namely that it would eliminate the sensitive decisions faced by schools in the dual system on whether to prepare children for O-level or CSE, decisions sometimes taking place at the end of their third year of secondary education. It would therefore be administratively more convenient to have a single system, eliminating the necessity for providing separate CSE and O-level instruction and hypothetically allowing for more flexible option organisations whenever they occur. The two types of grades at present pertaining to examination boards would be removed, thus alleviating some confusion amongst those unfamiliar with the system.

Davidson (1973) implies a paradox between the demand for a variety of courses suited to individual teachers' and pupils' needs and the call for a single system, arguing that the 16+ proposals, with the same fundamental principles as its two forerunners, will produce more problems.

The proposals of the Schools Council were evaluated by an

independent committee, chaired by Sir James Waddell, which concluded that a common system of examination for all candidates, for whom the GCE O-level and CSE examinations are intended, could be implemented without educational detriment (Waddell, 1978). The central issue in the debate on 16+ has been on the question of whether there should be a common examination or a common system. A common examination for most boards includes common papers taken by all candidates; common papers taken by all pupils, but containing questions of varying degrees of difficulty, structured to become gradually more demanding; common papers taken by all candidates but allowing them to select certain questions with pre-stated weight markings. A common system would contain a common paper taken by all candidates with alternative papers of different degrees of difficulty, where pupils could opt for an easier alternative paper with a lower mark tariff.

For modern languages the Waddell Report recommended an approach involving a choice between alternative papers because the range of skills is wide and certain concepts may not be within the grasp of many pupils. The committee maintained that by this means, candidates would be able to perform to the limits of their ability whilst the examiners would be permitted to include items appropriate to some pupils, without distorting the curriculm for others. However, the JMB consortium representing some of the northern boards have adopted a common examination policy in order to eliminate the necessity for choice between papers. Park (1973, p. 101) argues that if a choice of paper is offered, problems of reliability occur in describing grades on a common scale when equating scores on more than one paper of different standards of difficulty. His second criticism of the common system is the issue of who makes the option, the pupil or the teacher, prior to the examination. He asserts that, realistically, it should be the teacher, who would by implication then be perpetuating the former dual system.

The Waddell committee further recommended that a central co-ordinating body should be established with the responsibility for establishing national criteria for syllabuses, examinations and assessment, to ensure comparability of standards between the boards.

Although not as controversial as the 'N' and 'F' proposals, the recommendations on 16+ have generated some public debate which seems to be focused on the question of standards, with the opponents of the new system fearing that the high standards assured by the GCE O-level would inevitably be diluted. The Report takes great care to point out that representatives from many walks of life were members of its commitee, in order to obtain as wide a perspective as possible, and also to ensure that the opinions of parents, trade unionists, industrialists and specialists from further and higher education were reflected. One advantage inherent in the proposals is that for the first time in the English system there would be a means of ensuring comparability between examination boards and there may be some optimism at the possibility that standards would consequently be at least maintained.

It is not surprising that discussion should centre around any proposal for changes in either the curriculum or means of assessing its impact on pupils, particularly in modern languages where the previous decade has witnessed much reappraisal, summarised by Buckby (1973, p. 62): 'This is a period of transition in language teaching, when many things are changing: the number and range of pupils learning languages, the content and method of teaching and examinations.' At the time of writing discussions are taking place on the criteria for the proposed change to 16+, focusing on the Buckby committee, who have proposed that a 'point' would be awarded for passing sections of the examinations devoted to the four common language skills at two levels (basic and extended). This provides a possible optimum of eight 'points' which would be assessed as 'grade one'. Seven points would achieve a grade two, six a three and so on to grade seven for one point and unclassified for no points. This means that a grade three (equivalent to an O-level pass) would be possible without even taking the parts of the examination necessitating the writing of French, although the two higher grades of one and two require adequate performance in this aspect (Doe, 1982).

Almost all present attainment tests and examinations are built around what is commonly referred to as a norm-referenced approach. Here the indicator of competence is drawn up from a set of norms drawn from a typical population. The scores on a particular test are calculated, with pupils then being arranged in a rank order, from which the grades are allocated. Tests are produced in such a way that each item or question supposedly discriminates between the most able and least able pupils. Stones (1970) suggests that this approach puts the emphasis in the wrong place. He prefers a criterion-referenced approach in which the main issue is to assess skills and concepts, where the emphasis is on the achievement of pre-determined standards, rather than on the discriminative value of each part of the test. This suggestion has been proposed in an attempt to move away from an over-emphasis on individual differences and competitive assessments.

It was partly these reasons, and also a growing dissatisfaction by both teachers and pupils with the effects norm-referenced examinations were having on the curriculum, which prompted the initiation of the graded system of syllabuses and examinations. Page (1973) proposes an approach totally different in concept from the traditional examinations at 16+. He advocates a sequence of tests, at lower levels, graded in order to provide for even the least able pupils a realistic series of objectives which they are capable of mastering after a short period of study. This notion undoubtedly influenced the HMIs (1977, p. 3) who recommended:

> Pupils capable of following and benefitting from a modern language course designed to continue until the age of 16 should be identified at an early stage and, once embarked on such a course, should be given every encouragement to complete it. Other pupils should at least follow a shorter course which is complete in itself. Precise linguistic objectives should be determined for pupils following the longer and the shorter courses. These should be realistic, taking account of the pupils' aptitudes and needs, and should place greater stress upon the listening and reading skills than has hitherto been the case.

The initial groundwork on the scheme was prepared by the York and Oxfordshire groups, who produced a fairly well defined list of behavioural objectives, requiring the pupil to cope effectively with the sorts of situation he was likely to meet on a visit to France or when meeting French-speaking people in this country, for example, finding one's way, going to a café and restaurant or shopping. Learners should also be able to read short stories and letters written in simple French (Buckby, 1980).

The introduction in foreign language teaching of the notion of behavioural or performance objectives originated in the USA as an attempt to build an efficient systems-analysis approach to the languages curriculum.

In theory behavioural objectives would appear to have their advantages. They enable teacher and pupil to understand the nature of the task. They both would seem to understand what they are going to do and why, and the notion of knowing what criteria must be matched in order to make progress is an essential concept of performance objectives. 'The teacher . . . decides in advance what features of the unit he intends to stress in his class and what degree of proficiency he wants the students to develop with respect to these features' (Allen and Valette, 1972, p. 21). The objective is always stated in terms of the learner's performance or behaviour. This would appear to be treating language at a very superficial level and implies that the learning of a foreign language can be reduced to a number of small components which are accumulated.

Leading theorists maintain that language learning is more than a compilation of segments. Rivers (1976) refers to language learning at two levels: the basic knowledge of structures and vocabulary, which must be practised continually in the context of the production of meaningful communication, and the opportunity for the pupil to express himself through the language within his own experience of the foreign language. This must be real practice in the giving or receiving of the spoken or written form. A situation should be established where the pupil is participating in an interchange, where he can give full expression to his personality and it is here in the natural interaction between pupils and teachers, using the medium of the foreign language, that the pre-determination of an established level of attainment is inappropriate. She argues the need to control language at two levels. The first level is the basic learning of the patterns of the language, which demands commitment and motivation on the part of the teacher and the pupil, and it is here that the approach of performance objectives and the related concept of testing may be applicable. The second level, which is the more significant, is the natural, spontaneous use of the new language for the expression of personal meaning. It would be easy to believe that this second level should only be tackled at an advanced stage of learning. This premiss would seem to be implied by the proponents of the objectives approach, but here they would appear to be missing the point. If language use and creativity is to be fully developed, it must be integrated into every stage of language learning. It is at the level of creativity and self-expression that specification is most difficult, and if these communicative activities are to be encouraged it cannot be decided in advance what features the pupils will use and the level of attainment they will exhibit.

The problem of assessing creativity in language is a valid one. Valette (1967, p. 31) asserts: 'Until we know precisely what we intend to teach we cannot measure our success.'

Perhaps natural, spontaneous use of the language is more important than a pre-specified outcome which can be easily assessed. A performance objective explains the purpose for requiring a particular form of behaviour, the conditions under which this behaviour will occur and the criterion by which the pupil will demonstrate that he has achieved the required behaviour. To accept behavioural objectives as a strategy for teaching languages, a high degree of credibility must be ascribed to the belief that language is merely patterned behaviour and that the role of the language teacher is to manipulate pupils, so that they behave accurately and openly by the criteria of the test compilers.

It is the creative aspect of language use that the graded test approach would appear to fail to account for. Creative, innovative use of language does take place within a restricted framework to which the pupil's responses must conform if he is to be comprehended and thus to communicate effectively. The practice in the manipulation of language elements is important at an elementary or lower level. At this stage pre-specification of performance objectives could prove to be valuable. This is, however, only one of the first steps, for the pupil must realise the possibilities of application of what he has learned and apply the structures to those he has previously assimilated for some purpose of his own. It is very easy for the teachers to believe that because the pupil has displayed the suitable behaviour, i.e. achieved mastery of a particular situation, he has succeeded. Indeed, in terms of the objective he has set, he may well have, but it is vitally important that if it is to become an integral part of the pupil's communication system and he is to become self-reliant, it must be exploited by the teacher.

To develop skill in communication in the foreign language, the pupil must have continual practice in communication, not merely performing well in exercises or tests, no matter how skilfully they may have been designed. The ultimate aim of language teaching is to hear pupils using the second language without prompting and without embarrassment for communicating their own needs. This is language control and when the pupil has become conversant at this level he will be able to progress on his own, experiencing freedom of expression beyond the limitations of pre-specified criteria. It would, therefore, appear that the use of behavioural objectives is a debatable exercise beyond the level of rudimentary skill development. This does not imply certain priorities or certain subject-matter content or even the order in which events are taught should not be identified. It is an important pre-requisite of every teacher's role that he has an obligation to plan what he is going to do and delineate as clearly as possible the areas he is going to cover. The complexity of the teaching process can only be met with adaptable, flexible and varied procedures.

Lawton (1978) outlines the profile system of assessment. He believes that a composite grade in a subject gives no detail about the level of the specific abilities of a pupil. A more meaningful approach is to compile a detailed record for each pupil, which not only shows the level he has reached in cognitive skills but also demonstrates the affective criteria of performance, which are important in reinforcing motivation. There is a strong lobby for the expansion of such patterns of assessment in the 1980s, which some believe could lead to much-needed revitalisation in the popularity of foreign languages (for example Morrison, 1980, p. 119).

In conclusion, testing evaluation and assessment are invaluable to the language teacher, pupil and parent, provided they are conscientiously and thoughtfully applied. Initially, the content of the test prepared, no matter what language skill it may be testing, must be appropriate to the learner. In the early stages of language learning, testing would probably instigate passive responses, as opposed to productive ones, from the pupil, although this would undoubtedly depend largely upon the aims and objectives of the department and the courses used. Then, as the pupil becomes familiar with the more complex aspects of the language, tests would be more suitably conducted through known material but with varying approaches.

Both the teacher and the pupil should benefit from well constructed, valid and reliable tests. The pupil would, after testing, be able to re-assess his own goals in relation to the subject and later reap the benefits of his self-appraisal, should the test reveal weaknesses. However, all too often, children view tests and examinations as hindrances, rather than a device for helping them. The teacher, giving tests with a purpose in mind, should then evaluate both his pupils' performance and his own teaching method with a view to adapting or changing one, the other or both. Open-minded teachers formulate the philosophy of learning and its assessment as a multi-dimensional approach, and language teachers in particular are sharing a feeling that effective procedures need to be based on the consideration of many factors and that methodological decisions are open to new adaptations and contributions from different theories. It is naturally hoped that teaching and assessment activities will motivate pupils to learn and in consequence enable them to realise that it is not merely the result that is important but the means of achieving it. The important factor in all testing, evaluation and assessment is that any feedback from the results must be acted upon.

## References

Allen, E. and Valette, R.M. (1972) *Modern Language Classroom Techniques*, Harcourt, Brace, Jovanovich, New York

Appelt, W. (1968) 'Zur Rolle von Muttersprache und Übersetzung im neusprachlichen Unterricht', *Fremdsprachenunterricht*, Berlin, *12* (2), 50–2, 58

Brings, F. (1968) 'Zur Konstruktion eines informellen Sprachleistungstests', *Praxis des neusprachlichen Unterrichts*, Dortmund, *17* (4)

Buckby, M. (1973) 'A Syllabus for Modern Languages at 16-plus', *Audio-Visual Language Journal*, *11* (1), 62

——— (1980) 'A Graded System of Syllabuses and Examinations', *Modern Languages in Scotland (20)*, 75–81

Calvert, F.I. (1965) *French by Modern Methods*, Schofield and Sims, London

Castigliano, L. (1971) 'Il controllo della preparazione', *Scuola e lingue moderne*, Modena, *7* (9), 212–22

Centre for Information on Language Teaching (CILT) (1970) *Examining Modern Languages*, Reports and Papers 4, London

Davidson, J.M.C. (1973) 'A Common System of Examination at 16+: Some Reactions to the Schools Council Bulletin No. 23', *Modern Languages*, *LIV* (1), 16

Davies, A. (ed.) (1968) *Language Testing Symposium: a Psycholinguistic Approach*, Oxford University Press, Oxford

Doe, B. (1982) 'New Exams Criteria to Widen Competence', *Times Educational Supplement*, 8 January, 9

Dyson, A.P. (1972) *Oral Examining in French*, Modern Languages Association, London

Harding, D.H. (1967) *The New Pattern of Language Teaching*, Longman, London

Her Majesty's Inspectors (1977) *Modern Languages in Comprehensive Schools*, HMSO, London

——— (1978) *Assessing the Performance of Pupils*, D.E.S. Report on Education, *93*, HMSO, London

Hodgson, F.M. (1956) 'Prose Composition in the First Five Years of the School Course', *Modern Languages*, *37* (3), 104–16

Huebener, T. (1965) *How to Teach Foreign Languages Effectively*, New York University Press, New York

Hutchings, G. (1970) 'Colourless Green Ideas: Multiple Choice Vocabulary Tests', *English Language Teaching*, *25* (1), 68–71

Kelly, A.V. (1977) *The Curriculum: Theory and Practice*, Harper and Row, London

Lado, R. (1961) *Language Testing*, Longman, London

Lawton, D. (1978) *Theory and Practice of Curriculum Studies*, Routledge and Kegan Paul, London

Libbish, B. (ed.) (1964) *Advances in the Teaching of Modern Languages*, vol. 1, Pergamon, London

Macintosh, H.G. (ed.) (1974) *Techniques and Problems of Assessment*, Arnold, London

Mackey, W.F. (1965) *Language Teaching Analysis*, Longman, London

Modern Languages Association (MLA) (1975) 'M.L.A. Report on the Proposed 16+ Examination: an Evaluation of the Feasibility Studies', *Modern Languages*, *56*, (2), 98

Morrison, H.R. (1980) 'Pupil Profiles', *Modern Languages in Scotland* (August), 113–22

Moys, A., Harding, A., Page, B. and Printon, V.J. (1980) *Modern Languages at Sixteen Plus. A Critical Analysis*, CILT, London

Otter, H.S. (1968) *A Functional Language Examination*, Oxford University Press, Oxford

Page, B.W. (1973) 'Another Look at Examinations', *Audio-Visual Language Journal*, *11* (2), 127–30

Park, B. (1973) 'A Common Examination System at 16+ in French', *Modern Languages in Scotland* (February), 101

Pidgeon, W. and Allen, D. (1974) *Measurement in Education*, BBC Publications, London

Rivers, W.M. (1969) *Teaching Foreign Language Skills*, University of Chicago, Chicago

——— (1976) *Speaking in Many Tongues*, Newbury House Publications, Rowley, Mass.

Robinson, P. (1970) 'The Compilation, Adaptation and Choice of Second Language Tests', *English Language Teaching*, *25* (1), 60–8

——— (1971) 'Oral Expression Tests', *English Language Teaching*, *25* (3), 260–6

Rowe, G. (1969) 'Language Testing at Universities', *Babel*, Melbourne, *5* (2), 14–17

Stones, E. (ed.) (1970) *Readings in Educational Psychology: Learning and Teaching*, Methuen, London

Truchot, C. (1971) 'Les Tests de Langue: réévaluation critique', *Langues Modernes*, *65* (2), 103–12

Valette, R.M. (1967) *Modern Language Testing: a Handbook*, Harcourt, Brace, New York

——— (1969) *Directions in Foreign Language Testing*, Modern Languages Association, New York

Waddell, J. (1978) *School Examinations*, HMSO, London

Wright, R.M., Ramsay, A.L., Richards, D.F. (1974) 'Joint Council of Language Associations. A Report of Discussions on a Common System of Examinations at 16+', *Modern Languages*, *55* (2)

# 10 THE DEMANDS AND NEEDS OF THE UNIVERSITIES, INDUSTRY AND COMMERCE

D.E. Ager

## Demands and Needs

Industry and commerce are evident 'end-users' of the product, the students, created and fashioned in the educational system of the country. Universities are not end-users in this sense; although some of the products of secondary schools and sixth-form colleges pass to universities, the three or four years they spend there are a further stage in their education and training and from one point of view the process merely delays their entry on to the labour market.

The main traditional arguments for so delaying one's entry into the world of work are that career growth potential is thereby enhanced; a longer period of education leads to earlier and faster promotion and a more senior final position; at the same time leisure, whether enforced or voluntary, can be organised more effectively, becoming personally more satisfying and productive. The individual becomes a better person as well as a richer one.

In the 1980s these arguments remain valid, but the social and economic background against which they stand, and in particular the extent to which public funds will remain available to permit *any* choice for the individual between leaving school at 16+, leaving the sixth form at 18+, or leaving university at 21+, renders the debate academic for many.

In so far as languages are concerned, very different considerations apply to the three different points of entry to the labour market, and we shall consider all three with reference to employment in this chapter. The universities are not employers of students, yet their demands and the pressures they generate have affected the whole nature of learning in the schools, not least in languages. Their importance to secondary schools and sixth-form colleges will remain high; their influence, it is to be hoped, will be and remain beneficial.

The stark opposition between 'education', with all that implies for the development, the intellect and the character, and 'training', with the associated concepts of relevance, applicability of knowledge, and the ability to do rather than to be, continues to surface in many discussions concerning modern languages, partly, one may suspect, because this subject above all others marks out, in the schools, the field for debates about selection, about the viability of mixed-ability teaching, and also about early arts–science specialisation. This is a field for simple and simple-minded, not to mention political, dichotomies, and false oppositions between communicative needs and the development of accuracy in language use; between the defined, limited syllabus and the creative use of language; between writing and speaking even, have not helped to clarify the issues; in fact the whole debate on 'standards' as it applies to languages is more confusing than helpful at a time when 90 per cent of children now start a language where 25 per cent did before.

The development of a rounded personality, able to take a productive place in society, should perhaps remain, after this type of dust has settled, as the sole statable aim of education in modern languages at whatever stage. Perhaps such rounded personalities may then find themselves in actual employment; in so far as languages are concerned whatever the specific syllabus followed and whichever language is studied, the types of employment involved are not restricted by the choice of this subject to a small range of openings. This great advantage enables language learning to sit on both sides of the divide as well as on the fence; languages *can* be regarded as a purely educational subject; *or* as a purely vocational one; *or again* as a mixture of the two. But this great advantage does not mean that teachers of languages can shrug off their responsibilities to maintain this openness; neither schools nor universities can ignore either the world of work or the world of the spirit.

After 16+, in the United Kingdom, education is voluntary and costly to the individual in lost earnings, perhaps in tuition fees, and in the need to maintain himself in a world in which part-time work is frowned on. The participation rate in higher education, defined as the proportion of the age group which takes up places in universities and polytechnics, is abysmally low in the UK – 12–14 per cent, as compared to 25 per cent in France, Germany or the USA. Such a lack of trained and educated manpower has its inevitable consequences and its immediate return in the shape of Toxteth and Brixton riots as well as in the consistent takeover of British business by more expert foreign management, ranging from the Americans to the Japanese. Socially, too, higher and further education is still limited; in the 1980s working-class Britons do not come forward to take up opportunities available to them, and education as such is neither prized nor sought after, as witness the relative ranking of the Department of Education and Science in the Whitehall hierarchy, or the speed and size of the reductions in public expenditure on education, which have gone without the outcry attending even proposed cuts in defence spending.

Such problems are epitomised in the modern language scene: one can't learn a language without going abroad, and this costs money; as a subject its most obvious requirements are time and manpower, both expensive – and reducing expenditure on foreign language assistants in the schools or on colloquial assistants in the universities is an obvious, and attractive, economy in hard times. Investment in language learning is investment in people; those who are best at languages are also best at many other school subjects. Inadequate numbers of working-class kids get the chance to follow language courses, either through lack of parental pressure or that of potential employers or because of the apparent remoteness of the learning context. By contrast, knowledge of language can appear to many to be a positive good in its own right; if education is not prized, knowledge of a language is.

Universities and industry both reflect the values of the society in which they are located, and both also impose their own requirements on the secondary school system. Neither does so in an organised and systematic fashion and those with responsibility for teaching languages, particularly to students between the ages of 11 and 19, are fully justified in complaining for example that the university examining boards at O- and A-level are over-fussy on minor points, steadfastly refusing to accept any connection between the language knowledge they test and the realities of communication in or with a foreign environment. Although a university professor may protest that so-called 'university' examining boards are in fact teacher-dominated, it remains true that one determined Black Paper writer waving slogans of 'culture', 'standards', 'intellectual merit' can effectively, and very easily, halt any change.

Another traditional, but still serious, criticism of university dominance of the educational system is that the prestige of the university entrance game, particularly to Oxford and Cambridge, subordinates any and all educational aims to the pressure to train students to jump hurdles specifically designed by these prestigious institutions to keep the majority of applicants out; and such pressure affects many children from age 13 on, when selection by subject choice starts.

Industry often seems to condemn the educational system for not producing more 'usable' products:

> Changes are necessary in the education system and its curricula to allow for foreign language learning to be carried to a higher level (i.e. not to present it simply as an option which can be pushed aside at an early stage) without other subjects having to be sacrificed in its favour. (Barclay's Bank International, 1979, p. 87)

> The teaching of languages in this country was widely criticised by the companies interviewed during the survey. University courses and modern language graduates received the most severe comment. The implication seemed to be that firms would employ more linguists if there were more candidates with commercial and technical fluency as distinct from literary knowledge. (BETRO Report, 1979, p. 1)

> It is important that in the continuing review of examination syllabuses, full account should be taken of industry's need for practical language skills. (BOTB Report, 1979, p. 16)

Unfortunately such comments are often contradictory or require such massive re-drafting of the education system that they appear impracticable; thus the often repeated demand for some ability in a range of languages conflicts with the need for a high level of competence; and the suggestion that spoken language is of more use to industry conflicts with the demand for specialised commercial and technical vocabulary, although it is accepted that this vocabulary can be rapidly acquired in post on a basis of a more generalised competence in the language.

Thus re-stating some of the criticisms of 'end-users', and some of the replies, is only helpful if we have some notion of where to go from here; it is clear that debate, particularly between industry and the schools, is helpful and clarifies the issues; but both industry and the schools need to know what outcomes are practical and possible. Likewise the universities, exercising pressure on the schools and themselves subject to pressure, have to take stock of their priorities and policies. The other partners in the educational system of the country, the local and national educational authorities, parents and other citizens, although they exercise pressure on educational providers, hover around the outskirts of these discussions, which are essentially about the content, rather than the form, of education, although HMI and others are becoming bolder in their views on the curriculum, and individual Ministers have already allowed their own subject preferences to affect their provision of resources, as for instance with Sir Keith Joseph and the Social Science Research Council.

In a perfectly organised world demands such as those we have been discussing would be based on an analysis of the real needs of industry, of commerce, of the universities. In our imperfect world such analyses do not exist, and most governments have steadfastly refused to plan education on manpower requirements – the nearest we have to such planning is represented by the University Grants Committee, perhaps by the new National Advisory Board for local authority higher education, or by the Advisory Committee on the Supply and Education of Teachers. Even with a full needs analysis for different sectors, it would of course be impossible to specify precisely the number of O-level successes in French which the country needs, or the number of places in university Japanese departments which should be supported; to a certain extent supply breeds demand anyway, as two surveys at Aston have shown (Ager, 1977; Ager, Clavering and Galleymore, 1978), and planning is political anathema to some parties. Yet without some better information to go on we shall doubtless continue to have mindless 'cuts' or mindless 'expansion'.

## The Needs of Universities

Defining the ideal university entrant at age 18 is no easy task. Genuine qualities of intellect are often hidden beneath poor – or good – teaching and it is well nigh impossible for selectors to distinguish between the well prepared, well presented person of modest attainments and the badly taught genius. Certainly the badly taught or badly advised person of modest attainments will need considerable motivation and qualities of personality and drive to carry him this far and further. Selectors, too, are human and fallible, and many Admissions Tutors remain convinced that a southern English accent necessarily correlates with high intellectual ability. Before considering the needs of university language departments, therefore, it might be helpful to consider the mechanics of the actual admission process, if only to identify the problem areas and dispel some illusions.

For all universities except Oxford and Cambridge the process is entirely within the system laid down by the Universities Central Council on Admissions (UCCA), and takes place in three stages. First the intending student completes a form, giving information about himself, his studies and public examinations (usually O-levels) taken to date; his school, usually the head teacher, adds a report on him, usually but not always of both a personal and an academic nature, and this form is despatched to UCCA, which sends copies to each of the five universities (strictly courses) which the student has chosen and may have ranked in order of his preferences. The second stage requires the universities to select those students to whom they will give a conditional offer of a place (the conditions usually being success at specified grades and subjects in A-level); the student then confirms one offer and holds another as a reserve. When the A-level results are published in the middle of August, the student who holds a confirmed conditional offer is *automatically* accepted if he has achieved the exact requirements specified; otherwise he can be accepted or passed on to his reserve university or back to the UCCA office, which will attempt to match up empty places remaining in departments with qualified students prepared to reconsider their choice of university, of department, or of course. Although the system is better than a lottery, and is considerably fairer than that which preceded it or that which still operates in Oxbridge, it still retains a number of features of multi-layer chess, and no one would pretend that the result is always perfect for student or department.

Our concern is with the second stage as it relates to the nature of university studies of languages, although for individual departments the first stage and the third are if anything more important in the admissions process, if one accepts that university departments are in competition for the best students. The definition of 'best' is usually in terms of A-level scores, and counting the three best a particular student may achieve and awarding a points count of 5 for an A grade, 4 for a B and so on, the best possible student is one who has scored 15 points (3 grade A subjects) and the minimum acceptable score for university entrance is 2 (2 grade E subjects). One part of the Admissions Tutor's task – and a more important part since the 1981 round of university cuts was in essence based on this – is to maintain the department's 'average score', and to maintain it fairly near to the average for that subject across the country: for languages this average is 10 to 11 'points' (BCC to BBC), while for most subjects it is about 8 points.

Disregarding these more mechanical and mundane aspects of the admissions process, and assuming general intelligence and suitable motivation for higher education on the part of the candidate for admission, does the ideal university entrant in languages have any specific characteristics? Is there any particular stock of attitudes, interests, experience or knowledge which makes one eighteen-year-old more potentially successful than another? Success in this discussion is definable in academic terms – a good degree (2.1 or better).

The personalities of successful students seem to vary enormously. The hard-working introvert and the apparently lackadaisical extrovert seem to obtain first-class degrees with equal frequency. The glib are usually but not always found out, and the tongue-tied often balance their drawbacks with prolific written skills. One would like to be able to say that the balanced human being who enjoys his university career most also makes the most successful student; this is not always so. Notably extreme attitudes do however seem to have some correlation with poor performance. Particularly is this true in languages, where an understanding of and sympathy with representatives of a foreign culture seem to be a pre-requisite, while superior attitudes towards foreigners, including those living in the UK, are not conducive to success and attitudes of inferiority – inverse snobbery, for example – are equally damaging. Extremes seem also to affect performance, not merely in those aspects of courses in which judgement is at a premium – in writing essays on social, economic or literary topics, for example – but also in much of the language work itself; success in the process of getting under the skin of the relevant foreign society is revealed in the way one uses the foreign language as well as in what one says.

Many students at age eighteen are accomplished musicians, sportsmen, actors, artists; in language learning interests oriented towards other people and involving interaction do seem to be more supportive than those which are appropriate to the life of a recluse. None the less and notwithstanding this, the ability to read both intensively and extensively and to gain enjoyment from so doing is an abiding interest which is likely to have a positive spin-off in the language-learning process. Every student of course in any subject needs to be able to absorb quantities of information; the language student is unique in that he looks not only at the content of the information but also at its manner. Strangely, many foreign language students seem to have difficulty in applying their language interests in their own language; whereas one would think that a game of Scrabble or a wet afternoon passed in tracing a particular meaning through the dictionary would be a matter of some excitement for the potential language student, such interests are rarely met.

It is obviously helpful if the potential languages students has spent some time abroad. The experience, not merely of meeting and talking to foreigners in their own tongue, but also of acting on one's own behalf within a strange and sometimes confusing society, of taking responsibility for one's own actions, seems helpful in the development of that maturity of approach and the inner poise which are helpful to the arts student generally. Many students have had experience of exchange visits, camping holidays, or school attendance abroad; many universities will be delighted for their first-year students all to have spent at least six months and preferably a year in the foreign country before entering upon their studies.

University courses vary greatly. Most now place considerable stress upon competence in the language itself; some concentrate on literary studies, others on the political, social and economic context of foreign society. Some courses concentrate on one language, others combine studies of two; yet others combine a language with another subject such as politics or chemistry or business administration, in varying proportions – hence 'joint' or 'combined' honours courses are usually two subjects each of equal weight; 'major' and 'minor' courses usually imply a ratio of two-thirds to one-third, or three-quarters to one-quarter, between the two subjects involved; and 'single honours' courses are made up of the one subject – but quite often this is accompanied by a subsidiary (or it may be called a minor) subject over at least one or two years of the course. Most language courses now include a year abroad as an integral component – that is, it is impossible to obtain a degree without taking the year abroad; and very few language courses now ignore or downgrade the oral component, some even including interpreting and other specialised skills in their final examinations. Details of the range of courses now available are well described in the range of CRAC Degree Course guides, which include descriptions of all degree courses at universities, polytechnics and higher education colleges.

It may therefore seem somewhat surprising that there can be any common view between universities as to what a student should know before he enters on a degree course in languages; it may even seem surprising that there is any common ground at all between different language departments. Yet common ground there is: not merely do members of different departments act as external examiners to each other's courses, and participate in the subject panels of the Council for National Academic Awards (CNAA), which approves the syllabus and teaching arrangements for courses held in polytechnics and other colleges which do not have the right to award their own degrees, but also the professional bodies representing the different subjects have prepared documents indicating the broad outlines of this subject knowledge. The Association of University Professors of French, the Conference of University Teachers of German, and the Scottish Universities French Language research project have thus produced at least tentative descriptions, varying in detail, of the items of concrete knowledge which are appropriate to university entrants, and this movement towards definition of knowledge in language coincides with movements elsewhere in the language teaching profession towards defined syllabuses and achievement certificates. Gone are the days when achievement at A-level would only be defined as 'more than at O-level and less than at degree level'.

University selectors should therefore be well informed as to the amount of the foreign language which should be known by potential entrants. They should be aware that the knowledge required in language has three main facets: a firm basis of grammar and a reasonable vocabulary; a good practical command of the spoken and written language; and a sensitivity to language use. These three are not acquired in sequence: all go together; and progress in one such facet only is inadequate without progress in the others. This latter consideration is just as true in the case of those who learn a language for specific purposes as it is in those, like our A-level and degree student, who need to cover a range of language uses. Likewise it is difficult to classify language knowledge in terms of the now traditional distinctions between grammatical, notional and functional syllabuses for learning; we may specify grammatical items or individual skills or individual tasks we wish students to perform, but unless A-level is re-organised so that a profile of achievement may be given for each student, we are left at the end with an overall average and only six grades within which to recognise this achievement. Hence the simplistic belief on the part of Admissions Tutors that a grade A or B at A-level should enable a student of French, for example, to demonstrate language knowledge in all three aspects mentioned has little basis in fact.

A potential university student of French should none the less be able to understand the following passage, to realise that it is written in a journalistic style but in a formal manner, well expressed and rather removed from more normal everyday French; and he should be able himself to use, creatively and actively, most of the words and expressions it contains. He should be able to give the gist of a passage such as this in French, either speaking or writing his summary; might be able to translate it reasonably accurately into English, and should be able to compose and write a similar length passage in French on a similar theme, though not at this level of sophistication.

> La place du policier est au cœur de la société. Ni en marge ni à côté, mais en plein dedans. Seulement voilà: investi d'une parcelle de pouvoir qui le suit à chacun de ses pas, ses gestes, ses attitudes, sa manière de vivre et de se comporter restent d'une certaine façon liés à sa fonction. Pareil à un autre homme, il est regardé différemment. Il n'a pas le droit de trébucher puisqu'il possède celui de sanctionner les imperfections de ses concitoyens. C'est pourquoi le forfait d'un policier, ou même le simple accident qualifié aussitôt de 'bavure', choque, perturbe, scandalise puisqu'il écorne cette confiance que le citoyen accorde tacitement au policier comme le passager de l'avion au pilote, et pour la même raison: c'est qu'il ne peut pas faire autrement. . . (*Le Figaro*, 5 January 1982, p. 32)

If we thus specify that the potential entrant to a languages department 'ought' to be able to handle language of this type – and we can even go so far as to say that we would expect him to have some problems in understanding words like *investi*, *trébucher*, *sanctionner*, *concitoyens*, *forfait*, *bavure*, *écorne* – we are assuming both that the schools will continue to prepare students for an examination much like the present A-level and that the universities will continue to assume a level of previous language knowledge of this type. Whether such confidence is well placed or not it is difficult to say; it is certainly not clear whether language knowledge alone is adequate or appropriate to the needs of the universities.

A facile distinction is often still made between content and language, and many A-level marking schemes attempt to distribute credit differently for these elements. Despite the expressed view, for example of the Association of University Professors of French, that 'content' in terms of literary studies or historical/political studies is not a main requirement for entry to university departments, the examination still values this content highly and the literature paper, for example, may well count up to one-third of the marks awarded. It is worth repeating, therefore, that very few university language departments expect or insist on specific knowledge of literary history, of critical approaches and techniques, or of social, political and economic history; the only compulsory element is the language, and indeed any reading material specified in an A-level syllabus is there, as far as the universities are concerned, solely for purposes of linguistic exemplification and practice.

This fact may well be rather depressing, particularly to those of us who believe that language bears an intimate relationship to a speech community and that it is henceforth impossible to divorce understanding of the language from understanding of that community. Much effort has therefore been expended in establishing a 'content' element at A-level which will enable that certificate to be an appropriate proof of broad understanding of the community; to date, however, the A-level boards seem ultra-cautious about introducing a paper which might require skills not possessed by the majority of the teaching force, which requires breadth as well as, or even perhaps instead of, depth of understanding, and which might also underline the role of A-level as a School Leaving Certificate, in certifying that the student understands a total community rather than merely a fraction of its cultural inheritance. None the less 'experimental' syllabuses and 'alternative' papers exist in a number of boards which do not require the traditional set books, and it is to be hoped that this movement will bring about some change.

**The Needs of Industry and Commerce**

On present O-level and CSE arrangements, and under the 16+ proposals, 60 per cent only of sixteen-year-olds in this country take an examination before leaving school. At age 18+, only 25 per cent of the total age group, and at age 21, only 7–10 per cent of the age group have taken A-levels or first degrees respectively. People leaving the educational system at these ages form the qualified manpower to feed British industry, and among its other concerns the educational system must consider how it is preparing students to enter employment.

Employers themselves as individuals, and occasionally in groups and associations, have specified what they are looking for in potential employees, and their views are documented in various reports summarised in Wilding (1980). The present chapter has also had the benefit of advice from the Director-General of the Engineering Employers' Federation, Mr A. Frodsham (now retired), and the Chairman of Cadbury-Schweppes, Sir Adrian Cadbury, although the responsibility for its formulation remains with the author.

Very few, if any, jobs are reserved to those with a good knowledge of foreign languages as their sole qualification. Those that are so reserved, in translating, teaching, librarianship, research and personnel work, some aspects of broadcasting and journalism, government service and some secretarial work, usually require skills of a high order – at least a degree in the relevant language. Often additional skills are required as well – 'language cannot be the first qualification we look for. It cannot take the place of technical knowledge or selling ability – it must be an additional skill within the range of a rounded person's accomplishments' (Frodsham, 1980, p. 4).

In many cases the knowledge sought is that of a specific language within the context of a specific profession – accountancy, personnel, engineering, sales. Needs of this type have been recognised abroad, too, and much of the teaching of English as a Foreign Language which now takes place throughout the world is devoted to the special needs of individuals or groups, airline pilots, civil engineers, computer specialists; and equipment sales abroad are now often made as 'package deals' with a training period included for operatives to become familiar not only with the machinery but also with its specialised communication needs and jargon.

Industry and commerce often seem, however, not to be aware of their own needs in languages. The evidence of many reports is that export is more profitable than home sales, for two main reasons. Local market conditions vary greatly from one country to another, and balancing income from one area against that from another is clearly advantageous, particularly where the product range is adaptable; having all one's eggs in the home market means less flexibility and a more rigid pricing policy. Second, particularly in manufacture, the sort of volume of production which can now be achieved can very quickly saturate the comparatively small UK market. British Leyland's truck division can supply all the commercial vehicles which the UK can take and replace them all every five years; since our competitors are allowed to operate freely in our home market, British Leyland can either reduce its manufacturing base, export, or stop making trucks altogether. It is not for us here to comment on its decisions, but if the UK is to maintain any manufacturing base at all with the manufacturing processes now regarded as normal, we must export.

Faced with this sort of choice, it is sad to see that industry often relies on its traditional sources of linguistic 'expertise' – agents, translations, consultants, interpreters, often pin-money earners and less than professional *ad hoc* helpers. Crash language courses, offered to mid-career executives who frequently have tremendous difficulty in language learning, present a further problem, although it may well be that better early teaching in language-related subjects could help: 'I have a suspicion that one of our problems is our lack of familiarity with our own language. If we were "taught" English better, it would be easier for us to go on crash courses in other languages, for example' (Cadbury, 1982).

The public educational system is poor at making its potential contributions known: 'The study group concludes that firms are not making adequate use of the language training facilities already available. Better liaison between firms and educational establishments is needed' (BOTB Report, 1979, p. 2) and it might well be alleged that industry should be better aware of the need to have available and to develop adequate communication skills in the selling function. The educational system has available skills and resources which could well be developed or oriented to meet commercial needs; much of education in the higher and further education sectors is already geared to providing directly applicable skills, yet commerce still feels that it is not being adequately helped.

There is a need to define and articulate precisely the requirements involved and one can only welcome initiatives such as that taken by the CBI's Understanding British Industry scheme in encouraging language teachers to enter industry for short periods; movement in the other direction, too, would be helpful.

## O-Level and CSE

At 16+, industry and commerce need to be able to call upon a variety of languages. A pool of expertise in French, in German, in Italian, in Spanish is better than the British educational system's traditional insistence upon French alone as the first foreign language. Ideally some understanding of the new trading languages – Arabic, Japanese, Chinese – would be helpful; realistically, however, some understanding of foreign languages by all employees and a range of available languages is sought.

Industrialists would be happiest with at least some introduction to foreign languages for all. Perhaps some knowledge of two or more foreign languages, by all, even to a lower level than that traditionally required by O-level, would be more useful than the more normal concentration on one language by something like a third of all children. Some introduction to foreign language study for all seems hence advisable, and industrialists seem to welcome the fact that over 90 per cent of children now start a foreign language course.

A sympathetic understanding of the foreign society is also looked for, as evidenced in a successful visit abroad, for example, particularly if the visit was not merely for holiday purposes or too short to be effective. Appreciation of foreign customs and habits, at a rather higher level than the bitty and uncontrolled scatter of facts which used to be offered in some European Studies and CSE courses, is regarded as helpful and indeed essential. Such customs and habits should not be regarded as the weird ways of strange beings but as acceptable alternatives to the British way of life; one just does not use Christian names in business in Continental Europe or Japan!

The spoken language, as well as or even instead of the written, is currently needed, and much stress is placed on communicative skills, by which is meant the ability to get a message across and to understand the gist of a conversation, accurately and with as much detail as possible. Attention to 'finicky points of grammar' is not thought to be of major importance. Understanding of the contemporary language in its accepted normal form is looked for; this is often contrasted with the outdated and archaic styles required in traditional O-level examinations and could also be contrasted with popular and vulgar forms.

From the educationalist's point of view these may appear limited requirements, not dissimilar to the views of employers on a subject such as mathematics, for example. Mathematics, however, is regarded as a directly applicable subject which should be taught in such a way that the potential insurance agent or trainee or apprentice can make direct use of this specific skill on his first working day. As far as most industrialists and commercial people are concerned, languages at 16+ are required first as general evidence of intellectual ability and learning potential; if any immediately practical use is looked for it will be in the spoken contemporary language, and in a general understanding and communication of a direct message.

In two other ways, also, foreign language knowledge seems helpful to employers: a general understanding of language structure 'cannot be gained in any other way' than by following a foreign language course. Such an understanding of language structure 'does help people to express themselves clearly' and 'those who understand a foreign language . . . avoid ambiguity and structure their ideas in a logical form in their own language' (Cadbury, 1982).

Within Britain's multi-racial society there is also now some demand for knowledge of, or at least awareness of, the languages of immigrant communities. A multi-racial work-force inevitably has communication difficulties; add to that the problems caused by employment legislation and the health and safety provisions governing workplaces, and the need for clear and instant understanding is evident to any employer. Future foremen, chargehands and workmates have responsibilities to and for each other; and although it is essential that the 16+ school leaver has both a good spoken and written command of English – and this applies particularly to the immigrant himself – some knowledge of the other tongues spoken now, or at least of the culture and customs now accepted, within Great Britain would be helpful for all.

It is highly unlikely that a sixteen-year-old school leaver will actively use foreign languages for some years. The problem, however, for many apprentices and shop-floor workers is that they do not remain apprentices and shop-floor workers; they become fitters and sales representatives and as such may well have to travel

222 The Needs of Universities, Industry and Commerce

in later life. At this stage, at age 25, 35 or 45, their school French is suddenly called upon to perform miracles, often at short notice and with little time for preparation. In these circumstances foreign language education can do little to respond to the precise needs of the individual; it can, however, prepare him to travel and provide him with a usable basis for later work, and it can provide him with the confidence to cope with a strange environment, Almost above all else, then, the 16+ leaver needs to have an experience of success, to know that he can perform and to know what he can perform.


**After the Sixth Form**

For the 19+ entrant to the world of work, additional, and sometimes different, aspects of language use are significant. Most employers are agreed that at A-level literary studies should be replaced by social studies or by a better standard of knowledge and use of the language itself. Industrialists accept that they are not the best judges of the detailed curriculum and syllabus to be offered in schools, and many would reject the inherent philistinism of simply jettisoning what many schoolteachers regard as the cultural or even intellectual content of A-level studies. However, from the point of view of usable language competence, literary studies, particularly if they concentrate on texts of centuries prior to the twentieth, are not seen as relevant to the needs of communication in practical contexts: 'the ability to read the *Figaro* is of more value than the understanding of a play by Molière' (Frodsham, 1982).

Many employers feel that the stress on the written language, which is characteristic of A-level, should be replaced by a stress on oral competence. Among the many arguments advanced for this point of view is the belief that the present usable standard of A-level is too low for effective use; more time devoted to obtaining better standards in spoken language would result in a greater ability to establish and maintain contact from person to person, although it is accepted that a drop in written standards might well be the price to pay. Facile contrasts between communicative ability and accuracy are only too easily proposed at this stage; employers do not, however, look for inaccurate command of the spoken language but for accurate, careful and competent command of the spoken, and as far as possible of the written, language, relevant to the communication tasks involved.

A-level itself is often thought to be unfortunately designed in being a single subject examination, making no provision for the needs of those who do not wish to specialise in a particular subject. It would be helpful if at the age of 19+, more of the students who intend to follow numerate careers were also able to display a satisfactory command of foreign languages; if it were possible for those reading science subjects to maintain at least some practical contact with language in the sixth form, or if an alternative syllabus for A-level itself could be devised which would marry a foreign language with a non-arts subject – business studies, applied mathematics, economics – many industrialists would be delighted. As there are at least five or six different syllabuses available for physics at A-level, even with one examining board, and no one physics syllabus covers all the ground which it is necessary or desirable for physicists to cover at this level, no obvious objection is seen to a A-level syllabuses in foreign languages which could offer a selection of topics to accompany language competence; certainly a French geography A-level seems no more objectionable, and in fact much more acceptable, than a French literature A-level.

Many industrialists would in fact like *all* potential employees at 19+ to have studied language after the O-level stage. It is from this level of recruitment that many middle managers come and many of these will have to take responsibility for contacts at technician or production level with overseas factories, distributors or suppliers, and are currently separated far too early from language studies. This is particularly true of those going into science-based careers; hence the welcome from thoughtful employers for language components in BEC courses and for the Alternative Ordinary schemes such as that funded in its development phase by BP at Oxford.

Such views are those of manufacturing industry; in commerce and particularly in the financial world, requirements are at the same time simpler and yet infinitely more complex. Here it seems that the needs are for openness towars foreign societies, towards alternative systems, civilisations and cultures. Many of the services which advanced societies can offer less advanced countries lie in the financial domain, and contacts here will in the future be with non-English-speaking countries, many in the Far East, which already have well developed fiscal systems and trading patterns of their own. Understanding the oriental mind is no easy task for the lad from Rochdale, and although it is unlikely that the local school can teach Mandarin or Bahasa Indonesia, it is certainly to be hoped that it can prevent ossification of the intellect and closure of the understanding. And knowledge of one language makes the job of acquiring another less of a daunting task.


## After Higher Education

For those entering the employment market at 21+, industrialists and commercial leaders have stressed their preference for non-literary language studies. In reply, however, the point has been made that literary studies enable, at least in the case of the older civilisations such as that of France, a point of contact with the educated native speaker. A principal task for the export salesman is that of establishing personal contact, and in such a context having something to talk about is as important as being able to speak; since in France almost every adult who has obtained his Baccalauréat will have covered, if only in extracts, the history of his own literature and will be able to discuss main lines of cultural development, any businessman wishing to establish and maintain useful contacts will do well to be aware of these: 'A knowledge of literature and history can transform your relationship with a Frenchman; they are rightly proud of their cultural tradition and are pleased by a foreigner's awareness of it' (Cadbury, 1982). The same comment does not, however, apply to Germany or Japan, and the point is made that few Britons even at this level know much about Shakespeare and even fewer anything about Wordsworth. 'Perhaps a knowledge of current affairs is the most useful subject' (Frodsham, 1982). A deliberate concentration on studies which are remote from the daily concerns of the twentieth-century citizen, however, is regarded as excessive; and those universities which insist on such studies as proof of training of the mind are not thought to be sensible by most employers.

Particularly favoured by employers are graduates who have combined their study of a language with some other subject. Many joint honours degrees, whether in French and German, German and Business Administration, French and Engineering, now exist and have grown in popularity within universities during these past ten years. Employers are well aware of the actual and potential value of new recruits combining both language and other skills.

It is recognised that specialist linguists must come from a university background. In so far as their language skills are concerned, they will be expected to be competent in a range of manipulative skills including reading, writing, translating, interpreting and summarising and are often required to act within organisations as experts not merely in relation to their own foreign language but also to others as well. Such expectations can border on the ridiculous; there are anecdotes of the French graduate who was expected to translate from and into German and Spanish as well; but none the less limited and narrow-minded specialisation – narrow-mindedness of any sort – is not expected from the language graduate.

Employers' expectations may be high in other areas, too; the idea that a newly qualified graduate can conduct a telephone sales campaign or that he can instantly translate specialised research articles in engineering is difficult to eradicate. Conversely, if a newly qualified graduate cannot carry out such activities within a year or so of entering a commercial environment, employers have some reason to question his capabilities and his training.

Most industrialists feel that foreign language training should also be made available to *all* undergraduates, no matter what the subject, and many regret the passing of the compulsory language component in science-based degrees, and of the foreign language entrance qualification to universities: 'Engineers without the ability to communicate effectively, and preferably in at least one foreign language other than English, may be at an increasing disadvantage in future years' (B. Finch in the *Guardian*, 9 February 1982).

Employers also look to higher and further education to provide language courses for existing executives. Here many are dissatisfied with the offerings of the educational system and hence turn to private language schools and other commercial organisations. The most frequent complaint about the educational system is its lack of flexibility; with the best will in the world an industrial and commercial concern is necessarily moving from one order to the next and is unable to plan ahead for its language or indeed any other requirements with the degree of foresight and long-range planning which many educationalists feel provides the only framework for adequate success in language learning. It is literally impossible for a firm to decide to train four or five executives in Japanese on the off-chance that a contract may arise in the two- or three-year time-span which adequate training requires. Hence the air of crisis and disorganisation which seems to underlie many commercial organisations and which renders the preparation of adequate language courses difficult for educational establishments; and hence also the apparent gullibility of firms who accept what seem to be obvious confidence tricks on the part of unscrupulous commercial language schools, promising certain success in 25 hours. The commercial environment is *necessarily* unstable, volatile and uncertain, and educational establishments who offer language courses know that their offerings have to be tailored accordingly.

## Conclusion

We are entering a new era of employment which is imposing strains on the public educational system of the country. Some additional strains are imposed by political ideologies and economic theories, many of which directly affect what is offered in the schools and universities. But traditional forms of pressure still exist.

The backlash effect of public examinations on the school syllabus and teaching methods has been considerable, and many responsible teachers feel that the best way of helping pupils face the future is to help them to obtain the best possible results at these examinations even though their form and content may be less than ideal. The debate on standards, too, imposes pressures on students and teachers alike to achieve within the existing examination framework and to resist changes to that framework. Economic pressure has raised the competition for university and polytechnic places, and at the same time has made many career choices irrelevant.

Surprisingly, in view of the employment situation, the requirements of industry and commerce in relation to languages have not been directly translated into changed syllabuses or altered examinations. The overall lack of openings and the confused picture emanating even from bodies such as the CBI may in part be responsible; a consistent and coherent change in language policy is unlikely unless all the relevant bodies are unanimous and their demands can be shown to relate both to their own needs and to what is possible.

The universities are not, in British society, expected to be unanimous. However, the body which *is* supposed to provide an overall plan for language provision in the universities, the UGC, together with the CNAA and the NAB, could be expected to identify the needs of higher education and translate these into demands to be expressed to the secondary sector; at the moment, in languages, as in other subject areas, decisions on the amount and orientation of higher education to be made available depend on the demand for places coming from the schools, and on the cash made available by government in relation to its overall economic targets. The needs and demands of individual human beings, as so often, may well be ignored in the context of such pressures.

What, however, should schools and further education do about language teaching in order to enable students to cope with the various demands and pressures on them? Progress could come in four directions.

Languages are taught both for their own sake and also as a tool for other subjects. Unfortunately this latter area has been neglected and in many sixth forms it is well nigh impossible to persuade the head or the languages staff to mount continuation courses post O-level for those going on the science side. These short-sighted attitudes should change, and it is interesting to note that many independent schools now offer such courses, making good use of their more favourable staff-student ratios and of their closer contact with the business community's preferences.

Schools and examining bodies should look to the question of standards, without equating these with a retention of outdated syllabuses, inaccurate and incomplete syllabuses, or depth of study as opposed to breadth. Foreign languages are unique in that the measure of excellence is perfection; as Professor Hawkins has many times pointed out, it is possible to obtain 100 per cent in mathematics without being Einstein; it is impossible to obtain 100 per cent in French without being a Frenchman, and a bi-lingual one at that. Moves towards the certification of positive achievement, towards closer syllabus definition, towards the definition of authentic and appropriate communication tasks and skills, are surely to be welcomed.

A concentration on the contemporary and on the spoken language seems to be required by all. But this does not necessarily mean that audio-visual teaching methods are the only appropriate ones; nor does it mean that the necessary educational and training aims of getting things right – the endings right, the pronunciation right – have to be abandoned. There is no one successful methodology for teaching languages; but some obvious dis-incentives to learning could be avoided, such as too large classes or inappropriate timetabling. Teaching support is helpful and often essential – tape-recorders, *assistants*, visits; advisory services, in-service courses, courses for teachers in the subjects they teach as well as in the professional techniques of teaching; with adequate provision a flexible and expert teaching force can cope with changing circumstances. Particularly in view of suggestions about teaching a greater variety of languages in the schools, or teaching language or even linguistics, it is important that teachers are adequately informed of the continuing academic debates and of current research, and are able to take advantage of progress made.

What accompanies the language skills in the schools? At the moment somewhat of a rag-bag of disparate information, unsystematised and often incoherent, may be presented to CSE and O-level candidates, and examination texts for the latter in particular are still taken from the world of inane suburbia and endless country weekends. At A-level the France and Germany of today and the working world of those countries are too often still ignored. Perhaps a re-definition of reading skills may help; there are enormous difficulties to overcome, in which new technology may play a part – with satellite television, for example; but adequate and appropriate definitions of the content of language courses suitable for the 1980s and 1990s are not yet available. Industrialists and university departments are convinced that the centre of language courses should be and remain the language skills themselves, and that any content, whether literary, political, historical, scientific or commercial, should remain a background concern, illuminating and encouraging the active use of language until A-level standard is reached.

## References

Ager, D.E. (1977) *Language Training at Leyland International*, Department of Modern Languages, University of Aston, Birmingham (restricted)
———, Clavering, E., and Galleymore, J. (1978) *Foreign Languages in Industry, Commerce and Education: the Aston Experience*, Aston Modern Languages Club, Birmingham
Barclay's Bank International (1979) *Factors for International Success: the Barclay's Bank Report on Export Development in France, Germany and the United Kingdom*, Barclay's Bank International Ltd, London
BETRO (1979) *Language and Export Performance: a Study Prepared for the*

*BETRO Committee*, Royal Society of Arts, London
BOTB (1979) *Foreign Languages for Overseas Trade: a Report by the BOTB Study Group on Foreign Languages*, British Overseas Trade Board, London
Cadbury, Sir A. (1982) Private communication
Frodsham, A.F. (1980) Opening address in Aston Report, no. 1, University of Aston, Birmingham
———, (1982) Private communication
University of Aston/BOTB (1980) *Foreign Languages for Overseas Trade: Report of a Conference held on 22 March 1980* (Aston Report, no. 1), University of Aston, Birmingham
University of Aston/BOTB (1981) *The Language Key in Export Strategy: Report of a Conference held on 12 January 1981* (Aston Report, no. 2), University of Aston, Birmingham.
Wilding, C.M. (1980) *Languages, Education and Industry: a Summary of Reports and Conferences*, Department of Modern Languages, University of Aston, Birmingham

# NOTES ON CONTRIBUTORS

The following list is arranged in alphabetical order of surnames.

**Dennis Ager** taught French, German and Russian at Farnborough Grammar School for six years before becoming Lecturer in French at the University of Salford and then moving to Aston University as Professor of Modern Languages and Head of the Modern Languages Department. He was a member of the Standing Committee of the National Congress on Languages in Education (1978–80) and is currently one of the Governors of the Centre for Information on Language Teaching (CILT). His main interests are in French language, and particularly in the functional varieties of its contemporary written form; he has, of necessity, developed interests in the problems of language learning, of computational linguistics and other analytical procedures, and of the uses to which a knowledge of foreign languages may, and should, be put. He is author of *Styles and Registers in Contemporary French* (University of London Press, London, 1970), and of numerous articles.

**Nadine K. Cammish** is a Lecturer in the Department of Educational Studies at the University of Hull. Her main interests are modern language teaching methodology and comparative education, and she recently spent two years as French adviser in the Ministry of Education and Culture in the Seychelles. Her publications cover various aspects of materials development and methodology for the teacher of French and she is now working on language problems in developing countries.

**Frank Corless** taught in London at secondary and college of education levels before moving to the University of Southampton in 1975. As Head of French in a college of education, he developed a strong interest in advanced foreign language teaching which has led to publications on different aspects of theory and practice. He is currently working with Ralph Gaskell on a collection of French teaching/learning materials for use with post O-level students.
   As Lecturer in charge of Modern Languages in a Department of Education, he is concerned with methodology on a broad front; his

particular interests include the development of reading skills, working with texts and the implications for classroom practice of a communicative approach to language teaching.

**Ralph Gaskell** taught French for several years in secondary comprehensive and selective schools, first in England and then in Zambia, where he wrote a number of French radio series. Before taking up a post as Lecturer in French at Whitelands College, London, he spent a year at the Bureau pour l'enseignement de la Lange et de la Civilisation françaises à l'étranger in Paris, where he participated in writing French course materials for anglophone Africa. Recently, as Principal Lecturer at the Roehampton Institute, he has developed a particular interest in communicative approaches to language teaching and learning at all levels. With Frank Corless, he was a member of the French 16–19 Study Group which produced *French 16–19: a New Perspective* (Hodder and Stoughton, 1981). Currently Frank Corless and he are working on a French course for the post O-level stage which will be published shortly.

**Eric Hawkins** taught Spanish and French and after six years' war service in the infantry was headmaster of two grammar schools. Later he founded the Language Teaching Centre, York University, and was Professor of Education (Language Teaching). On his retirement from York he was elected Professor Emeritus.

He is author of textbooks in French and books on the curriculum. As chairman of the Schools Council Modern Languages Committee he edited Working Paper 28 (*New Patterns in Sixth Form Modern Language Teaching*). He also served as President of the British Association for Language Teaching (the Audio-visual Language Association), of the National Association of Language Advisers and (currently) is President of the Modern Languages Association. He was a member of several national commissions including Plowden (primary education) and the Rampton committee (education of ethnic minorities). He was awarded the CBE in 1973.

**Alan Hornsey** taught German and French in London and Rotherham before becoming Head of Modern Languages in the University of London Institute of Education. He has written extensively on German literature and the teaching of foreign languages, was editor of *Handbook for Modern Language Teachers* (Methuen, 1975) and is co-author of two French courses.

He is a former Chief O-level Examiner in German and President of the Association of Teachers of German, and is at present Chairman of the Standing Committee of the National Congress on Languages in Education and the Languages Advisory Committee of the Royal Society of Arts Examination Board.

**David Nott** taught French for seventeen years (eight years as Head of Department) at Manchester Grammar School. Since 1981 he has been Lecturer in Modern Languages in the School of Education of the University College of North Wales. He was co-author of the sixth-form French course *Actualités françaises* (Hodder and Stoughton, 2nd edn, 1976 and 1978) and has edited Vailland's *325,000 francs* (Hodder and Stoughton, 1975) and Sartre's *Les Mots* (Methuen, 1981). He was guest editor of *Language Teaching 16–19: a Handbook* (1977, reprinted from the British Association of Language Teaching *Journal*) and was a member of the study group that published *French 16–19: a New Perspective* (Hodder and Stoughton, 1981). He has served on numerous bodies connected with foreign language teaching and assessment; since 1972 he has been a member of the Executive Committee of the British Association for Language Teaching, and a member of the Bureau of the Fédération internationale des Professeurs de Français since 1978.

**Geoffrey Richardson** taught French and German (latterly as Head of Modern Languages) in the West Riding of Yorkshire before being appointed Lecturer in Education (Modern Languages) at the University of Leicester in 1955.

Since 1965 he has been a Senior Lecturer in the University of Hull Department of Educational Studies. He has considerable experience as examiner in French at A-level and as Chief Examiner for both GCE O-level and CSE French. He is co-author of a number of books for the teaching of modern languages in schools, and a writer for various journals.

His particular interests in the field of modern language methodology include assessment, motivation, 'Direct Method' teaching, and the role of the visual element, which was the field of his MA thesis for the University of Sheffield.

**Graham Soles** has taught modern languages in public, grammar and comprehensive schools in Yorkshire and was Head of Modern Languages at the Graham Comprehensive School, Scarborough. After completing his MA degree in Education at the University of Hull in 1979 he became Research Officer for the Language Teaching Research Project of the Language Teaching Centre at the University of York.

He has also worked on the Schools Council sponsored project, 'Self Evaluation and the Teacher in 1980'. He is now Head of Modern Languages, Hipperholme Grammar School, Halifax.

# GLOSSARY AND ABBREVIATIONS

A short list which may be of assistance to readers unfamiliar with the English organisations and institutions mentioned, or with the terms used to describe them.

AVLA: the Audio-Visual Language Association aimed to provide information for and further the interests of all teachers and students of the audio-visual approach. The work of AVLA and of its journal, *AVL Journal*, has since 1977 been taken over by BALT, the British Association for Language Teaching, whose organ is the *British Journal of Language Teaching*.

BALT: *see* AVLA.

CBEVE: The Central Bureau for Educational Visits and Exchanges.

CILT: The Centre for Information on Language Teaching and Research. Established in 1966 as the UK advisory service on modern language teaching and research, CILT collects and co-ordinates information about all aspects of modern languages and the teaching of them, and makes this information available for the benefit of education in Britain.

CSE: The Certificate of Secondary Education. The school examination taken at about 16 years of age which has been variously described as 'designed to record the performance of the average and above-average pupil', 'usually taken by the less academic', and as 'catering for the next 50 per cent of pupils if it is estimated that the "top" band of 20 per cent present themselves for GCE O-level'. It exists in three modes:

> Mode 1 in which the syllabus, the examination papers and the marking are externally controlled by the examinations Board;
> Mode 2 in which the school offers a syllabus approved by the Board, which is also responsible for the marking of the examination papers; and
> Mode 3 in which the schools set and mark their own examination, subject to external moderation.

> (See Schools Council Examinations Bulletins, especially Bulletin No. 1, *The CSE*, HMSO, 1963.)

Comprehensive schools: secondary schools which cater for the educational needs of all normal children irrespective of their level of attainment on entry.

DES: The Department of Education and Science, as the Government department responsible for primary, secondary and further education in England and Wales, is the main policy and executive body in Education.

GCE: The General Certificate of Education awarded on the results of external examinations set and marked by examining Boards in England and Wales.

Grammar school: formerly a secondary school offering largely academic courses for the most able pupils as selected at the age of 11. Now in process of disappearing as a separate part of secondary education, as a result of the spread and growth of comprehensive schools (qv).

HMI: Her Majesty's Inspectorate is composed of inspectors (HMIs) who are normally recruited from the teaching profession. They are attached to the DES and allocated to regional divisions of England and Wales, where they inspect schools and other institutions and provide a major source of advice to schools, LEAs and to the DES as to curriculum, policy etc. by their reports and personal contacts.

LEA: Local Education Authority. Education in England and Wales is administered locally by county, borough, or city councils which appoint the education committee, the Director of Education and his staff and are responsible for the education in schools and colleges within their areas.

Middle schools: admit pupils from the primary schools and cater for varying age-ranges between 8 and 14.

MLA: The Modern Language Association of Great Britain was founded to assist teachers and students of modern languages and to secure better recognition for their subject. Its journal, *Modern Languages*, is published quarterly.

Nuffield Foundation: supports research into education within the British Commonwealth and, most importantly perhaps for modern languages, was responsible for the Language Teaching Materials Project which produced such courses as *En Avant*, *Vorwärts* and *Adelante*.

OHP: the overhead projector.

Primary schools: provide for pupils from the age of 5 to 11.

Schools Council for the Curriculum and Examinations: an independent body funded by the DES and LEAs which undertakes research on curriculum development, teaching methods and examinations at school level. The findings form the basis of advice to the Secretary of State on examinations policy.

Secondary schools: provide for pupils aged 11 and over.

Secondary Modern schools: offered a wide range of courses, some non-academic, some leading to CSE and GCE, to pupils who had not been selected for the Grammar schools at age 11. Now in process of disappearing as a separate part of secondary education, as a result of the spread and growth of comprehensive schools (q v).

STM: the Short-term Memory, a hypothetical stage in the memory process whereby a limited amount of information can be held briefly in store for immediate use.

16+ examination: it was proposed in 1980 that the present separate systems of CSE and GCE O-level examinations should be replaced by a single, common system.

# INDEX

240   *Index*

University Grants Committee (UGC)
    211, 227
university language courses 214–15
utterances: 'medium-orientated' 48;
    'message-orientated' 48


Valdman, A. 62–3
Valette, R.M. 187
validity *see* tests
Viëtor, W. 23–7 *passim*, 34–9 *passim*,
    46, 47, 124
visits and exchanges 135–6
vocabulary sheets 155

vocational arguments for FL learning
    119
Vygotsky, L.S. 120


Waddell committee 199
wall pictures 173
Walter, B. 29, 30, 38, 40, 41, 45
whole-class work 96
Wilkins, D. 19, 80


York study 58
Yuan Ren Chao 120